UNITED NATIONS
ENVIRONMENT PROGRAMME

ENVIRONMENTAL EFFECTS OF OZONE DEPLETION AND

ITS INTERACTIONS WITH CLIMATE CHANGE:

2002 ASSESSMENT

Pursuant to Article 6 of the Montreal Protocol on Substances that Deplete the Ozone Layer under the Auspices of the United Nations Environment Programme (UNEP)

Copies of the report are available from

United Nations Environment Programme (UNEP)
P. O. Box 30552
Nairobi , Kenya
Email: Ozoneinfo@unep.org
Website: http://www.unep.org/ozone

and

U.S. Global Change Research Information Office
CIESIN, Columbia University
P.O. Box 1000
61 Route 9W
Palisades, New York 10964, USA
Tel.: +(1) (845) 365-8930
Fax: + (1) (845) 365-8922
Email: help@gcrio.org
Online document request: www.gcrio.org/ordering/

Published March 2003 by the Secretariat for The Vienna Convention for the Protection of the Ozone Layer and The Montreal Protocol on Substances that Deplete the Ozone Layer United Nations Environment Programme (UNEP)

UNEP, Environmental Effects of Ozone Depletion: 2002
Assessment, United Nations Environment Programme

ISBN 92-807-2312-X

ENVIRONMENTAL EFFECTS OF OZONE DEPLETION AND ITS INTERACTIONS WITH CLIMATE CHANGE: 2002 ASSESSMENT

Introduction

The four earlier assessments on Environmental Effects of Ozone Depletion, between 1989 and 1998, dealt almost exclusively with increasing ultraviolet radiation and its impacts. The present assessment gives an update on these same problems, but with a special emphasis on the interactions with climate change, at the request of the 11th Meeting of the Parties to the Montreal Protocol. Depletion of the stratospheric ozone layer and climate change are dealt with in separate international conventions. Although both processes are aspects of global atmospheric change, the measures needed for phasing out ozone depleting chemicals and for limiting the increasing greenhouse effect are distinctly different. Even if separated in this fashion, it is becoming increasingly clear that the two processes have many interactions. For the time period that these two threats co-exist, there is a strong likelihood that their interactions will have consequences for the environment.

Some of these interactions take place within the atmosphere and influence the UV radiation reaching the earth's surface, resulting in effects on health, ecosystems and materials. In other cases, a particular effect of UV radiation, e.g., on phytoplankton in the oceans, may even play a role in the large-scale interactions between climate change and ozone depletion. In addition, a specific biological system or material may be affected by increased UV radiation in combination with rising temperatures, changing precipitation or other aspects of climate change; these various factors may interact with each other in an additive, antagonistic or synergistic way.

Climate models that simulate future ozone levels have improved but still remain highly uncertain. Several models predict delays in recovery of the ozone layer, ranging from almost zero to a decade or more or even to further ozone depletion late in the century. This calls for an analysis of the consequences of a prolonged period of increased UV-B radiation on health and the environment.

Changes in snow and ice cover arising from global warming can modify the UV radiation received at the Earth's surface. The penetration of UV radiation into the sea and freshwaters is dependent on the concentration of dissolved organic matter in the water, which is modified by both UV radiation and temperature. Oceanic productivity is also influenced by temperature and UV radiation; the changed productivity in turn leads to changes in sulphur emission from the ocean, potentially altering the transmission of sunlight to the surface. The induction of skin cancer by solar UV radiation is likely to increase with global warming. Increasing temperatures are also expected to exacerbate the UV-related problems in air quality, and UV-induced damage to materials.

Research and understanding of most of these complex processes is still in an initial and uncertain phase, but it appears that some of these will have environmental impacts. In the following chapters, new information on the effects of increased UV radiation will be discussed in more detail, with special attention given to the role of interactions between ozone depletion and climate change.

Jan van der Leun, Xiaoyan Tang, Manfred Tevini

United Nations Environment Programme
PO Box 30552
Nairobi, Kenya
http://www.unep.org/ozone
http://www.unep.ch/ozone

TABLE OF CONTENTS

EXECUTIVE SUMMARY

ENVIRONMENTAL EFFECTS OF OZONE DEPLETION AND ITS INTERACTIONS WITH CLIMATE CHANGE: 2002 ASSESSMENT

Ozone and UV Changes

- **Atmospheric ozone remains depleted**. Antarctic ozone losses have remained similar each spring in recent years. In the Arctic, the ozone losses can be substantial, but only during winters when stratospheric temperatures fall below a critical threshold. Outside the Polar regions, ozone losses are less severe. Relative to 1980, the 1997-2000 losses in total ozone are about 6% at southern mid-latitudes on a year-round basis. At northern mid-latitudes the ozone losses are about 4% in winter/spring season, and 2% in summer/autumn. In the tropics, there have been no significant changes in column ozone. Globally, the annual average ozone loss is approximately 3%. These changes are in broad agreement with model calculations.

- **Although the quality, quantity, and availability of ground-based UV measurements continue to improve, a global-scale assessment from them is not yet available.** The complicated spatial and temporal distributions of the predominant variables that affect ultraviolet radiation at the surface (for example, clouds, airborne fine particles, snow cover, sea ice cover, and total ozone) continue to limit the ability to describe fully surface ultraviolet radiation on the global scale, whether through measurements or model-based approaches.

- **Spectral surface ultraviolet data records, which started in the early 1990s, are still too short and too variable to permit the calculation of statistically significant long-term (i.e., multi-decadal) trends.** However, long-term increases in peak UV levels have been observed at a few sites, and the measured increases are in agreement with model calculations. Progress has been made inferring historical levels of UV radiation using measurements of ozone from satellites in conjunction with measurements of total solar radiation obtained from extensive meteorological networks.

- **Long-term effects on UV radiation from changes in cloud and snow cover have been observed.** At two of three sites in Canada the increases in UV-B radiation were as expected from the changes in stratospheric ozone concentrations that have occurred, while at another site the UV-B trend was much larger as a result of additional long-term changes in snow cover and cloud. This indicates potentially complex interactions between climate change and UV-B radiation. Cloud reflectance measured by satellite has shown a long-term increase in some regions (e.g., in Antarctica), which would tend to reduce the UV-B radiation. In other regions (e.g., in the tropics) there have been decreases in cloud cover. These changes in cloud cover are not yet satisfactorily explained by models. Future changes in cloud cover and tropospheric air quality (especially aerosols) may modify significantly the UV exposures experienced at the Earth's surface.

- **Anthropogenic aerosols play a more important role in attenuating UV radiation than has been assumed previously.** Comparisons between UV measured at the Earth's surface and satellite data indicate that satellite estimates are too large in polluted locations, and thus aerosols are more important than previously thought. The effects of pollution originating from urban and industrial areas may extend over wide geographical areas.

Episodes of biomass burning, which contribute to enhanced particulates and gas composition, can decrease UV-B at the Earth's surface and in the troposphere.

- **Future changes in well-mixed greenhouse gases will affect the future evolution of ozone through chemical, radiative, and dynamic processes.** In this highly coupled system, an evaluation of the relative importance of these factors is difficult; studies are ongoing. Stratospheric cooling (due mainly to projected carbon dioxide increases) is predicted to increase ozone amounts in the upper stratosphere. However, a reliable assessment of these effects on total column ozone is limited by uncertainties in lower stratospheric response to these changes.

Health

- **New studies continue to confirm the adverse effects of UV-B radiation on the eyes, skin, and immune system.** Although no new health effects have been discovered, many improvements have been made in understanding the mechanism of action of UV-B, thereby reducing the level of uncertainty in predictions regarding the health consequences of ozone depletion.

- **Studies on the ocular effects of UV radiation strengthen the association between UV-B exposure and the development of age-related cortical cataract.** New epidemiological studies confirm the role of UV radiation in the formation of cortical cataract, and studies in various animal models strongly implicate UV-B radiation as the primary cause of this condition.

- **New animal models for UV-induced cutaneous melanoma and basal cell carcinoma have been developed.** These models are being used to determine how UV radiation causes or contributes to the development of these skin cancers. Interestingly, induction of melanoma in a transgenic mouse model occurred only when animals were exposed to UV radiation early in life. Similar results were obtained in an opossum model. These findings support those from epidemiological studies suggesting that exposure to UV radiation early in life is an important risk factor in the subsequent development of melanoma. In both models, UV-B, rather than UV-A radiation seems to play the more important role in melanoma induction.

- **Specific genes and biochemical pathways in cells that contribute to skin cancer development have been identified.** Such studies improve our understanding of the involvement of UV radiation in skin cancer induction and may eventually allow the identification of persons at greatest risk of developing UV-induced cancers of the skin.

- **New studies indicate that the risk of skin cancer development can be reduced by certain interventions.** Regular use of sunscreens reduced the incidence of squamous cell cancers in adults, and applying DNA repair enzymes to the skin of persons with a genetic susceptibility to skin cancer reduced the development of precancerous lesions.

- **Research on the immunological effects of UV irradiation continues to improve our understanding of the mechanisms by which UV radiation reduces immune function.** However, many questions remain as to the significance of these effects for allergies, autoimmune diseases, vaccinations, and cancers of internal organs.

- **Studies in animal models of infectious diseases provide compelling evidence that UV-B radiation can increase the incidence, severity, and duration of a variety of diseases.** Some of these effects are subtle and thus will be difficult to detect in epidemiological studies of infectious diseases in human populations. Nonetheless, evidence continues to accumulate suggesting associations between sunlight exposure and reduced efficacy of vaccinations and exacerbation of infectious diseases, particularly those caused by herpes viruses (cold sores, and shingles).

- **Phase-out of the ozone-depleting chemical, methyl bromide, may lead to increased use and numbers of other pesticides**. In locations where these chemicals are well regulated, additional health risks are expected to be small. However, in locations where controls are lax, there is reason to be concerned that increased use may lead to additional health risks.

- **Interactions between global climate change and ozone depletion are likely to influence the risk of adverse effects of UV-B radiation on health**. This influence could be either positive or negative and thus introduces greater uncertainty into the estimates of health effects. For example, increased temperature could increase the incidence of skin cancer, but it might also alter behavior by reducing the hours spent outdoors. Global climate change may also extend the period of ozone depletion, which would further increase the incidence of skin cancer. Changes in the geographic distribution of pesticide use resulting from climate change could introduce adverse health effects in some regions and reduce them in others. Similarly, shifts in the geographic distribution of vectors harboring infectious agents, coupled with impaired immune function, could have a greater impact on infectious diseases than anticipated from ozone depletion alone.

Terrestrial Ecosystems

- **Interaction of ultraviolet radiation with other global climate change factors may affect many ecosystem processes.** Examples of such processes and attributes that may be modified include plant biomass production, plant consumption by herbivores including insects, disease incidence of plants and animals, and changes in species abundance and composition. In these and other studies there is a need for long-term experiments.

- **A meta-analysis, with quantitative and statistical information has been used to assess how well overall research predicts common trends and results from different species of plants from experiments conducted outdoors using UV lamp systems.** This analysis showed that of the physiological and morphological traits, overall significance of elevated UV-B was found for decreased plant height and leaf area, increased phenolic compounds and sometimes reduced shoot mass.

- **Fungi and bacteria exposed to sunlight can be directly damaged by enhanced UV-B.** The species composition and biodiversity of bacteria and fungi growing on plants can be changed by UV-B. Biodiversity can be either increased or decreased. For pathogens, elevated UV-B can either increase or decrease the severity of disease development in plants.

- **Exposure of plants to enhanced UV-B can result in altered disease and herbivory intensity.** UV-B often decreases the intensity of insect herbivory and this likely involves plant tissue chemical changes, such as altered phenolic chemistry. The influence of UV-B on pathogen attack on plants can involve both changes in host plant chemistry and direct effects on pathogens. This can either increase, or decrease pathogen attack in different species of plants.

- **Common higher plant responses to elevated UV-B may be lessened by elevated CO_2.** In cases where enhanced UV-B reduces plant growth (height, leaf area and sometimes shoot mass), elevated CO_2 can often overcome these reductions.

- **Water limitation may decrease the sensitivity of some plants to enhanced UV-B.** Plants, especially those of agricultural use, experiencing drought stress are often less responsive to enhanced UV-B. Plants from some environments, such as Mediterranean scrub vegetation, may be more tolerant to drought stress if exposed to elevated UV-B.

- **The effects of UV-B on plant growth reductions are often accompanied by greater DNA damage.** UV-B can affect several critical macromolecules, such as nucleic acids, proteins and lipids. The mechanisms that mediate growth inhibition by UV-B under natural conditions are still poorly understood. However, correlative evidence suggests that DNA damage may play a significant role.

- **Increasing temperatures can promote repair of UV-B damage to DNA, although combining extreme temperatures and enhanced UV-B can cause unexpected results.** DNA damage is repaired more effectively if not limited by low temperatures. Thus, repair is promoted by warming under certain circumstances, and this may lessen the inhibitory effects of UV-B on plant growth. Some responses to extreme temperatures will be modified in unexpected ways by enhanced UV-B; for example, there is evidence for substantially increased frost sensitivity of some subarctic heath species. There is a need for further research in this area in relation to climatic change trends.

Aquatic Ecosystems

Recent results continue to confirm the general consensus that solar UV negatively affects aquatic organisms. Reductions in productivity, impaired reproduction and development and increased mutation rate have been shown for phytoplankton, fish eggs and larvae, zooplankton and primary and secondary consumers exposed to UV radiation. UV-B related decreases in biomass productivity are relayed through all levels of the food web, possibly resulting in reduced food production for humans, reduced sink capacity for atmospheric carbon dioxide, as well as changes in species composition and ecosystem integrity.

- **It is at the ecosystem level where assessments of anthropogenic climate change and UV-related effects are interrelated and where there is the potential for both antagonistic and synergistic effects**. Recent studies have shown that these changes may lead to loss of ecosystem resilience. In some aquatic ecosystems the onset of spring phytoplankton blooms and spawning in invertebrates and vertebrates coincides with dramatic ozone depletion as well as shifts in several climate-related parameters.

- **Polar ecosystems are particularly sensitive to change, because the freeze/thaw boundary applies critical limits to subsequent environmental responses** including: air and water temperature; the timing, extent and duration of ice and snow cover; changes in the surface albedo; changes in water column colored dissolved organic matter (CDOM) concentrations; and the level of solar radiation and the extent of its penetration. Such changes, which may be driven by climate variability, may be more important for UV-B exposure levels and spectral balance between UV-B and visible radiation than ozone depletion.

- **Solar UV penetrating the top layers of the water column markedly affects zooplankton, as well as larval stages of primary and secondary consumers.** The effect of solar UV is strongly modified by other environmental factors, such as variability in cloud cover, water temperature, mutual shading in algal blooms and depth of mixing layer. Although the primary causes for a decline in fish and shellfish populations are predation and poor food supply for larvae, over-fishing of adults coupled with increased water temperature, pollution and disease, and exposure to increased UV-B radiation may contribute to that decline. For amphibians, climate-induced reductions in water depth at sites where eggs are laid have caused a high mortality of embryos due to increased exposure to solar UV-B and subsequent vulnerability to infection.

- **In addition to increasing solar UV-B radiation, aquatic ecosystems are confronted with other environmental stress factors including increased nutrient input, pollution, acidification and global climate change.** In turn, climate change will result in temperature and sea level change, shifts in the timing and extent of sea ice cover, changes in salinity and altered stratification of the water column, and wave climate and ocean circulation. These effects will be linked by pronounced feedback mechanisms, which are not yet completely understood. The resulting complex changes are likely to have significant impacts that will vary both spatially and temporally.

Biogeochemical cycles

- **Global warming and enhanced UV-B radiation interact to affect a range of biogeochemical processes.** On land, warming increases microbial activity, nutrient cycling, and greenhouse gas emissions from soils, whereas increased UV-B can retard or accelerate these processes. In aquatic systems, warming also increases microbial activity. The exposure of organisms to UV is amplified by increased water stratification and changed mixing of surface waters that are related to global climate change.

- **Interactions between UV-B radiation and increased ocean temperatures affect sulfur emissions that influence the balance between incoming and outgoing radiation in the marine atmosphere.** Enhancements of sulfur transfer from the ocean to the atmosphere are linked to changes in ocean surface layer mixing, induced by global warming, increased UV-B exposure, and UV-B inhibition of bacterial growth. Oceanic sulfur emissions can influence cloud characteristics that in turn affect radiation in the marine atmosphere.

- **There is new evidence that UV accelerates decomposition of the colored organic matter that runs off from land into the ocean.** Previously, it was believed that land-derived organic matter was mainly lost by biological oxidation and burial in coastal zones where sedimentation is high. Now, it is known that UV plays a central role in the removal of this organic matter.

- **The exchange of trace gases between terrestrial systems and the atmosphere is influenced by changes in UV-B.** Additional research on UV-induced carbon monoxide production from dead plant matter in terrestrial ecosystems indicates that the global annual carbon monoxide input from this source to the atmosphere is significant. Solar UV-induced nitrogen oxide production has been observed in snowpacks located at diverse sites in Greenland, Antarctica, Canada and the northern United States. The UV-driven emissions of carbon monoxide and nitrogen oxides may change local concentrations of tropospheric ozone.

- **Important components of the terrestrial nitrogen cycle are sensitive to enhanced UV-B radiation.** In the Northern Arctic, where unavailable nitrogen severely limits plant growth, nitrogen fixation by free-living blue-green algae was retarded by enhanced UV-B. Potential nitrogen fixation by symbiotic algae in a sub-Arctic lichen species was also reduced in the long term. In addition, enhanced UV-B increased nitrogen immobilized by soil bacteria in the Subarctic, making nitrogen less available for plant production.

- **Enhanced UV-B radiation accelerates the decomposition of colored dissolved organic matter (CDOM) entering the sea via terrestrial runoff**, thus having important effects on oceanic carbon cycle dynamics. UV-induced changes in visible light absorption by CDOM can affect the accuracy of estimates of coastal oceanic productivity based on remote sensing of ocean color.

- **Several important sources of natural ozone depleting halogenated substances have been identified in the terrestrial biosphere and explain deficits in global budgets.** Calculations of global atmospheric budgets of methyl bromide and methyl chloride indicate large missing sources. Recent experimental data indicate that natural emissions of these gases from terrestrial ecosystems, particularly salt marshes, account for a significant part of these missing sources. Emissions appear to result from an active process strongly related to diurnal incident light levels. Methyl chloride and methyl bromide participate in ozone-depleting processes.

Air Quality

- **The effect of stratospheric ozone depletion on tropospheric ozone trends is significant, but small compared to the anthropogenic emissions in air-polluted areas.** Model and experimental studies suggest that the impacts of stratospheric ozone depletion on tropospheric ozone are different at different altitudes and for different chemical regimes. A measurable effect on concentrations will be expected only in regions where local emissions make minor contributions. The vertical distribution of NO_x, as well as the emission of volatile organic carbons and abundance of water vapour, are important influencing factors.

- **Risks from the effects on humans and the environment of trifluoroacetic acid (TFA) and chlorodifluoroacetic acid (CDFA) produced by atmospheric degradation of HCFCs and HFCs are judged to be minimal.** TFA has been measured in rain, rivers, lakes, and oceans, the ultimate sink for these and related compounds. Anthropogenic sources of TFA other than degradation of HCFCs and HFCs have been identified.

- **Interactions between ozone depletion and climate change will have an impact on tropospheric hydroxyl (OH) radical concentration, the "cleaning" agent of the troposphere.** Stratospheric ozone depletion leads to an increase in concentration of the OH radical in the troposphere. Increases in the concentration of gases such as volatile organic compounds will act as a sink for OH in the troposphere. Aerosols can also act to reduce UV-B in some circumstances and hence reduce OH. Changes in cloudiness and temperature will also have an effect. All of these can be influenced by climate change. The net change in air quality and chemical composition in the troposphere will depend on the balance between these effects.

- **Changes in the aerosol content of the atmosphere resulting from global warming may affect ozone photolysis rates and hence reduce tropospheric ozone concentrations.** Model and field studies show that a reduction in the ozone photolysis rate and ozone production in the troposphere is to be expected in the presence of increased absorbing aerosols in the troposphere.

Materials

- **Climate change is likely to modify the rates of UV-induced degradation of natural and synthetic materials.** In regions of the world with high UV-B levels, increase in the ambient temperature will have a marked influence in increasing the rate of light-induced degradation of materials. This is particularly true of plastics and wood used in building construction. Increased humidity can also have a similar effect on some materials when coupled with high UV, especially at the high ambient temperatures.

- **New varieties of commodity plastics with improved properties are emerging and these too can be stabilized effectively with existing light stabilizers.** Recent improvements in catalysts have lead to the discovery of metallocene plastics (polyethylenes and polypropylenes) that have improved properties including slightly better UV resistance compared to the conventional varieties. Commonly used conventional light stabilizers were found to be effective in stabilizing these varieties of thermoplastics as well.

- **Recent data suggest synergistic improvement in light-stabilizer effectiveness when mixtures of conventional HALS stabilizers are used in plastics.** Hindered amine light stabilizers (HALS) are commonly used as a light stabilizer with common plastics. Mixtures of two or more of these were recently reported to perform even better as light stabilizers of plastics. Increasing the light stabilizer effectiveness is important to minimize the cost of stabilization of plastics formulations against the damage caused by UV radiation and climate change.

CHAPTER 1. CHANGES IN BIOLOGICALLY ACTIVE ULTRAVIOLET RADIATION REACHING THE EARTH'S SURFACE

R. L. Mckenzie[a], L. O. Björn[b], A. Bais[c], And M. Ilyas[d]

[a] *National Institute of Water and Atmospheric Research, NIWA Lauder, PB 50061 Omakau, Central Otago, New Zealand*

[b] *Department of Cell and Organism Biology, Lund University, Sölvegatan 35, SE-22362, Lund, Sweden*

[c] *Laboratory of Atmospheric Physics, Aristotle University of Thessaloniki, Campus Box 149, GR-54006 Thessaloniki, Greece*

[d] *Sheikh Tahir Astro-Geophysical Centre, University of Science of Malaysia, 11800 USM Penang, Malaysia.*

Summary

Since publication of the 1998 UNEP Assessment, there has been continued rapid expansion of the literature on UV-B radiation. Many measurements have demonstrated the inverse relationship between column ozone amount and UV radiation, and in a few cases long-term increases due to ozone decreases have been identified. The quantity, quality and availability of ground-based UV measurements relevant to assessing the environmental impacts of ozone changes continue to improve. Recent studies have contributed to delineating regional and temporal differences due to aerosols, clouds, and ozone. Improvements in radiative transfer modelling capability now enable more accurate characterization of clouds, snow-cover, and topographical effects.

A standardized scale for reporting UV to the public has gained wide acceptance. There has been increased use of satellite data to estimate geographic variability and trends in UV. Progress has been made in assessing the utility of satellite retrievals of UV radiation by comparison with measurements at the Earth's surface. Global climatologies of UV radiation are now available on the Internet.

Anthropogenic aerosols play a more important role in attenuating UV irradiances than has been assumed previously, and this will have implications for the accuracy of UV retrievals from satellite data. Progress has been made inferring historical levels of UV radiation using measurements of ozone (from satellites or from ground-based networks) in conjunction with measurements of total solar radiation obtained from extensive meteorological networks.

We cannot yet be sure whether global ozone has reached a minimum. Atmospheric chlorine concentrations are beginning to decrease. However, bromine concentrations are still increasing. While these halogen concentrations remain high, the ozone layer remains vulnerable to further depletion from events such as volcanic eruptions that inject material into the stratosphere. Interactions between global warming and ozone depletion could delay ozone recovery by several years, and this topic remains an area of intense research interest.

Future changes in greenhouse gases will affect the future evolution of ozone through chemical, radiative, and dynamic processes. In this highly coupled system, an evaluation of the relative importance of these processes is difficult; studies are ongoing. A reliable assessment of these effects on total column ozone is limited by uncertainties in lower stratospheric response to these changes.

At several sites, changes in UV differ from those expected from ozone changes alone, possibly as a result of long-term changes in aerosols, snow cover, or clouds. This indicates a possible interaction between climate change and UV radiation. Cloud reflectance measured by satellite has shown a long-term increase at some locations, especially in the Antarctic region, but also in Central Europe, which would tend to reduce the UV radiation.

Even with the expected decreases in atmospheric chlorine, it will be several years before the beginning of an ozone recovery can be unambiguously identified at individual locations. Because UV-B is more variable than ozone, any identification of its recovery would be further delayed.

Ozone Changes

Since the previous assessment in 1998,[3, 4] there have been improvements in assimilating global ozone data from several sources, resulting in a more cohesive picture of how ozone has changed since the early 1990s when one of the few satellite sensors measuring long-term changes in global ozone failed (NASA's Total Ozone Mapping Spectrometer, TOMS, on the Nimbus 7 satellite). These re-analyses[6] show that the pattern of change since 1994 has been essentially a continuation of that before the eruption of Mt Pinatubo. Ozone changes continue to be insignificant in the tropics. At mid-latitudes, ozone depletion appears to be levelling off. In the Arctic, ozone has been highly variable, and in Antarctica it has remained similar to that during the 1990s. Because the ozone changes have not been monotonic, and with the expected future recovery, a linear trend analysis of ozone change is no longer appropriate.

The Antarctic ozone hole has continued to appear each spring. In 2000 its area, defined as the region where ozone is less than 220 DU, reached a record maximum size of 29 million km^2 (about twice the size of the Antarctic continental land mass), with a maximum depleted mass of 57 megatons (Mt) but it then rapidly dissipated much earlier than usual. During the spring of 2001, the area and depleted mass were 25 million km^2 and 54 Mt respectively (slightly less than the record values of the previous year). As in recent years, the hole persisted well into November, leading to potentially larger UV radiation effects (Chapter 3).[7-9] The Antarctic ozone minimum in recent years has been about 90-100 DU, which is less than 40% of the minima typical for Antarctica in the late 1970s, before the ozone hole first developed. The minimum recorded ozone column occurred in 1993 when other factors (e.g., aerosols from the volcanic eruption of Mt Pinatubo) contributed to a particularly severe depletion of ozone.

In the Arctic, ozone depletion remains less severe than in the Antarctic, with minimum ozone amounts typically in the range 200-250 DU. The extent of ozone depletion in the Arctic is more dependent on year-to year variability in wind patterns. Depletions are more severe when the Arctic stratosphere is cold in the winter/spring. In the cold spring of 2000, the accumulated loss of ozone near 20 km altitude, where ozone depletion was most severe, reached roughly 20% by mid-February. This is a moderate chemical loss compared to Arctic winters during the last decade, when ozone losses as high as 70% have been observed at some altitudes.

Outside the Polar Regions, ozone losses are less severe. Relative to 1980, the 1997-2000 losses in total ozone are about 6% at southern mid-latitudes on a year-round basis. At northern mid-latitudes the ozone losses are about 4% in winter/spring, and 2% in summer/autumn. In the tropics, there have been no significant changes in column zone. The annually averaged global ozone loss is approximately 3%.[6] These changes in ozone are broadly consistent with the changes predicted by atmospheric models.

There remain unresolved differences between satellite and ground based measurements of ozone. For example, the TOMS instruments currently overestimate ozone at high latitudes, especially in the Southern Hemisphere summer.[10]

At any single observation site, the year-to-year variability in ozone hinders our ability to detect long-term trends in ozone. Similarly, it has been demonstrated that any detection of future ozone recovery (and of consequent UV recovery) will not be possible for several years or even decades. Mid-latitudes of the Southern hemisphere appear to offer the earliest possibility of detection of recovery.[11] To detect global trends in ozone, it is necessary to use large spatial averaging such as from the global network of ground-based spectrometers, or from satellite data.

Polar ozone-depleting processes are now better understood, but uncertainties remain about ozone depletion processes at mid-latitudes. These processes could influence how global warming affects future ozone depletion. The importance of long-term changes in dynamics, possibly forced by changes in climate, in driving ozone change is now better appreciated.

Factors Affecting UV Radiation Received at the Earth's Surface

Variability in ozone is not the dominant factor affecting UV-B radiation received at the surface. The dominant factor is the angle of the Sun's rays through the atmosphere. This angle is often given in terms of the solar zenith angle (SZA - which is the angle between the vertical and the center of the solar disc). When the SZA is small, the light path through the atmosphere is small, so absorption is minimised. For this reason the maximum UV-B irradiances occur in the tropics at times when the Sun is directly overhead. In these regions ozone amounts are also relatively low. At mid- and high latitudes the UV-B irradiances in winter are much smaller than in the summer. Consequently even with extremely low ozone amounts, as under the springtime Antarctic ozone hole, UV-B irradiances only rarely reach the levels that are normal in the tropics.[7, 12] Variability in cloud cover is the second major factor influencing surface UV-B. The importance of these factors is illustrated clearly by results from a network of erythemal UV sensors that cover a wide range of latitudes in Argentina,[13] and from global analyses based on satellite data (e.g., Figure 1-4).

The effect on surface UV of ozone depletion depends on the wavelength range of interest, shorter wavelengths in the UV-B region being more sensitive. For many processes of environmental interest, a reduction in ozone of 1% leads to an increase in damaging radiation of 0.2 to 2 %, depending on the wavelength-dependence of the sensitivity, as described by the so-called Radiation Amplification Factor (or RAF).[14]

Other factors affecting surface UV radiation include seasonal variations in Sun-Earth separation, extinctions by aerosols, altitude, and surface reflectivity (albedo). Several of these are discussed later.

UV Information to the Public

There have been significant improvements in the delivery of UV information to the public. An internationally standardized UV Index has been defined,[15] by which information on UV intensities is disseminated to the public (see box).

UV Index

The internationally agreed UV Index scale is defined in terms of the erythemally weighted UV irradiance (i.e. "skin-reddening", or "sunburning" irradiance). The erythemal weighting function, which is applied to the spectrum, involves an arbitrary normalization to unity at wavelengths shorter than 298 nm, so erythemally weighted UV is not strictly defined in terms of an SI unit. Furthermore, when UV information was first provided to the public, another normalization (a multiplication by 40 m^2/W) was applied to provide a number, called the UV Index. With this normalization, the maximum UV Index in Canada (where the unit was first used) is about 10 for normal ozone conditions.

UV Index = $40\int I(\lambda)\, w(\lambda)\, d\lambda$,

where

λ is the wavelength in nm,

$I(\lambda)$ is the irradiance in W $m^{-2}nm^{-1}$, and

$w(\lambda)$ is the erythemal weighting function

    which is defined as:

$w(\lambda) = 1.0$ for $250 < \lambda \leq 298$ nm

$w(\lambda) = 10^{0.094(298-\lambda)}$ for $298 < \lambda \leq 328$ nm

$w(\lambda) = 10^{0.015(139-\lambda)}$ for $328 < \lambda \leq 400$ nm

$w(\lambda) = 0.0$ for $\lambda > 400$ nm

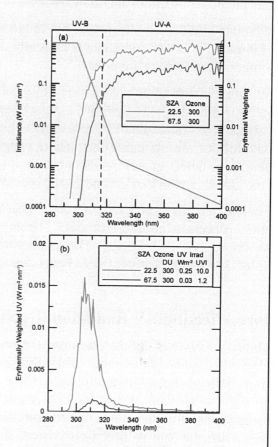

The upper panel shows the spectral UV irradiance for two sun angles; with an ozone column amount of 300 DU. The erythemal weighting function is shown on the right axis. The lower panel shows the corresponding spectra of erythemally weighted UV. The UV Index is the integral under these curves multiplied by 40 m^2/W.

Although there are uncertainties about the biological applicability of this erythemal action spectrum, its advantage is that it is mathematically defined and therefore its detailed shape is unambiguous. This is important in the UV region where the steeply sloping spectrum spans several orders of magnitude. Although the UV Index was developed to represent damage to human skin, it may be applied to other processes, since many biological UV effects have similar action spectra. Since the UV Index is based on the erythemal action spectrum, its sensitivity to ozone change is the same as for erythema. For small reductions in ozone, the change in UV Index can be estimated by the radiative amplification factor, where for each 1% reduction in ozone the UV Index increases by approximately 1.1 % (i.e., the RAF for erythema is 1.1, as detailed elsewhere).[14] However, this formulation underestimates the change for large changes in ozone. In that case the power law formulation of the sensitivity is required, as noted previously.[14]

In reality, the UV Index is an open-ended scale. In the tropics, at unpolluted mid-latitudes in the Southern Hemisphere, and at high altitudes it often exceeds a value of 12.[13, 16, 17] Outside the protection of the Earth's atmosphere the UV Index is ~300 (depending on the lower wavelength limit of the integration). To calculate the UV Index, estimates of ozone are required as inputs to a radiative transfer model. Atmospheric dynamical forecasts are sometimes used to predict how the ozone will change between the measurement time and the prediction time. Corrections to account for reductions by clouds are applied by some reporting agencies, but not all. The use of satellite derived ozone and cloud fields (see below) has improved the timely delivery of UV Index information to the public.

Measurements of UV at the Surface

Ground Based Measurements

There has been a significant improvement in the geographical coverage of instruments to measure UV,[13] and in their quality control and quality assurance. The UV data are now more readily available through international data archives such as the World Ozone and UV Data Centre (WOUDC, see http://www.msc-smc.ec.gc.ca/woudc/) in Canada, and the European Database created through EU research projects (EDUCE, see http://www.muk.uni-hannover.de/EDUCE). In combination with radiative transfer models, these measurements have confirmed the expected inverse correlation between ozone and UV-B. In addition, the effects of other variables are now better understood.[6]

Data Availability, Quality Control and Quality Assurance

Recent international intercomparisons between spectroradiometers have demonstrated agreement within limits comparable to the uncertainties in maintaining irradiance standards via lamp transfer standards.[18] Progress has been made using Langley analyses of spectra to derive a calibration based on solar extraterrestrial spectra.[19, 20] This procedure avoids the need for radiometric calibrations via quartz halogen lamps (such as 1000 W FEL lamps calibrated by the National Institute of Standards and Technology (NIST)), which are difficult to maintain and use. However, it has not yet been successfully applied at the shorter wavelengths in the UV-B region at many sites.

Results from more recently established UV monitoring networks (e.g., in Europe and South America) are contributing to the characterisation of geographic differences.[13, 21-26]

Altitude Effects

The effect of altitude on UV irradiance has been better quantified. In practice the altitude effect depends on differences in surface albedo and boundary layer extinctions by aerosols and tropospheric ozone, so it cannot be represented by a single number. Even when these effects can be ignored, it has been found that the altitude effect is a strong function of the solar zenith angle and wavelength. For erythemally weighted UV, irradiances increase by approximately 5 to 7 percent per kilometer (for the same overhead ozone column), with the greatest increase occurring at SZA ~ 60-70°. To correctly model the effect at Mauna Loa Observatory, it was necessary to consider the effects of sky irradiance scattered from below the observatory.[17] Recent measurements in Europe, which included aerosol and albedo effects, showed much larger and more variable increases.[27] Aircraft measurements in the free troposphere over Greece have revealed larger altitude gradients than at pristine sites.[28]

Surface Albedo Effects

The presence of snow cover in the surrounding area can increase UV irradiances appreciably,[29, 30] even when the snow is several kilometers away from the observing site.[31, 32] Furthermore, increases in effective surface albedo due to reflectances from air below the observing site can also be important.[17] An implication of these findings is that three-dimensional radiative transfer models are needed to accurately model UV irradiances in mountainous regions. Codes suitable for this purpose are being developed and are becoming available.[33-36]

Cloud Effects

Cloud effects are important. The mean attenuation of UV-B by clouds is typically in the range 15-30%. There have been improvements in the measurement of clouds from automated imagers at the Earth's surface. Progress has been made relating these cloud images to satellite-derived cloud patterns and to the UV radiation received at the Earth's surface.[37] There is evidence for long-term changes in cloud in some regions, as discussed later.[38]

Aerosol Effects

Aerosols can have a marked effect on the UV-B radiation received at the surface. In some locations aerosols can scatter more than 50% of UV-B radiation out of the direct beam.[39] In Mexico City, poor air quality has been shown to be responsible for reductions of ~20% in erythemal UV in the city centre compared with the suburbs.[40] The optical properties of aerosols, as measured in the Eastern USA, have been shown to have a strong impact on UV-B at the surface. In extreme cases during the summertime, aerosol extinctions can result in reduction of the UV Index by up to 5 units, representing reductions of approximately 50%. More typically however, the deduced reductions are less than 20%.[41]

Recent work suggests that anthropogenic aerosols (e.g., from urban pollution) that absorb in the UV-B region may play a more important role in attenuating UV-B irradiances than has been assumed previously.[42] Measurements in the Los Angeles region have shown that near-surface absorption is much larger in the UV-B than in the visible region. Direct measurements of aerosol absorptions and single scattering albedos of aerosols will be helpful in resolving the importance of aerosols.

Comparisons between satellite-derived UV and measurements from four cross-calibrated ground-based spectrometers have revealed inconsistencies in satellite-derived UV. The discrepancy is probably related to the inability of the satellite sensors to correct for extinctions in the lowermost region of the atmosphere (i.e., in the "boundary layer"). Only at the pristine site was there good agreement within the experimental errors. At more polluted sites, the satellite-derived UV estimations were too large.[43]

These findings, and the much larger altitude gradients of UV reported in polluted regions, suggest that boundary layer extinctions from man made pollutants may be more important attenuators of UV than has previously been recognised.

As discussed later, the effects of urban pollution may extend over wide geographical areas. Recurring episodes of biomass burning, which contribute to increased particulates and altered gas composition, can lead to reduced UV-B at the surface and in the troposphere, [22, 44, 45] but with attendant increases in other health risk factors.

Actinic Fluxes

For many biological and photochemical processes, including atmospheric photochemistry, irradiances falling on a horizontal surface are not the most relevant quantity. It has been shown that the irradiance on surfaces of different orientations can differ markedly from that on a horizontal surface. In particular for surfaces directed towards the sun, or for vertical surface facing the sun at large SZA, irradiances can be significantly greater than on a horizontal surface.[46, 47] For many applications, the target is insensitive to the direction of incoming radiation, and for those cases actinic flux (sometimes called scalar flux, or scalar irradiance, or fluence rate) rather than cosine-weighted irradiance may be more appropriate. However, such measurements have not been generally available until quite recently.[48, 49] Progress has been made in converting irradiance to actinic flux and this work offers the prospect of deriving historical changes from the more extensive database of irradiance measurements.[50-52]

Long-Term Changes in UV Measured from the Ground

The complicated spatial and temporal distributions of the variables that affect ultraviolet radiation at the surface (for example, clouds, airborne fine particles, snow cover, sea ice cover, and total ozone) continue to limit the ability to describe surface ultraviolet radiation on the global scale, whether through measurements or model-based approaches. The spectral surface ultraviolet data records, which started in the early 1990s, are still too short and too variable to permit the calculation of statistically significant long-term (i.e., multi-decadal) trends.

Many studies have demonstrated the inverse correlation between ozone and UV. However, the detection of long-term trends in UV is even more problematic than the detection of ozone trends because in addition to its dependence on ozone, UV radiation at the surface is sensitive to clouds, aerosols, and surface albedo, all of which can exhibit large variability.

In Moscow, changes in atmospheric opacity from clouds and/or aerosols were probably responsible for a reported gradual decrease in UV from the 1960s to the mid 1980s, followed by an increase back to 1960s levels by the late 1990s.[53]

One of the longest time series of UV-B data available is that from Robertson-Berger (RB) meter measurements from Belsk, Poland. An analysis of data over the period 1976 to 1997 in all weather conditions shows an increase in sunburning UV of 6.1 ± 2.9 percent per decade, which is attributed mainly to ozone change.[54]

An increase in peak UV in response to decreasing ozone has been detected in New Zealand, as shown in Figure 1-1[5, 55] However, the trend has not continued in the last two summers. In these two summers, ozone amounts at this site have been slightly higher than in the summer of 1998/99. Furthermore, both years were rather cloudy over the summer period that is most critical for this analysis. This shows that year-to-year variability in cloud cover can have a significant effect even for peak irradiances.

A 10-year record of UV measurements in Thessaloniki, Greece indicates significant increases in erythemal UV irradiance and in irradiance at the lower UV-B wavelengths (e.g., 305 nm) which is partly caused by ozone decreases and partly by the cleaning of the atmosphere by air-pollution abatement measures.[56] Other medium term dynamical effects, such as the Quasi Biennial Oscillation (QBO) in atmospheric wind patterns with a period of about 2 years, are also significant.[57, 58] Long term changes and year-to-year variability have also been observed in Antarctica.[59]

Broadband UV-B monitors are generally less suitable for trend detection since their calibration is less direct and the quality assurance of long-term calibrations is more problematic. Recently it has been shown that the spectral response functions of some broad band instruments in common usage for measuring sunburning UV are sensitive to relative humidity.[60] The largest sensitivity is in the UV-A region, where instrument response varies, sometimes reversibly, over time scales of hours.[10] The implication of this finding is that in instruments where desiccant is not replenished regularly, readings may have large time-dependent errors between calibrations.

Inferring UV Changes from Indirect Methods

A limitation on trend detection is the relatively short time period for which suitable UV measurements are available. However, methods have been developed to estimate the effects of

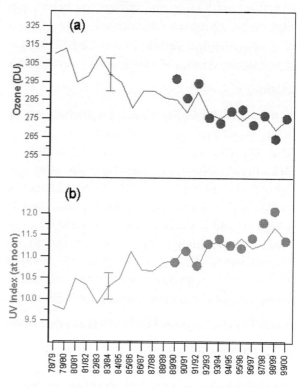

Figure 1-1 (a) Mean ozone (Dobson Units, 1 DU = 2.69×10^{16} molecule cm^{-2}), and (b) estimated UV Index at Lauder New Zealand for the summers of 1978-79 through 1999-2000. Summer is defined as the period from December through February. The solid line in (a) shows the changes in summertime ozone that have occurred since the 1970s. The solid line in (b) shows the deduced changes in clear-sky UV expected from these changes in ozone. The dots (from 1989-90 on) show measured values of ozone and the summertime peak UV Index, both derived from the UV spectroradiometer.[5]

clouds on UV from total solar radiation measurements (i.e., pyranometer data) and so to derive long-term estimates of UV using historical pyranometer data in conjunction with ozone measurements. Initially these used ozone data from satellite, so enabling estimation of long-term changes from 1978 to the present.

A recent study of this kind in Canada used a longer time series of ozone data from a network of ground-based instruments to derive trends from the mid-1960s at Toronto, Churchill and Edmonton.[1] Trends in UV for individual wavelengths and weighted spectral intervals have been determined for the period from 1965 to 1997 (see Figure 1-2).

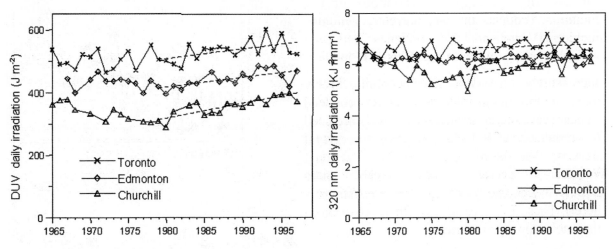

Figure 1-2 Mean summer (May-August) daily UV irradiation for Toronto, Edmonton, and Churchill, Canada.[1] Left Panel: damaging UV radiation (DUV), as defined by the American Conference of Governmental Industrial Hygienists – National Institute of Occupational Safety and Health (defined in [1]). Right panel: 320 nm, which is insensitive to ozone change.

Trends in the daily total values and noontime values are essentially the same, and trends at wavelengths of 310 nm or less and for the erythemally weighted UV are all statistically significant at the 2-sigma level. In addition to the estimation of past hour-by-hour UV irradiance, the data can be used to quantify and distinguish between trends in UV that are caused by factors other than long-term changes in total ozone. Churchill had statistically significant trends at all wavelengths, including those with insignificant ozone absorption. The positive trends at these wavelengths are due to the combined effect of an increase of days with snow cover and a decrease in hours of cloudiness that occurred at Churchill over the period (1979-1997). Although the increases in damaging UV were rather modest, there was a more marked increase in the occurrence of extreme events such as the number of hours that the UV Index exceeded a threshold value (see Figure 1-3).

Statistical methods, using pyranometer data in conjunction with ozone measurements, have also been applied in other geographical regions to deduce long-term increases in surface UV in several parts of Europe[61, 62] as well as in the Arctic and Antarctic.[59] These increases are in agreement with those expected from changes in satellite-measured ozone. At the South Pole, the deduced springtime increases from 1979 to 1996 in 300 nm radiation are ~300% during spring, while at Barrow Alaska corresponding increases of ~100% have been inferred. Increases in biologically weighted UV would however be much less than those at 300 nm.

By selecting for clear sky data only, large statistically significant increases have been reported over a 30-year period in Bavaria. This was achieved by deriving statistical relationships between UV and ozone and using diffuse/direct ratios from pyranometers to characterize aerosol extinction classes.[63] Significant increases at the longer wavelengths indicate that not all of the change is due to ozone depletion.

Estimations of UV from Satellite Observations Satellite methods provide the greatest potential for assessing geographical variations in UV radiation. Products that are currently available include UV dose and UV irradiances. Both are available with or without the effects of clouds.

Increasingly these data are becoming freely available through the Internet, and are produced in near real time. In some cases models are used to predict ozone and cloud patterns for several days into the future (e.g., by NOAA, National Weather Service see web site http://www.cpc.ncep.noaa.gov/products/stratosp here/). These UV forecasts are then provided to the public through the media.

From these data, global climatologies of UV, such as that shown in Figure 1-4, can be derived. The dominant feature here is the strong latitudinal gradient, with highest doses of UV occurring in the tropics. As noted below, however, questions remain about the absolute accuracy of these products.

Methods have recently been developed to generate regional-scale maps of surface UV radiation, including cloud effects, using satellite data of higher spatial and temporal resolution, along with ancillary geophysical data.[64]

Measurements from satellite also provide the potential for deriving accurate trends in UV since only a single sensor needs to be characterized for the lifetime of that satellite instrument, and since the global coverage offers

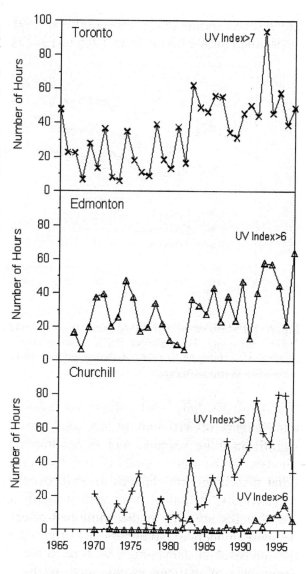

Figure 1-3 Number of hours when the hourly mean UV index exceeded 7 at Toronto, 6 at Edmonton, 5 and 6 at Churchill.[1]

the potential to average out variability caused by changing cloud patterns. However, the insensitivity to changes in tropospheric extinctions currently limits the ability of satellite data products to be used in trend studies.

In one study, satellite-derived estimates of erythemal UV incident in Australia showed larger increases in the tropics than at mid-latitudes over the period 1979-1992, due to the combined influence of changes in ozone and clouds.[65] Another study of satellite-derived erythemal UV trends in the Northern Hemisphere (1979-91) showed marked regional differences. At latitudes 30-40 °N, trends were larger over oceans, while at 40-60 °N they were larger over continental areas. The largest trends were seen over northeast Asia where they exceeded 10% per decade for May-August.[66]

A study using satellite data has demonstrated that long-term changes in cloud cover have occurred in some regions.[67] For example, according to this analysis, cloud cover has increased in parts of Antarctica, and this would have suppressed some of the increase in UV expected from ozone loss over the same period.[6, 67, 68]

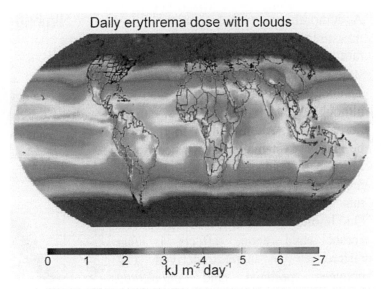

Daily erythrema dose with clouds

Figure 1-4 Global climatology (1979-1992) of mean daily erythemal UV dose (from the NCAR web site http://www.acd.ucar.edu/TUV/).

Comparisons between UV Measured at the Ground and from Satellite

The determination of surface UV from satellite observations is essentially a model calculation. Key atmospheric variables such as ozone and cloud reflectance, which are available from the satellite-borne sensors, are used as input parameters to the model calculation. In the case of satellite instruments that measure backscattered ultraviolet radiation, one of the difficulties is the insensitivity to radiation that penetrates deep into the troposphere. Consequently, it is necessary to make assumptions about the radiative transfer in the boundary layer. In this region, local differences in ozone, clouds, and aerosols can be important. One example of these difficulties is that satellite-derived ozone amounts can be overestimated in regions where the tropospheric ozone component is lower than assumed in the retrieval algorithm. This is most likely the cause of the overestimation[10] of satellite-derived ozone in the southern hemisphere summer. This ozone error would tend to translate to lower than expected estimates of surface UV. A second issue relates to the assumption that the complement of the reflected component is transmitted to the surface. With complex broken clouds, three-dimensional effects also become important, particularly in analyses at high spatial and temporal resolution. A further limitation of polar orbiting satellites is that there is generally only one overpass per day, whereas studies with geo-stationary satellite data have demonstrated that several cloud images over the midday period are desirable for determining UV dose.[64] Finally, satellite sensors are not yet capable of measuring extinctions from the ubiquitous non-absorbing aerosols in the boundary layer. As discussed above, these aerosol extinctions can have a marked effect on UV at the surface.

There have been several intercomparisons between UV measured at the ground and satellite-derived UV.[69-71] Difficulties in these studies include (1) uncertainties in the ground-based measurements, and (2) the assumption that the specific ground location is representative of the entire satellite pixel, which typically covers a much larger geographical area.

A comprehensive study compared UV measured over several years at four mid-latitude sites using cross-calibrated, state-of-the-art spectrometer systems.[43] The conclusion from that study was that although broad patterns of UV can be derived from satellite data there could be large systematic differences (see Figure 1-5). In some regions, UV measured at the ground is ~40% less than that derived from satellite data. One implication from these tropospheric aerosol and ozone effects is that differences in satellite-derived UV between polluted and unpolluted locations (e.g., mid northern latitudes versus mid southern latitudes) will be suppressed.

Interactions Between Ozone Depletion and Climate Change

Since the 1998 assessment, there has been an increased awareness of the importance of linkages and feedbacks between climate change (global warming) and ozone depletion.

Surface warming and ozone depletion are different aspects of global change. The former is an increase in surface temperature due to a buildup of radiatively active gases (i.e., gases that

absorb outgoing infra-red radiation), especially CO_2. The latter is primarily due to a release of gases that catalytically destroy ozone, especially chlorine and bromine, from CFCs and halons photolysed in the stratosphere. Some of these linkages are illustrated schematically in Figure 1-6. A complete inventory of the many processes is outside the scope of the present document and is discussed elsewhere,[6, 68] but a few examples are used to illustrate the complexity of these issues.

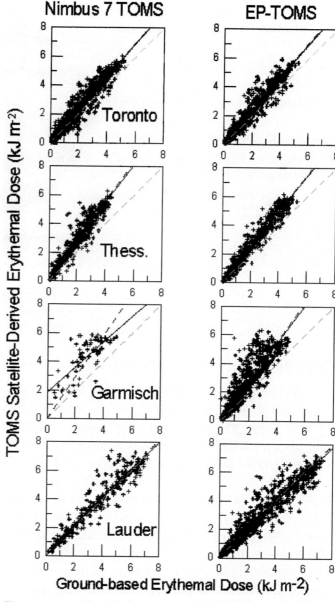

Figure 1-5 Scatter plots of TOMS-derived erythemal UV as a function of UV measured at four sites: Toronto, Canada (43.4°N); Thessaloniki, Greece (40.5°N); Garmisch-Partenkirchen, Germany (47.5°N), and Lauder, New Zealand (45.0°S). Note the more intense UV at the Southern Hemisphere site. The red line is the ideal regression line. The solid black line is the best-fit regression, and dashed black line is the best-fit line through the origin.

The effects of global warming on UV radiation are twofold. The first effect results from global warming influencing total ozone. The second effect results from climate changes that affect UV through influences on other variables such as clouds, aerosols, and snow cover.

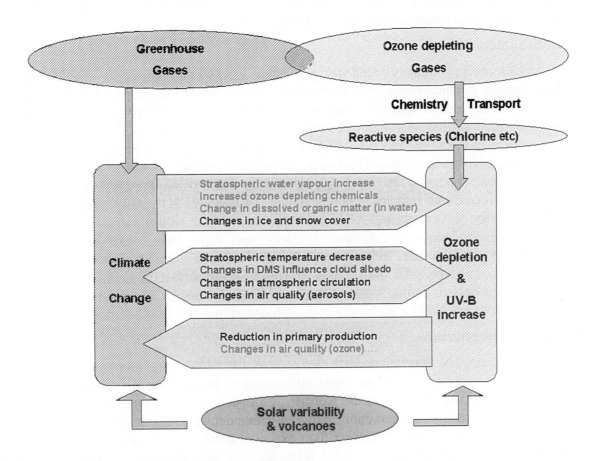

Figure 1-6 Interactions between ozone depletion and climate change. The sense of the interaction is given by the direction of the arrow. For example, the top horizontal arrow shows examples of how Climate Change influences Ozone Depletion and UV-B. Processes that exacerbate the change are in red, processes that ameliorate the change are in blue, and processes that may act both ways are in black (DMS is dimethyl sulphide). Adapted from Clark.[2]

Chemical Interactions

Ozone itself is a minor greenhouse gas, as are the CFCs and their substitutes. Several other gases involved with the chemistry of ozone depletion are also greenhouse active. These include water vapour, methane (CH_4), and nitrous oxide (N_2O), which are increasing and will ultimately lead to increases in stratospheric gases (e.g., NO_2), which catalytically destroy ozone. Some models predict that this could potentially delay any recovery of ozone, and may even lead to increased ozone depletion late in the century.[72, 73] Observed increases in stratospheric NO_2 are larger than the increases in N_2O at the surface, which is thought to be its major source gas.[74, 75] Another chemical feedback is concerned with the decreased stratospheric temperatures that occur as a result of future global warming at the surface. This will tend to slow down the reactions that destroy ozone at mid latitudes, and may thus aid future ozone recovery.[76] However, at high latitudes ozone depletion proceeds much more rapidly through heterogeneous chemistry on the surfaces of crystals composed of ice and acids (i.e., polar stratospheric clouds, or PSCs), which occur only when the temperature is below a critical threshold. Some models have suggested that this feedback could delay the start of any ozone recovery in Polar regions by a decade or more.[77] However, more recent studies predict much shorter delays.[6]

Radiative Interactions

There are also several radiative feedback processes. Increases in temperature can for example lead to changes in cloud cover, rainfall patterns, ice accumulation, surface albedo, and ocean circulation. Furthermore, radiative changes caused by depletion of stratospheric ozone have offset some of the global warming that would have otherwise occurred.[68] In the event of an ozone recovery in the future this would therefore exacerbate future global warming. The direct radiative forcing from changes in UV-B that result from changes in ozone[78] are not significant since only a small fraction of the incoming solar energy falls within the UV-B range. However, changes in UV-B radiation influence photochemical reactions in the troposphere. Models predict a global decrease of tropospheric OH in the future, which would affect the lifetimes of greenhouse gases. Long-term changes in cloudiness have been observed from satellite observations in recent decades, with increases at high latitudes,[67] and decreases in the tropics.[38] Atmospheric models have so far been unable to reproduce this effect, reducing our confidence in the ability of models to predict future changes.[79] Changes in solar output and possible future volcanic eruptions are likely to influence both global warming and ozone depletion.

Dynamical Interactions

Other feedbacks involve interactions with atmospheric dynamics. One numerical climate model predicted that there would be longitudinal differences in the patterns of recovery; with larger ozone depletions being expected in the Northern European sector.[80] It has also been postulated that there may be dynamical interactions between ozone depletion and greenhouse warming that can act synergistically to produce larger than expected trends in both surface temperature and stratospheric ozone.[81, 82] On the other hand, it has also been postulated that changes in dynamics associated with global warming may accelerate the atmospheric removal of CFCs, thus advancing ozone recovery by 5 to 10 years.[76, 83]

Biospherical Feedbacks

Other feedbacks can involve the biosphere (Chapters 4 and 5).[9, 84, 85] For example, increasing UV can reduce the productivity of oceanic phytoplankton. This can produce two feedbacks. Firstly, it reduces the oceanic sink for carbon in atmosphere (production of carbonates which fall to the sea floor). Secondly, it can influence the production of dimethyl sulphide (DMS), which is an important source of condensation nuclei.[85] This, in turn affects cloud-droplet size, cloud-reflectivity, and hence planetary albedo.

Concluding Remarks on Feedbacks

The study of interactions between ozone depletion and global warming has been an active area of research since the 1998 assessment. At that time, there was strong emphasis on a single study,[77] which suggested that interactions with global warming could delay the recovery of ozone at polar latitudes by 10 years or more. However, subsequent studies with more complex models show smaller delays, and the current consensus, based on these models, is that polar ozone should begin to recover within the current decade.[6] There are also contrasting views on future ozone recovery at mid-latitudes. Some models predict that ozone recovery could be delayed and inhibited by interactions with increases in water vapour[86, 87] and increases in greenhouse gases, particularly in the latter part of the current century.[72, 73] However, the emerging consensus is that over the first half of the current century, increases in greenhouse gases will contribute to cooler stratospheric temperatures which will in turn lead to a decrease in the rate of catalytic destruction of ozone outside polar regions.[76, 88, 89] The temperature changes will lead to changes in atmospheric circulation. These changes will aid the mixing of long-lived CFCs from the troposphere to the stratosphere, which will increase their rate of photochemical destruction, again contributing to a faster recovery of ozone. Changes in polar ozone can also lead to changes in tropospheric circulation patterns, which in turn affect surface climate.[90]

These interactions are complex, and our understanding of the relevant processes may not yet be complete. It seems that, while current ozone depletion is dominated by chlorine and bromine in the stratosphere, in the longer term (~100 years) the impact of climate change will dominate, through the effects of changes in atmospheric dynamics and chemistry. The results are also sensitive to the assumed scenarios of future changes in greenhouse gases. A useful introduction to understanding these linkages has been prepared by Environment Canada.[91] (the document is also available from http://pda.msc.ec.gc.ca/saib/ozone/docs/ozone_depletion_e.pdf).

Influence of Solar Variability

The Sun's output is not constant over time, and solar UV-C radiation changes significantly over the 11-year solar cycle. This UV-C does not penetrate as far as the Earth's surface, but changes in UV-C cause ozone changes of ~3%. Counter-intuitively, the UV-B received at the surface is therefore expected to be a minimum when the solar output is a maximum. However, there may be other climatic impacts of solar variability as well (e.g. changes in cloud cover), and changes in surface UV due to solar variability have not yet been verified by observations. The Sun also exhibits variability on much longer time scales. For example, during the 17th century the Sun was less active (fewer sunspots), leading to the possibility of significantly greater UV-B during that period.[92]

Expectations for the Future

The Montreal Protocol is having a beneficial effect on global ozone. Modelling studies have demonstrated that ozone column amounts at high latitudes in the Southern Hemisphere are now 5% more than they would have been without the Montreal Protocol.[93] However, the largest benefits will be realised in years to come, as the stratospheric chlorine loading decreases. The concentrations of most anthropogenic precursors of ozone depletion are now decreasing (though bromine is still increasing at present). However, because of large year-to-year variability in ozone, it will be several years before we can detect whether an ozone recovery is occurring.

Although most practicable strategies to mitigate ozone depletion are already in place, there is much to be done to understand atmospheric processes fully. Polar processes are now better understood, but the situation is less promising at mid-latitudes. For example, (1) the observed rate of decline of ozone at mid latitudes is larger than predicted, (2) the large downward step in ozone at mid southern latitudes in the mid-1980s is not understood, (3) hemispheric differences in the effect of the eruption of Mt Pinatubo are not fully understood (large reduction in Northern Hemisphere ozone following the eruption, but very little change in Southern Hemisphere ozone), (4) the extent to which high-latitude ozone depletion affects ozone at mid-latitudes is still not fully resolved, and this could have a strong influence on how global warming affects future ozone levels. The importance of long-term changes in dynamics, possibly driven by changes in climate, in driving ozone change is now better appreciated.[6]

An incomplete understanding of processes that have occurred in the last decades and the resultant inability of models to track these changes reduce our confidence in the ability of the models that are currently available to predict future changes. Interactions between increased concentrations of greenhouse gases and ozone are being addressed in the Scientific Assessment of Ozone Depletion[6] through scenario studies using climate models. Figure 1-7 shows how UV may be expected to change over the period 1980 to 2050, owing to expected changes in ozone that will result with continued compliance to the Montreal Protocol. By the middle of the century, UV levels should be close to those in 1980.

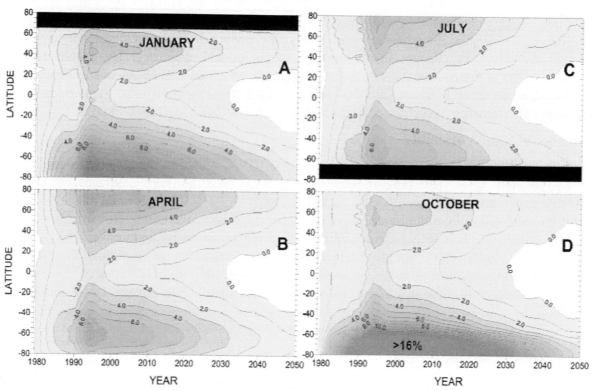

Figure 1-7 Projection of the departures (in percent) from 1980 UV noontime clear sky irradiance levels between 1979 and 2050 for the months of January (A), April (B), July (C) and October (D).[3, 4]

Although the outlook for future recovery of ozone and hence future recovery of UV-B is promising, the ozone layer will, as stated in the WMO Scientific Assessment report, remain vulnerable for the next decade or so, even with full compliance to the Montreal Protocol and its amendments and adjustments. Failure to comply would delay or could prevent recovery. UV-B intensities are likely to remain significantly higher than pre-1980 values for the next few years at least.

References

1   V. Fioletov, B. McArthur, J. Kerr and D. Wardle, Long-term variations of UV-B irradiance over Canada estimated from Brewer observations and derived from ozone and pyranometer measurements, *J. Geophys. Research*, 2001, **106**, 23009-23028.

2   E. D. Clark, Ozone depletion and global climate change: linkages and interactive threats to the cetacean environment, in *International Whaling Commission Scientific Committee, July 2001*, International Whaling Commission, 2001.

3   WMO (World Meterorological Organization), Scientific Assessment of Ozone Depletion: 1998 Global Ozone Research and Monitoring Project, Report No. 44, Geneva, Switzerland, 1999.

4   UNEP, Environmental effects of ozone depletion: 1998 assessment, UNEP Report No. Nairobi, p. 192.

5   R. L. McKenzie, G. E. Bodeker, B. J. Connor, P. V. Johnston, M. Kotkamp and W. A. Matthews, Increases in Summertime UV radiation in New Zealand: an update, in *Quadrennial Ozone Symposium* (Eds.: R. D. Bojkov and K. Shibasaki), EORC/NASDA, Tokyo, 2000, pp. 237-238.

6   WMO (World Meterorological Organization), Scientific Assessment of Ozone Depletion: 2002 Global Ozone Research and Monitoring Project, Report No. 47, Geneva, Switzerland, 2003.

7   J. F. Abarca, C. C. Casiccia and F. D. Zamorano, Increase in sunburns and photosensitivity disorders at the edge of Antarctic ozone hole, Southern Chile, 1986-2000, *J. Am. Acad. Dermatol.*, 2002, **46**, 193-199.

8   M. C. Rousseaux, C. L. Ballaré, C. V. Giordano, A. L. Scopel, A. M. Zima, M. Szwarcberg-Bracchitta, P. S. Searles, M. M. Caldwell and S. B. Diaz, Ozone damage and UVB radiation: impact on plant DNA damage in Southern America, *Proc. Nat. Acad. Sci.*, 1999, **96**, 15310-15315.

9   M. M. Caldwell, C. L. Ballaré, J. F. Bornman, S. D. Flint, L. O. Björn, A. H. Teramura, G. Kulandaivelu and M. Tevini, Terrestrial ecosystems, increased solar ultraviolet radiation and interactions with other climatic change factors, *Photochem. Photobiol. Sci.*, 2003, In press.

10   G. E. Bodeker, J. C. Scott, K. Kreher and R. L. McKenzie, Global ozone trends in potential vorticity coordinates using TOMS and GOME intercompared against the Dobson networks: 1978-1998, *J. Geophys. Res.*, 2001, **106**, 23029-23042.

11   E. C. Weatherhead, G. C. Reinsel, G. C. Taio, C. H. Jackman, L. Bishop, S. M. Hollandsworth Frith, J. DeLuisi, T. Keller, S. J. Oltmans, E. L. Fleming, D. J. Wuebbles, J. B. Kerr, A. J. Miller, J. Herman, R. McPeters, R. M. Nagatani and J. E. Frederick, Detecting the recovery of total column ozone, *J. Geophys. Res.*, 2000, **105**, 22201-22210.

12   S. B. Diaz, G. Deferrari, C. R. Booth, D. Martinioni and A. Oberto, Solar irradiances over Ushuaia (54.49°S, 68.19°W) and San Diego (32.45°N, 117.11°W) geographical and seasonal variation, *J. Atmos. Solar-Terr. Phys.*, 2001, **63**, 309-320.

13   A. Cede, E. Luccini, L. Nuñez, R. D. Piacentini and M. Blumthaler, Monitoring of erythemal irradiance in the Argentina ultraviolet network, *J. Geophys. Res.*, 2002, **107**, 10.1029/2001JD001206.

14   S. Madronich, R. L. McKenzie, L. O. Björn and M. M. Caldwell, Changes in biologically-active ultraviolet radiation reaching the Earth's surface, *J. Photochem. Photobiol. B.*, 1998, **46**, 5-19.

15   WMO, Report of the WMO-WHO Meeting of Experts on Standardization of UV Indices and their Dissemination to the Public, WMO Report No. Les Diablerets, Switzerland, 21-24 July 1997, p. 187.

16   M. Ilyas, A. Pandy and S. I. S. Hassan, UV-B radiation at Penang, *Atmospheric Research*, 1999, **51**, 141-152.

17   R. L. McKenzie, P. V. Johnston, D. Smale, B. Bodhaine and S. Madronich, Altitude effects on UV Spectral Irradiance deduced from measurements at Lauder, New Zealand and at Mauna Loa Observatory, Hawaii., *J. Geophys. Res.*, 2001, **106**, 22845-22860.

18   A. F. Bais, B. G. Gardiner, H. Slaper, M. Blumthaler, G. Bernhard, R. L. McKenzie, A. R. Webb, G. Seckmeyer, B. Kjeldstad, T. Koskela, P. Kirsch, J. Groebner, J. B. Kerr, S. Kazadzis, K. Lesczynski, D. Wardle, C. Brogniez, W. Josefsen, D. Gillotay, H. Reinen, P. Weihs, T. Svenoe, P. Eriksen, F. Kuik and A. Redondas, SUSPEN intercomparison of ultraviolet spectroradiometers, *J. Geophys. Res.*, 2001, **106**, 12509-12526.

19   J. R. Slusser, J. Gibson, D. S. Bigelow, D. Kolinski, P. Disterhoft, K. Lantz and A. Beaubien, Langley method of calibrating UV filter radiometers, *J. Geophys. Res.*, 2000, **105**, 4841-4849.

20   J. Gröbner, R. Vergas, V. E. Cachorro, D. V. Henriques, K. Lamb, A. Redondas, J. M. Vilaplana and D. Rembges, Intercomparison of aerosol optical depth measurements in the UVB using Brewer spectrophotometers and a Li-Cor spectrophotometer, *Geophys. Res. Lett.*, 2001, **28**, 1691-1694.

21   J. P. Diaz, F. J. Exposito, C. J. Torres, V. Carreno and A. Redondas, Simulation of mineral dust effects on UV radiation levels, *J. Geophys. Res.*, 2000, **105**, 4979-4991.

22   V. W. J. H. Kirchhoff, A. A. Silva, C. A. Costa, N. Paes Leme, H. G. Pavao and F. Zaratti, UV-B Optical Thickness Observations of the Atmosphere, *J. Geophys. Res.*, 2001, **106**, 2963-2973.

23   F. Zaratti, R. Forno, J. Garcia and M. Andrade, Erythemally-weighted UV-B variations at two high altitude locations, *J. Geophys. Res.*, 2002, **In Press**.

24   D. Meloni, G. R. Casale, A. M. Siani, S. Palmieri and F. Cappellani, Solar UV dose patterns in Italy, *Photochem. Photobiol.*, 2000, **71**, 681-690.

25   V. L. Orce and E. W. Helbling, Latitudinal UVR-PAR measurements in Argentina: extent of the 'ozone hole', *Global and Planetary Change*, 1997, **15**, 113-121.

26   S. Cabrera, S. Bozzo and H. Fuenzalida, Variations in UV radiation in Chile, *Photochem. Photobiol.*, 1995, **B28**, 137-142.

27   J. Gröbner, A. Albold, M. Blumthaler, T. Cabot, A. De la Casiniere, J. Lenoble, T. Martin, D. Masserot, M. Müller, R. Philipona, T. Pichler, E. Pougatch, G. Rengarajan, D. Schmucki, G. Seckmeyer, C. Sergent, M. L. Touré and P. Weihs, Variability of spectral solar ultraviolet irradiance in an Alpine environment, *J. Geophys. Res.*, 2000, **105**, 26991-27003.

28   C. Varotsos, D. Alexandris, G. Chronopoulos and C. Tzanis, Aircraft observations of the solar ultraviolet irradiance throughout the troposphere, *J. Geophys. Res.*, 2001, **106**, 14843-14854.

29   R. L. McKenzie, K. J. Paulin and S. Madronich, Effects of snow cover on UV irradiance and surface albedo: A case study, *J. Geophys. Res.*, 1998, **103**, 28785-28792.

30   K. Minschwaner, New observations of ultraviolet radiation and column ozone from Socorro, New Mexico, *Geophys. Res. Lett.*, 1999, **26**, 1173-1176.

31   M. Degünther, R. Meerkötter, A. Albold and G. Seckmeyer, Case study on the influence of inhomogeneous surface albedo on UV irradiance, *Geophys. Res. Lett.*, 1998, **25**, 3587-3590.

32   M. Degünther and R. Meerkötter, Influence of inhomogeneous surface albedo on UV irradiance: Effect of a stratus cloud, *J. Geophys. Res.*, 2000, **105**, 22755-22762.

33   K. F. Evans, The spherical harmonics discrete ordinate method for three-dimensional atmospheric radiative transfer, *J. Atmos. Sci.*, 1998, **55**, 429-446.

34   D. W. Mueller, Jr and A. L. Crosbie, Three-dimensional radiative transfer with polarization in a multiple scattering medium exposed to spatially varying radiation, *J. Quant. Spectros. Radiat. Transfer*, 1997, **57**, 81-105.

35   W. O'Hirok and C. Gautier, A three-dimensional radiative transfer model to investigate the solar radiation within a cloudy atmosphere. part I: Spatial effects, *J. Atmos. Sci.*, 1998, **55**, 2162-2179.

36   W. O'Hirok and C. Gautier, A three-dimensional radiative transfer model to investigate the solar radiation within a cloudy atmosphere. part II: Spectral effects, *J. Atmos. Sci.*, 1998, **55**, 3065-3076.

37   R. L. McKenzie, K. J. Paulin, G. E. Bodeker, J. B. Liley and A. P. Sturman, Cloud cover measured by satellite and from the ground: relationship to UV radiation at the surface, *Int. J. Remote Sens.*, 1998, **19**, 2969-2985.

38   J. Chen, B. E. Carlson and A. D. Del Genio, Evidence for strengthening of the tropical general circulation in the 1990s, *Science*, 2002, **295**, 838-841.

39   A. di Sarra, M. Cacciani, P. Chamard, C. Cornwall, J. J. DeLuisi, T. Di Iorio, P. Disterhoft, G. Fiocco, D. Fuá and F. Monteleone, Effects of desert dust and ozone on the ultraviolet irradiance: observations at the Mediterranean island of Lampedusa during PAUR II, *J. Geophys. Res.*, 2002, **107**, 10.1029/2000JD000139.

40   L. R. Acosta and W. F. J. Evans, Design of the Mexico City UV monitoring network: UV-B measurements at ground level in the urban environment, *J. Geophys. Res.*, 2000, **105**, 5017-5026.

41   B. N. Wenny, V. K. Saxena and J. E. Frederick, Aerosol optical depth measurements and their impact on surface levels of ultraviolet-B radiation, *J. Geophys. Res.*, 2001, **106**, 17311-17319.

42   M. Z. Jacobson, Global direct radiative forcing due to multicomponent anthropogenic and natural aerosols, *J. Geophys. Res.*, 2001, **106**, 1551-1568.

43   R. L. McKenzie, G. Seckmeyer, A. Bais and S. Madronich, Satellite retrievals of Erythemal UV dose compared with ground-based measurements at Northern and Southern mid-latitudes, *J. Geophys. Res.*, 2001, **106**, 24051 -24062.

44   M. Ilyas, A. Pandy and M. S. Jaafar, Changes to the surface level solar ultraviolet-B radiation due to haze perturbation, *J. Atmos. Chem.*, 2001, **40**, 111-121.

45   J. R. Herman, P. K. Bhartia, O. Torres, C. Hsu, C. Seftor and E. Celarier, Global distribution of UV-absorbing aerosols from Nimbus 7/TOMS data, *J. Geophys. Res.*, 1997, **102**, 16911-16922.

46   R. L. McKenzie, K. Paulin and M. Kotkamp, Erythemal UV irradiances at Lauder New Zealand: relationship between horizontal and normal incidence, *Photochem. Photobiol.*, 1997, **66**, 683-689.

47   A. R. Webb, P. Weihs and M. Blumthaler, Spectral UV irradiance on vertical surfaces: a case study, *Photochem. Photobiol.*, 1999, **69**, 464-470.

48   R. E. Shetter and M. Müller, Photolysis frequency measurements using actinic flux spectroradiometry during the PEM-Tropics Mission: instrumentation description and some results, *J. Geophys. Res.*, 1999, **104**, 5647-5662.

49   A. Hofzumahaus, A. Kraus and M. Müller, Solar actinic flux spectroradiometry: a technique measuring photolysis frequencies in the atmosphere, *Appl. Opt.*, 1999, **38**, 4443-4460.

50   S. Kazadzis, A. F. Bais, D. Balis, C. S. Zerefos and M. Blumthaler, Retrieval of downwelling UV actinic flux density spectra from spectral measurements of global and direct solar UV irradiance, *J. Geophys. Res.*, 2000, **105**, 4857-4864.

51   R. L. McKenzie, P. V. Johnston, A. Hofzumahaus, A. Kraus, S. Madronich, C. Cantrell, J. Calvert and R. Shetter, Relationship between photolysis frequencies derived from spectroscopic measurements of actinic fluxes and irradiances during the IPMMI campaign, *J. Geophys. Res.*, 2002, **107**, 10.1029/2001JD000601.

52   A. R. Webb, R. Kift, S. Theil and M. Blumthaler, An empirical method for the conversion of spectral UV irradiance measurements to actinic flux data, *Atmos. Environ.*, 2002, **36**, 4397-4404.

53   N. Y. Chubarova and Y. I. Nezval, Thirty year variability of UV irradiance in Moscow, *J. Geophys. Res.*, 2000, **105**, 12529-12539.

54   J. Borkowski, Homogenisation of the Belsk UV-B Series (1976-1997) and Trend Analysis, *J. Geophys. Res.*, 2000, **105**, 4873-4878.

55   R. L. McKenzie, B. J. Connor and G. E. Bodeker, Increased summertime UV observed in New Zealand in response to ozone loss, *Science*, 1999, **285**, 1709-1711.

56   C. Zerefos, D. S. Balis, A. F. Bais, D. Gillotay, P. C. Simon, B. Mayer and G. Seckmeyer, Variability of UV-B at four stations in Europe, *Geophys. Res. Lett.*, 1997, **24**, 1363-1366.

57   C. Zerefos, C. Meleti, D. S. Balis, K. Tourpali and A. F. Bais, Quasibiennial and longer-term changes in clear-sky UV-B solar irradiance, *Geophys. Res. Lett.*, 1998, **25**, 4345-4348.

58   J. R. Herman, R. D. Piacentini, J. Ziemke, E. Celarier and D. Larko, Interannual variability of ozone and UV-B ultraviolet exposure, *J. Geophys. Res.*, 2000, **105**, 29189-29193.

59   S. Diaz, G. Deferrari, D. Martinioni and A. Oberto, Regression analysis of biologically effective integrated irradiance versus ozone, clouds and geometric factors., *J. Atmos. Sol.-Terr. Phys.*, 2000, **62**, 629-638.

60   M. Huber, M. Blumthaler and J. Schreder, Effect of ambient temperature and internal relative humidity on spectral sensitivity of UV detectors, in *SPIE 46th Annual Meeting,* **Vol. 4482** (Eds.: J. Slusser, J. Herman and W. Gao), SPIE, Washington DC, 2002, pp. 187-193.

61   J. Kaurola, P. Taalas, T. Koskela, J. Borkowski and W. Josefsson, Long-term variations of UV-B doses at three stations in northern Europe, *J. Geophys. Res.*, 2000, **105**, 20813-20820.

62   P. N. den Outer, H. Slaper, J. Matthijsen, H. A. J. M. Reinen and R. Tax, Variability of ground-level ultraviolet: model and measurement, *Radiat. Prot. Dosimetry*, 2000, **91**, 105-110.

63   L. Gantner, P. Winkler and U. Kohler, A method to derive long-term time series and trends of UV-B radiation (1968-1997) from observations at Hohenpeissenberg (Bavaria), *J. Geophys. Res.*, 2000, **105**, 4879-4888.

64   J. Verdebout, A method to generate surface UV radiation maps over Europe using GOME, Meteosat, and ancillary geophysical data, *J. Geophys. Res.*, 2000, **105**, 5049-5058.

65   P. M. Udelhofen, P. Gies, C. Roy and W. J. Randel, Surface UltraViolet (UV) radiation over Australia, 1979-1992: effects of ozone and cloud cover changes on variations of UV radiation., *J. Geophys. Res.*, 1999, **104**, 19135-19159.

66   J. R. Ziemke, S. Chandra, J. Herman and C. Varotsos, Erythemally weighted UV trends over northern latitudes derived from Nimbus 7 TOMS measurements, *J. Geophys. Res.*, 2000, **105**, 7373 - 7382.

67   J. R. Herman, D. Larko, E. Celarier and J. Ziemke, Changes in the Earth's UV Reflectivity from the Surface, Clouds and Aerosols, *J. Geophys. Res.*, 2001, **106**, 5353-5368.

68   IPCC, *Climate Change 2001: The Scientific Basis. Contribution of Working Group I to the Third Assessment Report of the Intergovernmental Panel on Climate Change.*, Cambridge University Press, Cambridge, UK, 2001.

69   P. M. Udelhofen, H. P. Gies and C. R. Roy, Comparison of measurements of surface UVR and TOMS UV exposures over Australia, in *SPARC 2000*, SPARC, CD/SPARC web page, P/4.18, 2000.

70   A. Arola, S. Kalliskota, P. N. den Outer, K. Edvardsen, G. Hansen, T. Koskela, T. J. Martin, J. Matthijsen, R. Meerkoetter, P. Peeters, G. Seckmeyer, P. Simon, H. Slaper, P. Taalas and J. Verdebout, Assessment of four methods to estimate surface UV radiation using satellite data, by comparison with ground measurements from four stations in Europe, *J. Geophys. Res.*, 2002, **107**, 10.1029/2001JD000462.

71   R. D. Piacentini, E. Crino, J. S. Flores and J. y. M. Ginzburg, Intercomparison between ground based and TOMS/EP satellite southern hemisphere ozone data. New results, in *Proceedings SPARC (Stratospheric Processes and their Role on Climate) 2000*, SPARC, CD/SPARC web page, P/2-3.2., 2000.

72   B. Rognerud and I. Isaksen, Model calculations of stratospheric ozone recovery, in *NDSC Conference*, Network for the Detection of Stratospheric Change, 2001.

73   L. K. Randeniya, P. F. Vohralik and I. C. Plumb, Stratospheric ozone depletion at northern mid latitudes in the 21st century: The importance of future concentrations of greenhouse gases nitrous oxide and methane, *Geophys. Res. Lett.*, 2002, **29**, 10.1029/2001GL014295.

74   J. B. Liley, P. V. Johnston, R. L. McKenzie, A. J. Thomas and I. S. Boyd, Stratospheric NO_2 variations from a long time series at Lauder, New Zealand, *J. Geophys. Res.*, 2000, **105**, 11633-11640.

75   C. A. McLinden, S. C. Olsen, M. J. Prather and J. B. Liley, Understanding trends in stratospheric NO_y and NO_2, *J. Geophys. Res.*, 2001, **106**, 27787-27793.

76   J. E. Rosenfield, A. R. Douglass and D. B. Considine, The impact of increasing carbon dioxide on ozone recovery, *J. Geophys. Res.*, 2002, **107**, 10.1029/2001JD000824.

77   D. T. Shindell, D. Rind and P. Lonergan, Increased polar stratospheric ozone losses and delayed eventual recovery owing to increasing greenhouse-gas concentrations, *Nature*, 1998, **392**, 589-592.

78   P. Bunyard, How ozone-depletion increases global warming, *The Ecologist*, 1999, **29**, 85.

79   B. A. Wielicki, T. Wong, R. P. Allan, A. Slingo, J. T. Kiehl, B. J. Soden, C. T. Gordon, A. J. Miller, S.-K. Yang, D. A. Randall, F. Robertson, J. Susskind and H. Jacobowitz, Evidence for large decadal variability in the tropical mean radiative energy budget, *Science*, 2002, **295**, 841-844.

80   P. Taalas, J. Kaurola, A. Kylling, D. Shindell, R. Sausen, M. Dameris, V. Grewe, J. Herman, J. Danski and B. Steil, The impact of greenhouse gases and halogenated species on future solar UV radiation doses., *Geophys. Res. Lett.*, 2000, **27**, 1127-1130.

81   D. L. Hartmann, J. M. Wallace, V. Limpasuvan, D. W. J. Thompson and J. R. Holton, Can ozone depletion and global warming interact to produce rapid climate change?, *Proc. Nat. Acad. Sci.*, 2000, **97**, 1412-1417.

82   M. P. Baldwin and T. J. Dunkerton, Stratospheric harbingers of anomalous weather regimes, *Science*, 2001, **294**, 581-584.

83   N. Butchart and A. A. Scaife, Removal of chlorofluorocarbons by increased mass exchange between the stratosphere and troposphere in a changing climate, *Nature*, 2001, **410**, 799-802.

84   D.-P. Häder, H. D. Kumar, R. C. Smith and R. C. Worrest, Aquatic ecosystems: effects of increased solar ultraviolet radiation and interactions with other climatic change factors, interactions with other climatic change factors, *Photochem. Photobiol. Sci.*, 2003, In press.

85   R. G. Zepp, T. V. Callaghan and D. J. Erickson, Interactive effects of ozone depletion and climate change on biogeochemical cycles, *Photochem. Photobiol. Sci.*, 2003, In press.

86   K. H. Rosenlof, S. J. Oltmans, D. Kley, J. M. Russell III, E.-W. Chiou, W. P. Chu, D. G. Johnson, K. K. Kelly, H. A. Michelson, G. E. Nedoluha, E. E. Remsberg, G. C. Toon and M. P. McCormick, Stratospheric water vapor increases over the past half-century, *Geophys. Res. Lett.*, 2001, **28**, 195-198.

87   N. Stuber, M. Ponater and R. Sausen, Is the climate sensitivity to ozone perturbations enhanced by stratospheric water vapor feedback?, *Geophys. Res. Lett.*, 2001, **28**, 2887-2890.

88   T. Nagashima, M. Takahashi, M. Takigawa and H. Akiyoshi, Future development of the ozone layer calculated by a general circulation model with fully interactive chemistry, *Geophys. Res. Lett.*, 2002, **29**, 10.1029/2001GL014026.

89   V. Ramaswamy, M.-L. Chanin, J. Angell, J. Barnett, D. Gaffen, M. Gelman, P. Keckut, Y. Koshelkov, K. Labitske, J.-J. Lin, R., A. O'Neill, J. Nash, W. Randel, R. Rood, K. P. Shine, M. Shiotani and R. Swinbank, Stratospheric temperature trends: observations and model simulations, *Rev. Geophys.*, 2001, **39**, 71-122.

90   D. W. J. Thompson and S. Solomon, Interpretation of recent Southern Hemisphere climate change, *Science*, 2002, **296**, 895-899.

91   A. Fergusson, Ozone depletion and climate change: understanding the linkages, Meteorological Service, Environment Canada Report No. Toronto, p. 34.

92   J. Rozema, B. van Geel, L. O. Björn, J. Lean and S. Madronich, Toward Solving the UV Puzzle, *Science*, 2002, **296**, 1621-1622.

93   T. Egorova, E. V. Rozanov, M. E. Schleisinger, N. G. Andronova, S. L. Malyshev, I. L. Karol and V. A. Zubov, Assessment of the Effect of the Montreal Protocol on Atmospheric Ozone, *Geophys. Res. Lett.*, 2001, **28**, 2389-2392.

CHAPTER 2. HEALTH EFFECTS FROM STRATOSPHERIC OZONE DEPLETION AND INTERACTIONS WITH CLIMATE CHANGE

F.R. De Gruijl[a], J. Longstreth[b], M. Norval[c], A.P. Cullen[d], H. Slaper[e], M.L. Kripke[f], Y. Takizawa[g] And J.C. Van Der Leun[h]

[a] Leiden University Medical Centre, Sylvius Labs., Wassenaarseweg 72, NL-2333 AL Leiden, The Netherlands

[b] Institute for Global Risk Research, LCC, 9119 Kirkdale Road, Suite 200, Bethesda, MD 20817, USA.

[c] Medical Microbiology, University of Edinburgh Medical School, Teviot Place, Edinburgh EH8 9AG, Scotland, UK.

[d] School of Optometry, University of Waterloo, Ontario N2L 3GI, Canada

[e] National Institute of Public Heath and the Environment (RIVM), PO Box 1, NL-3720 BA Bilthoven, The Netherlands

[f] University of Texas, M.D. Anderson Cancer Center, 1515 Holcombe Boulevard, Box 113, Houston, Texas 77030-4095, USA.

[g] National Institute for Minamata Diseases, 4058 Hama, Minamata City, Kumamoto 867-0008, Japan.

[h] Ecofys, Kanaalweg 16 G, NL-3526 KL Utrecht, The Netherlands.

Summary

The potential health effects of elevated levels of ambient UV-B radiation are diverse, and it is difficult to quantify the risks, especially as they are likely to be considerably modified by human behaviour. Nevertheless epidemiological and experimental studies have confirmed that UV radiation is a definite risk factor for certain types of cataract, with peak efficacy in the UV-B waveband. The causal link between squamous cell carcinoma and cumulative solar UV exposure has been well established. New findings regarding the genetic basis of skin cancer, including studies on genetically modified mice, have confirmed the epidemiological evidence that UV radiation contributes to the formation of basal cell carcinomas and cutaneous melanomas. For the latter, animal models have demonstrated that UV exposure at a very young age is more detrimental than exposure in adulthood. Although suppression of certain immune responses has been recognised following UV exposure, the impact of this suppression on the control of infectious and autoimmune diseases is largely unknown. However, studies on several microbial infections have indicated significant consequences in terms of symptoms or reactivation of disease. The possibility that the immune response to vaccination could be depressed by UV-B exposure is of considerable concern. Newly emerging possibilities regarding interactions between ozone depletion and global climate change further complicate the risk assessments for human health but might result in an increased incidence of cataracts and skin cancer, plus alterations in the patterns of certain categories of infectious and other diseases.

Introduction

The potential health effects of elevated levels of ambient UV radiation due to a depletion of stratospheric ozone have been under study for over 30 years, and the UNEP 1998 report[1, 2] presented an overall review. The present chapter focuses on the main research developments from 1997 to the present.

From the outset it should be pointed out that human behaviour with regard to sun exposure is of decisive importance in considering the health risks. This includes such parameters as the popularity of tanning, the taking of holidays in the sun, and the wearing of minimal clothing as soon as the sun shines. Epidemiological and experimental studies show that proper protective measures, such as wearing appropriate glasses or sunglasses, and sunscreens, can offer some protection. In addition, some dietary and therapeutic ingredients are known to influence the risks both positively and negatively. These modifying factors are not included here because of the uncertainties surrounding their current and future impact.

Although UV-B radiation is effectively attenuated by the stratospheric ozone layer, it is not fully blocked (see Chapter 1).[3] It is very strongly absorbed in tissues and penetrates only superficially into the body; thus it directly affects only the eye and the skin. Detrimental consequences for the eye could include impaired vision, since UV radiation has been reported to cause opacification of the lens (cataract). Effects of UV radiation on the eye are discussed in the first section below. The second section deals with the skin, summarising the acute effects of UV exposure and research developments with direct relevance to UV-induced skin cancers. Modulations in immune responses due to UV irradiation are then outlined, including the impact of these changes on the immunological control of certain diseases. In later sections, the potential effects of UV exposure on internal cancers and the possible health consequences of the substitutes for ozone depleting substances (ODS) are discussed. Finally, consideration is given to new research into environmental changes, in particular the interactions between global warming and stratospheric ozone depletion. Regarding health effects that could be caused by these interactions, little research has been done thus far, but an inventory of potential outcomes is attempted.

The Eye

In recent years, it has become increasingly apparent that the effects of UV radiation are much more insidious and detrimental to the eye and vision than had been suspected previously. The effects may be acute (usually after a latent period), long-term following an acute exposure, or chronic due to extended or repeated exposure to levels of UV radiation below those required for acute effects. All anterior structures of the eye and those adjacent to it are potential targets for solar UV radiation. Whereas the skin and eyelids may be irradiated by direct sunlight, the outer layers of the eyeball (corneal and conjunctiva), iris and crystalline lens are mainly exposed to reflected and scattered UV radiation.[4] Our earlier report[2] considered the possible direct and indirect effects on the cornea and conjunctiva (photokeratitis, photoconjunctivitis, climatic droplet keratopathy, pinguecula, pterygium and squamous cell carcinoma), and the iris, ciliary body and choroid (anterior uveitis, ocular malignant melanoma). This report concentrates on the lens of the eye since cataract is the sunlight-related eye disease (ophthalmoheliosis) with the most serious public health implications.

Lens Opacities

The lens of the human eye changes with increasing age: it loses its transparency, becomes opalescent and turns yellowish to brownish in hue. Its fluorescence increases,[5] and the internal scattering of light increases[6] resulting in reduced contrast, increased glare and decreased vision.

In addition to these general changes in the nucleus of the lens, localized changes in the cortex (opaque spokes) may occur and may increase in size and extend toward the visual axis of the eye, ultimately impairing vision. Such an advanced stage of lens opacity forms a cataract requiring surgical intervention. As it is related to age, it is sometimes unfortunately referred to as 'senile cataract'. The mechanisms underlying all of these age-related changes are not fully established, but in accordance with general views on aging, oxidation is involved, e.g. as a side effect of metabolic processes (see for example[7, 8]). As UV radiation can generate reactive oxygen, it is also suspected to contribute to the deterioration of the lens by oxidation.[9-11]

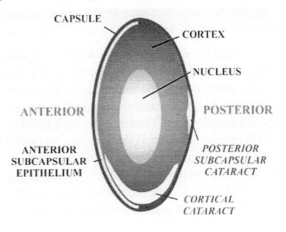

Three main types of age-related cataract can be distinguished on the basis of location (Figure 2-1): cortical cataract (CC) involving the cortex of the lens (Figure 2-2a), nuclear (sclerotic) cataract (NC) at the nucleus of the lens (Figure 2-2b), and posterior subcapsular cataract (PSC) at the extreme posterior cortex (Figure 2-2c).

Epidemiology

Globally cataract is a major cause of blindness. Cataract is adequately treated by surgery, but, where not treated, it often leads to permanent blindness with grave social/economic consequences; for instance, in 1998 an estimated 135 million people were visually impaired and 45 million people were blind worldwide with cataract as the leading cause [http://www.who.int/pbd/Vision2020/V2020slides/sld003.htm accessed 21 September 2002]. Epidemiological studies show that the aetiology of cataract is complicated and

Figure 2-1 Schematic cross section of the lens demonstrating various zones and forms of age-related cataract

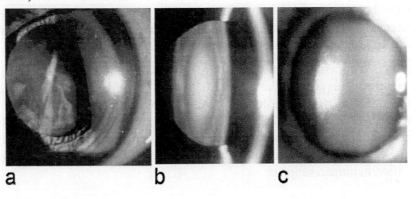

a   b   c

Figure 2-2. a) frontal view of a cortical cataract, b) cross sectional view (slit lamp) of a nuclear cataract, c) slit lamp view of a posterior subcapsular cataract

involves many risk factors. In considering all the risk factors, Taylor[12] concludes that the only effective preventive interventions are to stop smoking and to reduce ocular UV-B exposure.

The reported risks from sun (UV) exposure in population-based studies are quite moderate: generally, less than 2 fold increases of risk[13]). Assessments of personal, lifelong UV exposures in these studies (mainly from questionnaires) are, however, very inaccurate and inevitably lead to an underestimation of the relative risk. The best attempt made to record an accurate personal solar UV exposure history was in a study among watermen in Maryland,[14] and a highly significant correlation was found between exposure and CC. The impact of solar UV radiation is population-wide, and therefore a small relative risk translates into a substantial number of cases. One alternative to assessing personal UV exposure is to study populations living at latitudes with differences in ambient UV exposure. For example, good correlations have been established between cataracts and ambient UV exposure in the Aboriginal population in Australia,[15] and in the registered cataract operations in the USA.[16] Although overall (ambient) UV exposures can be accurately assessed, these correlations can be affected by many confounding factors, such as behavioural, ethnic and environmental differences.

Of people older than 40 years in Victoria, Australia, 12% were found to have CC, 13% NC and 5% PSC.[17] CC is relatively more prevalent than other types of cataract in populations living in temperate climates and the incidence increases toward lower latitudes. NC is more common in populations near the equator (tropical climates), e.g. comparing Iceland and Noto versus Singapore and Amami.[18] Despite the high prevalence of NC in the tropics, there is no evidence that NC is related to solar UV exposure. The relationship between CC and sun exposure was re-affirmed in a population-based study in Salisbury, Maryland.[19] A recent study in Iceland involving 1045 people older than 50 years reported a significantly increased risk for two different grades of cortical opacification in people who spend more than 4 hours per day outside on weekdays.[20] In all, there is sufficient evidence of an increase in cortical opacities, including CC, with increasing UV exposure to warrant advising the public on measures to decrease their ocular exposure.[21]

Experimental Evidence

The dependence of cataract formation on the wavelength of the UV radiation is important in establishing whether increases in ambient UV-B exposure due to ozone depletion will have an impact. Cataracts in humans develop slowly with age, and this process is difficult to investigate experimentally, especially in human subjects, but it can be done in isolated lenses and in animals. The problem with these experiments is that the catatacts are induced in a matter of hours, days or weeks. Careful comparisons show that the commonly UV-induced anterior subcapsular opacification in animals is not adequate to model the age-related cataracts observed in humans.[22] The wavelength dependence of cataract formation can be inferred from the basic mechanism, but knowledge on this subject is inadequate.

Much in agreement with an older study,[23] the wavelength dependence of cataract formation in rats was found to peak in the UV-B at 300 nm.[24] Similarly, the efficacy of inducing CC in pig lenses in culture was found to be greatest for wavelengths shorter than 300 nm (UV-B), and these were about 2000 times more effective than wavelengths around 365 nm (UV-A);[25] see Figure 2-3. Hence, the experiments on isolated lenses and in animals provide the best data on the wavelength dependence, and reveal the increased potential hazard of ozone depletion to CC formation in human subjects.

The Skin

Although there are several types of molecules in the skin that absorb UV radiation resulting in their modification or damage, cellular DNA is the primary target for many UV-induced effects. These range from acute outcomes such as sunburn, to chronic outcomes such as skin cancer. DNA molecules are of central importance to

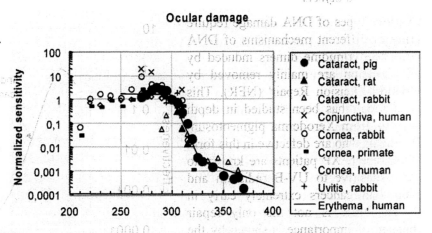

Figure 2-3 Wavelength dependencies measured for effects on the eye (symbols) compared to sunburn (lines); most recent data on cataract formation in solid symbols (cataract in pig[25] and in rat[24]) (courtesy of S. Madronich).

the cell: sections make up the various genes that carry the basic information with which a cell forms its proteins and thus controls its behaviour.

Acute Effects of UV exposure

Sunburn

A unique study in Punta Arenas, a city located at the southern tip of Chile, has documented the relationship between episodes of ozone depletion, increased terrestrial UV-B radiation and sunburn during the spring months.[26] The spring Antarctic "Ozone Hole" passes over or near this city each spring, and local data of sudden ozone depletion and the corresponding increase in UV-B radiation were available. There was a dramatic rise in the number of sunburn cases after sudden severe ozone depletion, coinciding with Sunday outdoor recreational exposure. Further detrimental consequences for this population and others at similarly affected latitudes are currently unknown, but are worthy of further consideration.

DNA damage

UV-B radiation causes very specific damage in a strand of DNA: chemically linking neighbouring pyrimidine bases to form pyrimidine dimers. The wavelength dependency of such damage closely follows that of inducing sunburn,[27] and effective repair in active regions of DNA lowers the sunburn sensitivity.[28] Focus on this type of alteration in DNA may have detracted from other, less direct, effects of UV radiation such as the generation of chemically reactive molecules, most notably those containing reactive oxygen, that cause oxidative damage to DNA. The oxidative damage is relatively more abundant at longer wavelengths, in the UV-A band, when compared to pyrimidine dimers which are more abundant at wavelengths around 300 nm.[29] The wavelength dependence of these types of DNA damage combined may explain the wavelength dependence of squamous cell carcinomas, see Figure 2-4.

Recent research has revealed that, in addition to point mutations in the DNA, UV-B induced DNA damage also gives rise to changes in larger sections of DNA, such as by deletions[31] and by faulty division leading to an excess of DNA in 'micro-nuclei' within cells.[32, 33] Because such defects in DNA can be caused by many other agents, it is not easy to establish a link between them and solar UV exposure.

DNA repair and defects

The various types of DNA damage require an array of different mechanisms of DNA repair. The pyrimidine dimers induced by UV-B radiation are mainly removed by 'Nucleotide Excision Repair' (NER). This form of repair has been studied in depth using cells from Xeroderma pigmentosum (XP) patients who are defective in this form of DNA repair. XP patients are known to be very sensitive to UV-B radiation and develop skin cancers extremely early in life. That NER is not the only repair mechanism of importance is shown by the increased skin cancer risk in patients with a milder form of XP, the XP-variant. These patients have no defect in NER, but they lack a proper corrective mechanism in the replication of UV-B damaged DNA (caused by a lack of an enzyme that is capable of copying DNA across a cyclobutane pyrimidine dimer).[34] This results in gross rearrangements in the genetic material of the cells (i.e., increases in 'sister chromatid exchanges' caused by yet another form of DNA repair, recombinational repair).[35]

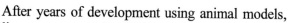

Figure 2-4 The wavelength dependence of induction of skin carcinomas[30] compared to that of direct DNA damage (pyrimidine dimers) and indirect, oxidative DNA damage (e.g., 8-oxo-G)[29] the DNA damage curves are shifted over the vertical axis by factors of 10 to coincide with the curve for skin carcinomas around 350 nm. Notice the correspondence between curve for skin carcinomas and the upper contour for total DNA damage

After years of development using animal models, liposomes containing DNA repair enzymes have now been tested on the skin of human volunteers. There was some acceleration in the repair of pyrimidine dimers but the UV induction of sunburn (the skin 'erythema' or redness) and 'sunburn cells' (apoptotic cells, i.e. cells undergoing programmed cell death) was not affected. However the UV-induced expression of genes important in suppressing immune responses was decreased.[36] In another experiment using different, light-activated, repair enzymes, the enhanced repair prevented the UV-induced suppression of an allergic skin reaction.[37] These latter experiments confirm that DNA is one very important UV target, and that DNA damage can initiate the immunosuppressive response to UV exposure (see section on UV-induced immunosuppression for further details).

Skin Cancer

Epidemiology and trends

Skin cancer is very common in people of Northern European descent and is by far the most frequent cancer in these people living in subtropical areas of the USA and Australia. In increasing order of malignancy and decreasing order of incidence, the three main types are basal cell carcinoma (BCC), squamous cell carcinoma (SCC), and cutaneous melanoma (CM) (cancer of skin pigment cells called melanocytes). To give one example of the scale of the problem, in Finland about 50 new cases of BCC occur per 100,000 people per year[38] whereas in Australia it is about 800 new cases per 100,000 people per year.[39] Epidemiological studies have shown that all 3 types are related to sun (UV) exposure.[40] The high incidences imply a large burden on health care systems. Except for CM, the mortality is generally low when compared to internal cancers, but successful therapy can leave a person disfigured, e.g. by surgery on the face where these tumours occur most frequently.

Reported trends with time in incidences of BCC and SCC vary substantially, but mainly increases are reported. For example both BCC and SCC incidences rose by about 50% from 1988 to 1998 in the south of Wales,[41] BCC by about 70% and SCC by about 15% from 1978 to 1995 in the Slovak Republic,[42] BCC by 20% and SCC by 90% from 1985 to 1995 in Australia.[39] In contrast, there have been no consistent increases in either BCC or SCC from 1985 to 1996 in Arizona, USA.[43] Large increases, up to a doubling over 10 years, have occurred in the incidence of CM during the last century,[40] but as reported earlier for CM mortality in the USA,[44] age-standardised mortality and incidence are levelling off, especially in women, in Northern Europe, Australia and Canada.[45-47]

Intervention studies

A recent randomised prospective cohort study in Queensland, Australia[48] showed that the daily use of sunscreens for 4.5 years by adults decreased the appearance of new SCC, but not BCC. This is in accordance with the finding that UV radiation contributes to the development of SCC at all stages during a lifetime, whereas UV radiation mostly affects early stages of BCC development.[2]

In a randomised multi-centre study on 30 XP patients, it was found that enhanced DNA repair by regular application of liposomes containing DNA repair enzymes to the exposed skin over a period of 1 year was of significant benefit to these patients. It decreased the rate of newly occurring actinic keratoses (precursors of SCC) to one third of the number in control patients.[49]

Regulatory pathways of cell growth and carcinogenic changes in man and animal models

With the rapid expansion of bio-molecular techniques, cancer research is making great advances in the understanding of how normal cells can become malignant, i.e., proliferate and spread uncontrollably. In general, a cancer cell arises from corrupted biochemical signalling pathways that control a cell's life cycle (i.e., division, maturation and death). The most permanent disruption stems from altered or lost genes that code for proteins involved in these signalling pathways. As discussed previously, UV-B radiation damages the DNA from which the genes are built up, and when repair fails to remove the damage, faulty copies of a gene may be passed to daughter cells. In general, a combination of genes has to be affected rather than a single gene in order for a cell to become malignant. Studies on oncogenic pathways indicate that the conversion of a normal cell to a cancer cell requires the modification of two or more pathways promoting cell survival and proliferation, on the one hand, versus growth suppression and cell death, on the other. After identifying such pathways, their targeting by UV radiation can be investigated.

Early changes in the genes involved in cancer (carcinogenic "events") can be detected or even quantified in terms of frequency of occurrence. A good example is the early occurrence in human skin of microscopic clones of cells that carry UV-B specific point mutations (at potential pyrimidine dimer sites) in the P53 tumor suppressor gene;[50, 51] these mutations are also found in a large majority of skin carcinomas (BCC and SCC). In animal experiments the relationship between these early carcinogenic events and the ultimate SCC can be studied in detail, and the causal link between the P53-mutant clones and SCC has been substantiated recently.[52] These developments open up new possibilities for improved quantitative risk models that incorporate such early events as predictors of future cancer risk.

There is epidemiological evidence and experimental proof in mice to demonstrate that chronic exposure to solar UV-B radiation causes SCC.[2] Although there is epidemiological evidence that sun exposure contributes to the formation of BCC and CM, there was virtually no animal data for

BCC, and only ambiguous animal data for CM until recently (see below). Details of the specific oncogenic pathways involved in BCC and CM have been revealed from studying familial forms of these cancers.[53, 54] Subsequently, non-familial (sporadic) skin cancers were investigated for abnormalities in these pathways and relevant genes. These aberrant genes have been introduced into mice which can then be studied for their tendency to develop these types of skin cancer, either with or without UV exposure.

BCC

A particular proliferative pathway (SHH) is activated in the vast majority of BCC,[55] often by mutations in the PTCH gene.[56] Some of these mutations are characteristic of UV-B induced mutations. Transgenic mice with one functional copy of the homologue (Ptc) of the PTCH gene contract more BCC more rapidly when exposed to UV radiation.[57] Most of these BCC lose the functional copy of the Ptc gene, and all BCC show activation of the SHH pathway. As in humans, a large fraction (40%) of the BCC also carry UV-B related mutations in the P53 tumor suppressor gene. These data show that UV-B radiation can play an important role in causing and enhancing the development of BCC, both by contributing to the activation of the proliferative SHH pathway (by loss of Ptc) and by rendering the P53 tumour suppressor protein dysfunctional.

CM

The tumour suppressor pathway involving the p16/INK4a protein is important in the development of CM.[58] The gene of p16/INK4a is mutated infrequently in CM, but the expression of the protein is aberrantly low in the majority of CM.[59] Although CM is readily induced in mice lacking p16/Ink4a by neonatal exposure to chemical carcinogens,[60-62] attempts using UV radiation have thus far not been successful.

The proliferative pathway in CM appears to involve RAS proteins. Earlier studies showed UV-B related activating mutations in *RAS* genes of CM from sun-exposed skin areas.[63] Recently, Davies et al.[64] reported that about 70% of CM carried an activating mutation in the gene that codes for BRAF, a protein which is activated by RAS. However, this mutation was not specific for UV-B radiation.

The hepatocyte growth factor stimulates proliferation of melanocytes (the normal pigment cells), and this protein also activates the RAS/BRAF pathway. Transgenic mice, overexpressing the hepatocyte growth factor in the skin, have melanocytes superficially in the skin (at the epidermal-dermal junction), a position at which they are found in human skin. In contrast, the melanocytes of normal mice (and other rodents) are located deeper in the skin (in the dermis and in hair follicles). Neonatal exposure of these transgenic mice to broadband UV radiation (including UV-B) was found to result in (metastatic) CM in adulthood. As in humans, these CM stemmed from superficial melanocytes.[65] Remarkably, chronic exposure throughout adulthood did not induce CM, but mainly SCC.[66] Similar results were obtained in a model using opossums (*Monodelphis domestica*) where 3 weeks of moderate UV-B exposure of sucklings resulted in metastatic CM in some of these animals later in life;[67] some of these CM carried UV-B specific mutations in the *Ink4a* gene.[68] A 100-fold higher UV-A exposure of the neonates did not induce CM,[69] and chronic UV-B exposure of adult animals induced melanocytic lesions, but no aggressive, metastatic CM.[67]

These data indicate that CM arise from a defective tumour suppressive pathway involving p16/INK4a and activation of a cell proliferation pathway involving RAS/BRAF. It is, however, not clear whether and to what extent UV-B radiation disrupts either or both of these pathways in the genesis of CM in humans. Evidence from these animal models support the hypothesis that UV exposure early in life is an important factor in the subsequent development of CM, consistent with epidemiological data, specifically those data obtained from migratory studies. Furthermore, studies in the two mammalian models support a role for UV-B radiation in CM, but provide no evidence in support of UV-A (E.C. De Fabo, personal communication). Thus, they do not support earlier studies in a fish model suggesting that UV-A radiation in full sunlight was more effective than UV-B radiation in inducing melanoma (for a review of UV-A and melanoma, see [70]).

UV-Induced Immunosuppression

It is well established that UV radiation can suppress immunity (reviewed in [71]). The consequences for the pathogenesis of infectious diseases, for the effectiveness of vaccination, for tumour rejection and for autoimmune diseases are largely unknown but accumulating evidence indicates that the impact could be considerable.

Although the sequence of events leading to suppression of immune responses is known to be complex, it is clear that it begins with molecules in the skin which absorb UV radiation and change their structure as a result. At present major roles are indicated for DNA and *trans*-urocanic acid (*trans*-UCA) as the initiators, the former becoming damaged and the latter isomerising to *cis*-UCA. As a result of these changes, many molecules located in the skin are produced, some of which are called cytokines. They act on various cell populations in the skin and lymph nodes, with the end result being effects on the functions of the two major T lymphocyte subsets which represent part of the white blood cells. The first subset called T helper 1 lymphocytes, required to control tumour growth, responses to simple chemicals, and intracellular infections such as those caused by viruses, is severely depressed. In contrast, the second subset called T helper 2 lymphocytes, needed to control extracellular infections such as those caused by many bacteria, is not depressed to the same extent, in the majority of systems analysed thus far.

The activities of these two subsets of lymphocytes are orchestrated by regulatory cells, the precise identities of which have recently been reported.[72, 73] These cell types, which are present in very small numbers, could be enriched from lymphoid tissues of UV-irradiated mice that had subsequently been immunised: small numbers of these T cells were capable of suppressing the response to the immunising material when placed in untreated mice. The molecular controls of "unresponsiveness" are of great interest currently and this work aids in our understanding of immunological regulatory pathways. In Figure 2-5, details of the steps leading from UV exposure to immuno-suppression can be found.

The Impact of UV-Induced ImmunoSuppression on Diseases

Herpes Viruses

For infectious diseases of human subjects, a role for UV radiation in affecting the control of a microorganism by altering the immune response of the host is most evident in the case of cold sores caused by herpes simplex virus (HSV). Here the evidence linking exposure to sunlight and reactivation of the virus from latency is very strong.[74] It is interesting in the context of HSV infections to note a recent study[75] reporting a seasonal variation in the incidence of shingles, caused by another herpesvirus, namely herpes zoster

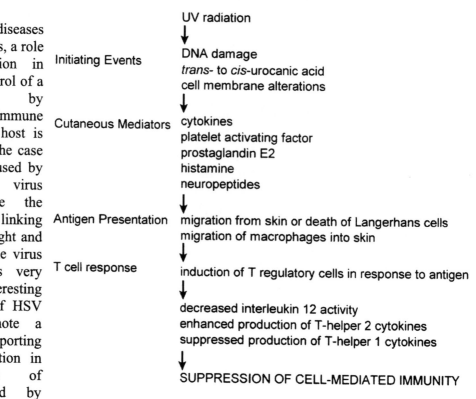

UV radiation
↓
Initiating Events — DNA damage
trans- to *cis*-urocanic acid
cell membrane alterations
↓
Cutaneous Mediators — cytokines
platelet activating factor
prostaglandin E2
histamine
neuropeptides
↓
Antigen Presentation — migration from skin or death of Langerhans cells
migration of macrophages into skin
↓
T cell response — induction of T regulatory cells in response to antigen
↓
decreased interleukin 12 activity
enhanced production of T-helper 2 cytokines
suppressed production of T-helper 1 cytokines
↓
SUPPRESSION OF CELL-MEDIATED IMMUNITY

Figure 2-5 Details of the steps leading to UV-induced immunosuppression

which is also the virus causing chicken-pox. Following chicken-pox, the virus remains deep in the nervous tissue until it reactivates to give the lesions of shingles, often many years later. The frequency of shingles was found to be higher in the late spring/summer months than in the winter months. A similar study has been undertaken in Lodz, Poland.[76] Again the number of cases of shingles was higher in the summer and showed a similar temporal pattern to ground level solar UV measurements. The number of zoster cases with lesions occurring on the exposed body sites (the face) varied significantly with season and peaked in July and August. In marked contrast, the majority of chicken-pox cases developed predominantly in the winter months, perhaps due to the more effective respiratory spread of the virus at this time of the year. For shingles, it could be speculated that the longer day and more sunlight in the summer lead to interference with the immune response to the virus and consequent reactivation. This hypothesis requires further testing.

Human Immunodeficiency Virus (HIV)

Various pieces of evidence indicate that UV exposure could affect the interaction of HIV with the host. A recent report adds further credence to this possibility.[77] HIV-positive patients were given a suberythemal dose of UV-B radiation. Their skins were subsequently examined for activation of HIV which was shown to occur, most likely through the production of gene-activating factors by the host.[77] An epidemiological study, in which viral load and various immunological parameters were followed over a period of 12 years in a cohort of HIV-infected homosexual men, showed a decreased number of CD4-positive T lymphocytes in the spring and summer months but no effect of seasonality on viral load.[78] In addition, other immunological markers followed different seasonal courses. It should be noted, however, that to date, clinical studies involving HIV-infected patients have revealed no effect of sunlight exposure or of phototherapy on disease (reviewed in [79]).

Vaccination

If UV radiation can modify immune responses to microbial antigens significantly, then various questions arise regarding vaccination. For example, does vaccination in the summer months generate less effective immunity than vaccination during the winter? Is vaccination of sun-exposed subjects less effective than vaccination of unexposed individuals? Should vaccination take place through sun-exposed body sites or should it be confined to sites which are normally covered? Is resistance to re-infection with a particular microbe lowered in the summer months? This aspect of UV-induced immunomodulation has not been investigated thoroughly as yet, although there has been interest for many years in the possible influence of season on sero-conversion in response to oral poliovirus vaccination. For example, one paper reported that, in Tel-Aviv, the rates of sero-conversion and the antibody titres generated were higher in children vaccinated in the winter compared with the summer.[80] The reason for this difference was not found: exposure to sunlight was not considered. Furthermore, a decrease in the immunogenicity and replication in the upper respiratory tract of live influenza A and B vaccines in the summer compared with the winter has been reported in a study based in Leningrad.[81]

A Dutch group has assessed the effects of artificial UV-B irradiation on immune responses to hepatitis B virus.[82] Volunteers were given whole body UV-B radiation with doses just below a sun-burning dose on each of 5 consecutive days, then vaccinated against hepatitis B virus. Although the UV-treated subjects demonstrated the typical immunosuppression observed following such exposures, such as suppression of the response to a simple chemical, the suppression did not extend to either antibody or T cell immunity specific for the virus. However it should be noted that the vaccine used was given together with the adjuvant aluminium hydroxide, which directs the response towards the type of immunity (T helper 2) not likely to be affected by UV radiation. In addition the vaccine is administered at a high dose to encourage a protective outcome in subjects who respond poorly. This dose may have overcome any suppressive effect of UV radiation. Finally the degree of immune response to the hepatitis B vaccine is recognised to correlate with the genetic background of the individual, and small differences in, for example, the genes encoding the mediators involved in UV-induced immunosuppression were not taken into account. Preliminary results indicate that subjects with a particular polymorphism in the interleukin-1 beta gene may demonstrate UV-induced suppression of their immune responses to the hepatitis B vaccine (Sleijffers et al, personal communication).

A very interesting study examined the effect of UV radiation in subjects who had been immunised against tuberculosis at some time in the past, using a BCG vaccine.[83] They were given suberythemal UV on a small area of their bodies and their immunological response to BCG tested in both this UV-exposed site and at a distant non-exposed site. Daily treatment with UV radiation for 5 consecutive days was sufficient to suppress the response at the exposed site but not at the distant site. It is not known if the depression in T cell responses induced by the UV radiation could lessen the protection offered by BCG vaccination significantly, and make individuals more prone to infection, or indeed to reactivation in the case of a persistent tuberculosis infection.

Knowledge of the immunological impact of UV radiation on vaccine effectiveness is lacking, in particular for vaccinations designed to stimulate T helper 1 responses.

Autoimmune Diseases

Several studies over the past 40 years have pointed out a marked positive correlation in the incidence of multiple sclerosis in the white Caucasian population with latitude. For example, in Australia, the prevalence of multiple sclerosis per 100,000 persons is 12 in North Queensland at latitudes of 12-23 degrees south, and 76 in Tasmania at a latitude of 43 degrees South. Recently, McMichael and Hall have suggested that this could be due to solar UV radiation levels that are negatively correlated with latitude.[84] Multiple sclerosis is known to have an immunological basis with increased autoimmune T lymphocytes reactive with nerve-specific protein (myelin). Therefore increased UV exposure could perhaps ameliorate the disease by suppressing T cell function. This suggestion has gained support recently in a report where a negative association of deaths from multiple sclerosis and residential and occupational solar radiation in the United States was found.[85] In contrast, deaths from non-melanoma skin cancer in the same population were positively associated with residential and occupational UV exposure. In the case of a second autoimmune disease, insulin-dependent diabetes mellitus, there are also reports of a latitude gradient in incidence. For example, in a large study of the Swedish population, there were 1.35 times more cases in the north of the country than in the south.[86]

Another autoimmune disease, systemic lupus erythematosus (SLE), is thought to involve a different type of T cell immunity, one which could be potentially enhanced by UV radiation causing exacerbations of symptoms. It has been reported that an increase in disease activity in 50% of photosensitive patients with SLE occurred following exposure to fluorescent lamps which emitted substantial levels of UV-B.[87] A recent study in Puerto Rico examined the correlation between taking photoprotective measures and clinical outcome in patients with SLE.[88] Although the wearing of a hat or long-sleeved clothes to protect from sunlight had no effect on the disease, individuals who regularly used sunblocks had lower renal involvement, thrombocytopoenia, hospitalisation and requirement for cyclophosphamide treatment than patients who had not used sunblocks. Thus the benefit of avoiding sun exposure in SLE is considerable, and it would be of great interest to monitor the immune response in such patients following sun exposure to confirm the suspected immunomodulatory effects on disease progression.

Respiratory Allergy

Concern has been expressed that UV exposure could exacerbate the symptoms of respiratory allergy, which is associated with enhanced T helper 2 responses. This hypothesis has not been tested in human subjects, but one study in mice indicated that UV irradiation did not enhance allergic reactions in the respiratory tract although it did modulate various systemic immune responses.[89]

Animal Models

To date approximately 15 animal models of infection have been developed, mainly using mice, in which the effects of UV radiation on immunity have been investigated (reviewed in [90]). The organisms range from viruses to worms, with some infections being skin-associated and others systemic with no skin involvement at any stage. In almost all cases the UV radiation caused suppression of resistance to the microorganism under investigation, the one exception being schistosomiasis.

Four models of particular interest have been described recently, all noting severe exacerbation of symptoms following UV exposure, with death ensuing in some instances. The first involved the malaria parasite. A single burning UV exposure one day before inoculation of mice resulted in the death of the infected animals, whereas, without the UV irradiation, the mice survived.[91]

The major immunological effect was attributed to a UV-induced alteration in the spectrum of cytokines normally induced in response to the parasite. The UNEP report in 1989[92] suggested that there may be a particular risk of greater incidence or severity of malaria if the terrestrial UV radiation exposure of human subjects increased. In the second model, prior exposure of mice to UV radiation was shown to enhance influenza virus infections.[93] Mortality was increased up to 2-fold and was UV dose-dependent. The UV-irradiated animals demonstrated greater weight loss and degeneration of the thymus, raising concerns that sun exposure may also affect the course of human respiratory viral diseases. In the third model, rats were infected intranasally with HSV which leads to encephalitis, accompanied by severe clinical symptoms such as paralysis.[94] UV-B treatment prior to such an infection increased the incidence and severity of the clinical signs. The viral load in the brain was greater and the specific immune response to the virus suppressed. Although HSV-encephalitis is rare in people, again the potential for UV exposure to have detrimental effects during the course of an infection is demonstrated. In the fourth model, mice were infected intradermally with *Borrelia burgdorferi*, the bacterium that causes Lyme disease. Exposure of the mice to UV radiation, either at the site of infection or at a distant site, decreased the immune response to the bacteria, increased the rate of dissemination from the skin to the bloodstream, and increased the severity of the arthritis that accompanies this infection.[95] Again, this study illustrates the potential of UV irradiation to adversely affect an infectious disease of relevance to humans. In addition, the subtlety of the effects (reduced immunity and increased disease severity) points out the difficulty in identifying such effects in human populations.

Extrapolation from Animal Models to Human Subjects

It is of considerable interest to relate the observed immunological effects of UV radiation in the animal models to human subjects. The biologically effective dose for UV-induced suppression of contact hypersensitivity in a mouse model as a function of latitude and of ozone depletion was first calculated.[96] Then, by using these data and by extrapolation from one animal model of infection, it has been suggested that exposure of people for about 100 minutes at mid-latitudes around noon on a clear day in summer would be sufficient to suppress their cellular immunity to a microbe significantly.[97] This conclusion has yet to be verified for a natural human infection. However the effective solar dose for the suppression of the immune response to a simple chemical in human subjects has been established recently and is equivalent to approximately 60 minutes of noonday summer sunlight at mid-latitudes[98] - of the same order as the theoretical extrapolation. Therefore it is likely that the doses of solar UV radiation required to suppress immunity to infectious agents are of the same magnitude as those experienced during common outdoor activities.

The Impact of UV-Induced Immunosuppression on Tumours

Several studies in the past have indicated that human subjects can be divided into those who are susceptible to the immunosuppressive effects of UV radiation and those who are resistant.[99] The former were thought to be at higher risk of developing skin cancer than the latter. More recently Kelly et al have shown that simulated solar radiation is highly immunosuppressive in every person tested.[98] A further report by the same group examined the relationship between sunburn and immunomodulation.[100] Suppression occurred in all subjects by exposure to solar irradiation equivalent to 1 hour of noonday summer sunlight at mid-latitudes one day before application of the chemical at the irradiated site. A correlation was demonstrated between erythema (redness) and suppression of immunity. However if the UV dose was reduced to below the minimum required to cause erythema of the skin, differences in immunomodulation were revealed, depending on the skin phototype of the individual. People who do not tan readily and are sun-sensitive (type I/II) were 2-3 fold more susceptible to immunosuppression than people who tan readily and are sun-tolerant (type III/IV). It is known that individuals with the former skin type are at greater risk of developing skin cancer than individuals with the latter skin type. Thus the greater sensitivity of pale skinned subjects for a given level of exposure may play a role in their increased risk of developing skin cancer.

Several studies have indicated an important role for mast cells in UV-induced systemic immunosuppression. Hart et al used strains of mice with differing susceptibilities to immunomodulation following UV radiation, and showed a correlation of susceptibility with the number of mast cells in the skin.[101] Thus a strain in which immunity was easily suppressed by UV exposure had a large number of mast cells while another strain, in which immunity was only suppressed by large UV-B doses, had about half that number. Mast cells contain granules containing histamine and other pharmacological mediators, which can be released upon sun exposure or other stimulation, thus affecting local immunity and cell trafficking. Most interestingly, a subsequent publication by the same group showed that human subjects with a past history of BCC had higher numbers of cutaneous mast cells than matched controls, suggesting a link between UV-induced immunosuppression and skin cancer.[102] There is preliminary evidence that *cis*-UCA, one of the initiators of UV-induced immunosuppression, may trigger mast cell degranulation.[103] In fact recent evidence suggests that *cis*-UCA may cause mast cell degranulation by mimicking the action of serotonin (J. Walterscheid, personal communication). However the relationship between UCA and the risk of developing skin cancer, if it exists, is not likely to be a straightforward one, as no difference in total UCA or the percentage of *cis*-UCA was found in subjects with a past history of CM and BCC compared with control subjects.[104, 105]

Finally a study by Beissert el al., has revealed that *cis*-UCA may be an important factor in photocarcinogenesis.[106] Mice chronically exposed to UV-B radiation were treated concurrently either with a monoclonal antibody effective in reversing the immunosuppressive effects of *cis*-UCA or a non-related monoclonal antibody. In the mice receiving the *cis*-UCA antibody, tumours took twice as long to develop as in mice receiving the unrelated antibody.

Other Systemic Effects from UV Exposure

UV exposure of the skin is known to cause effects throughout the body by substances released into the circulation or cells migrating to and from the skin. Over the last decade data have been collected indicating that solar UV exposure may influence the development of internal cancers. UV radiation is unlikely to cause internal cancers by direct DNA damage, but it may stimulate or suppress the outgrowth of internal cancers.

Immune suppression (such as that induced by medication in renal transplant patients) is a known risk factor for both SCC and non-Hodgkin's lymphoma (NHL). Like skin cancers, the incidence of NHL has been increasing. BCC and SCC appear to be associated with increased risk of NHL and chronic lymphocytic leukaemia (CLL)[107-110] suggestive of a common aetiological factor, presumably solar UV radiation. Similarly, NHL incidences were found to be higher in populations in sunnier areas,[111-114] though this relationship was not demonstrated in the United States.[115] Besides UV exposure, the impact of socio-economic factors on NHL risk needs to be taken into account (Langford et al., 1998, Schouten et al., 1996).[113, 116] Assessments of personal UV exposure have not revealed clear, significant assciations with NHL,[114] at most, they show trends of borderline significance with NHL and leukaemia.[117, 118] However, such exposure assessments may have been too crude or inadequate (e.g. assessing total instead of peak exposures) to reveal striking differences. An indication that sun (UV) exposure may affect lymphocytes adversely was found in the increase in mutation frequency in these blood-borne cells during the summer,[119] presumably due to the UV-induced release of a factor that stimulated lymphocyte proliferation. Furthermore, UV exposure of certain genetically modified animals (missing one copy of the *P53* tumor suppressor gene) greatly enhance the development of leukaemia in addition to causing SCC in the skin,[120] suggesting that UV exposure may enhance the development of lymphoid tumours in genetically predisposed individuals.

UV-B radiation contributes to the formation of vitamin D in the skin. This vitamin is not biologically active, but the 'vitamin D hormone' (1,25 di-hydroxivitamin D) derived from it is. The vitamin D hormone can inhibit the growth of various cancer cells (e.g. breast cancer) in cell culture, and some studies have demonstrated that the risk of certain types of cancer (colon, prostate and breast) increases with low dietary intake of vitamin D or with low levels of vitamin D metabolites in the blood (see [121] for an overview). It is possible that UV exposure could influence the blood level of the vitamin D hormone, but there is no simple direct relationship between vitamin D hormone and UV exposure because of the many regulatory feedback mechanisms. Following an earlier report of a very slight, but significant latitude gradient in prostate cancer across the USA,[122] a recent case-control study[123] showed that low levels of sun exposure are associated with a higher risk of prostate cancer. Within the group of prostate cancer patients, the individuals with the lowest level of UV exposure (within the lowest 25 percentile) developed their tumours at a median age of 68 years, whereas the others developed them at a median age of 72 years. It has also been suggested that a low level of vitamin D could contribute to the risk of developing insulin-dependent diabetes mellitus.[124]

Risks Associated with the Use of Substitutes for Ozone Depleting Substances

With the phase-out of ozone depleting substances (ODS) mandated under the Montreal Protocol and its amendments, a number of new chemical alternatives have been developed, and there has been increased usage of some older chemicals, often in venues different from their traditional usage. These increases in usage are likely to lead to increased human (and environmental) exposures that could have adverse consequences for both human health and the environment. Previous assessments have presented brief reviews of what was known about the toxicology of a number of these chemicals. As a consequence this review will focus on those chemicals not previously mentioned in earlier reports that are discussed in the most recent Technology and Economic Assessment Panel (TEAP) report.[125] A list of these chemicals with their CAS (Chemical Abstracts Service) numbers and their likely use is presented in Table 2-1.

Currently ODS substitutes are being used in six major areas: 1) Aerosols, 2) Refrigerants, 3) Fire-suppressants, 4) Solvents, 5) Foam-blowing agents, and 6) Pesticides, including fumigants, all of which are represented in Table 2.1. All of these uses have the potential for human exposure, mainly for occupationally exposed populations, but also for the public in general.

The largest use of aerosols still requiring ODS is in the metered dose inhalers used to deliver pharmaceuticals to the respiratory system. Substitutes for use in these inhalers are being introduced; their production and use will continue to increase as the essential use exemption for the ODS is phased out. Of all the substitutes under consideration to replace ODS, those to be used in metered dose inhalers will be under the greatest scrutiny for adverse health effects, and it seems likely that any risks associated with their use will be correspondingly small.

Quite the reverse is likely to be true of the chemical pesticides, most of which will see increased use because of the phase-out of methyl bromide. Pesticides and fumigants have been designed to be very toxic. Thus, exposures to substitutes for these agents are likely to result in higher risks than exposure to the same levels of the substitutes used in the other areas. However, pesticides for the most part are closely regulated (and all of those identified in Table 2-1 have seen considerable use) so presumably these exposures and their associated risks will also be subjected to a higher degree of control than those chemicals not regulated as pesticides. It should be noted, however, that there are parts of the world where stringent pesticide regulation is lacking. In these locations, misuse of the substitutes (or for that matter any chemical pesticide) has the potential for significant adverse effects.

The remaining four groups of chemicals are much more likely to pose risks to occupationally exposed populations than the general public, and even then the risks from most of these chemicals appear to be low. Most of the chemicals listed below as substitutes for refrigerants, fire suppressants, solvents and foam-blowing agents have a low degree of acute toxicity. Furthermore, although the database on these chemicals is somewhat limited, what is available suggests that they will also demonstrate a low degree of activity as carcinogens. The one possible exception to this low degree of toxicity is n-propyl bromide, a bromine-containing compound that is being marketed as a replacement for many of the solvent uses of CFC.

Table 2-1. CFC Substitutes

Common Name	Chemical Name	CAS No	Likely Use	Reference
HFC 245fa	1,1,1,2,3,3,3-heptafluoropropane	431-89-0	Medical aerosols Fire-fighting agent	www.fluorocarbons.org
HFC 365mfc	1,1,13,3-pentafluorobutane	406-58-6	Foam blowing Agent	"
n-propyl bromide				
HFC 43–10mee	1,1,1,2,2,3,4,5,5,5 decafluoropentane	138495-42-8	Solvent	
HFC-236fa	1,1,13,3,3-heafluoropropane	290-39-1	Fire-fighting Agent	
1-3 dichloropropene		542-75-6	Fumigant	
Chloropicrin	Trichlornitromethane	76-06-2	Fumigant	
Furfural		98-01-1	Pesticide	
methyl isocyanate		624-83-9	Pesticide	
methyl iodide		74-88-4	Pesticide	
Fosthiazate	phosphonothioic acid, (2-oxo-3-thiazolidinyl)-,)-ethyl S-(1-methylpropyl) ester	98886-44-3	Pesticide	
Enzone	Sodium Tetrathiocarbonate		Pesticide	
Avermectin		73989-17-0	Pesticide	
propargyl bromide		106-96-7	Pesticide	
potassium azide		20762-60-1	Pesticide	
sulfuryl fluoride		2699-79-8	Pesticide	
Ethyl formate		109-94-4	Fumigant	
propylene oxide		75-56-9	Fumigant	
Carbonyl sulfide		463-58-1	Fumigant	

Common Name	Chemical Name	CAS No	Likely Use	Reference
R-407C	mixture of HFC 32, HFC-134a & HFC-125		Refrigerant	
R-410A	mixture of HFC-32, HFC-125		Refrigerant	
R-404A	mixture of HFC-125, HFC-134a & HCFC-143a		Refrigerant	
R-500			Refrigerant	
R-1270	Propylene	115-07-1	Refrigerant	
HC-600a	Isobutane	75-26-5	Refrigerant	
Ethylene dichloride		107-6-2		
Phosphine		7803-51-2	Pesticide	

This chemical, which is becoming more and more widely used, is now recognized for its toxicity to the nervous and reproductive systems, as well as to the foetus.[125]

For a number of uses of ODS substitutes have not been identified.[125] Although some of these involve the use of CFC, e.g., the use of CFC-113 as a solvent in the production of fluoropolymer resins, most relate to the use of carbon tetrachloride as a solvent in the production of a various chemicals ranging from pharmaceuticals to a number of different kinds of polymers. Clearly when substitutes are found for these ODS they will need to be closely evaluated to ensure that one problem is not being substituted for another.

Possible Interactions between Climate Change and Ozone Depletion

At the same time as the world is anticipating at least another 50 years of depleted ozone, another threat, namely increased atmospheric CO_2 leading to global climate change (GCC), has been identified as having the potential to affect the world's environment for generations to come. For the time period when these two threats co-exist, the likelihood is great that interactive effects on human health will occur. This section will attempt to identify possible interactions between ozone depletion and GCC. It should be noted at the outset, however, that there are few experimental data from systems exploring the issue of how these threats may interact and how such interactions may affect human health. Thus most of the following discussion should be viewed as informed speculation. It should also be noted that one of the most likely impacts of both ozone depletion and GCC will be changes in human behaviour. Human behaviour will also change as nations develop economically. The inability to predict human behaviour adds a large degree of uncertainty to the prognostications provided below.

Impact of UV Radiation and Climate Change on the Eye

The prevalence of nuclear cataract is reported to be higher in tropical and subtropical regions where there is a high annual UV exposure rate coupled with high ambient temperature and infrared exposure. Unlike the skin, the temperature of the lens is more related to core body temperature than to external temperature, and little direct synergism of temperature with UV radiation would be anticipated. Other heat-induced systemic factors, which may indirectly affect lens nutrition and metabolism could, on the other hand, potentially accelerate cataract development.

A recent study evaluating the effect of environmental temperature on cataract progression in rats[126] found no interaction between UV radiation and environmental temperature in UV-induced cortical cataract (including anterior subcapsular cataract). This suggests that the higher prevalence of nuclear cataract in regions near to the equator may be due primarily to other factors. The role of ambient temperature in influencing these factors has yet to be adequately investigated.

Impact of UV Radiation and Climate Change on the Skin

Results from one atmospheric model suggested that cooling of the stratosphere could delay the recovery of the ozone layer by a decade or more.[127] Later models have led to a variety of conclusions, ranging from no delay at all to a resurgence of ozone depletion late in this century (see Chapter 1).[3] The possibility of a delayed recovery gives reason for concern about the consequences, especially in the long-term. Before this problem was noted, a scenario study had been made for the increase in skin cancer incidence due to ozone depletion during the entire present century.[2, 128] Under the most optimistic conditions of full and worldwide compliance with the Montreal Protocol and all its amendments, the excess incidence would peak about the year 2055 at 9% above the baseline incidence, and then gradually decline. A similar scenario study has been performed recently, but now including a delay in the recovery of the ozone layer by 15-20 years[129], Figure 2-6. This showed that the excess incidence at the time of the peak would increase to 15%, and the peak itself would shift from 2055 to 2065.

Experiments performed many years ago[130, 131] demonstrated that mice exposed to UV radiation at increased room temperature developed skin cancers at an accelerated rate. From the data given in these papers, van der Leun and de Gruijl[132] calculated an average increase in the carcinogenic effectiveness of the UV radiation with a 5% per degree C increase in temperature. This result was then applied to skin cancer in the human population – firstly, to the excess incidence caused by ozone depletion. The conclusion was that a 2 degree rise in temperature would increase the peak excess from the 9% calculated by Slaper et al.[128] to 11%, and a 4

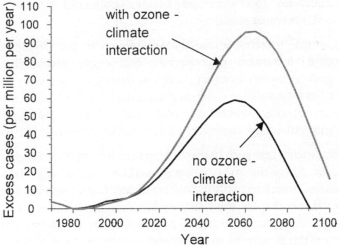

Figure 2-6 Increase in skin cancer incidence in the North-Western Europe, with ozone-climate interaction causing 15-20 years delay (worst case scenario) in recovery of the ozone layer, and without any delay from an ozone-climate interaction.[129]

degree rise would increase it to 13%. Secondly, the effect on the baseline incidence itself was considered, without any ozone depletion. A persistent increase of temperature by 2 degrees C was calculated to increase the baseline incidence by 21%, and a 4 degree C rise by 46%.

It should be noted that, while UV carcinogenesis in mice and humans is basically similar, there are important quantitative differences, and the same may be true for the influence of higher temperatures. Direct data relating temperature and UV carcinogenesis in human populations are not yet available. The experimental mice were exposed to the higher temperatures constantly, a procedure which is rather different from normal human behaviour where people are unlikely to experience increased temperatures all the time. It is also unknown at what stage the temperature exerts its critical influence. This could be during the exposure to UV radiation, or during the time between exposures, or both. The calculation is also complicated by the fact that the observed temperature influence was non-linear: in the mouse experiment there was little effect below the normal room temperature of 23 degrees centigrade, and a marked effect at the higher temperatures. Despite all these uncertainties, the influence of increased temperatures on carcinogenesis in the human population merits further consideration and could be of importance.

Impact of UV Radiation and Climate Change on the Immune Response

The potential consequences of GCC with regard to human health have been the subject of numerous reviews.[133-135] For the most part it seems that any increases in such effects that might occur will be in those diseases whose incidences are increased in the tropics or with warm weather in other places. However, it is also clear that in most locations, there will only be an effect of GCC on disease if the disease already exists at that location or in a location that is geographically contiguous. Although there has been much concern that malaria may increase with GCC perhaps in the developed nations as well as the developing ones,[135] it has been contended that most developed nations conquered the disease in their past and are unlikely to see a serious resurgence.

Longstreth[136] examined the diseases found in the US that showed a seasonal variation and identified a number of endpoints that could potentially be affected by the changes in temperature and/or humidity likely to be associated with GCC. These included a variety of infectious diseases, e.g., viral encephalitis, Hanta virus pulmonary syndrome, as well as a number of other health endpoints such increased asthma due to increased air pollution, shellfish poisonings, morbidity and mortality from extreme events, and heat stress.

To the extent that such diseases are increased by the changes in weather associated with GCC, it seems likely that many of them could be additionally exacerbated by elevated levels of UV radiation associated with a thinner stratospheric ozone layer. If climatic conditions become more favourable for the transmission of a particular endemic infectious disease, for example malaria, increased ambient UV radiation due to a depleted ozone layer may lead to more severe cases of the disease due to suppression of the immune system.

References

1   J. C. van der Leun, M. Tevini, X. Tang and R. C. Worrest, Environmental Effects of Ozone Depletion; 1998 assessment, United Nations Environment Programme, Nairobi, 1998, p. 192.

2   J. Longstreth, F. R. de Gruijl, M. L. Kripke, S. Abseck, F. Arnold, H. I. Slaper, G. Velders, Y. Takizawa and J. C. van der Leun, Health risks, *J. Photochem. Photobiol. B*, 1998, 46, 20-39.

3   R. L. McKenzie, L. O. Bjorn, A. Bais and M. Ilyas, Changes in Biologically active ultraviolet radiation reaching the Earth's surface, *Photochem. Photobiol. Sci.*, 2003, In press

4   D. H. Sliney, Geometrical assessment of ocular exposure to environmental UV radiation--implications for ophthalmic epidemiology, *J. Epidemiol.*, 1999, 9, S22-32.

5   J. A. Van Best, J. L. Van Delft and J. E. Keunen, Long term follow-up of lenticular autofluorescence and transmittance in healthy volunteers, *Exp. Eye. Res.*, 1998, 66, 117-123.

6   H. Sasaki, O. Hockwin, T. Kasuga, K. Nagai, Y. Sakamoto and K. Sasaki, An index for human lens transparency related to age and lens layer: comparison between normal volunteers and diabetic patients with still clear lenses, *Ophthalmic Res.*, 1999, 31, 93-103.

7   S. Fu, R. Dean, M. Southan and R. Truscott, The hydroxyl radical in lens nuclear cataractogenesis, *J. Biol. Chem.*, 1998, 273, 28603-28609.

8   Y. Berry and R. J. Truscott, The presence of a human UV filter within the lens represents an oxidative stress, *Exp. Eye. Res.*, 2001, 72, 411-421.

9   J. W. Eaton, UV-mediated cataractogenesis: a radical perspective, *Doc. Ophthalmol.*, 1994, 88, 233-242.

10   J. Dillon, UV-B as a pro-aging and pro-cataract factor, *Doc. Ophthalmol.*, 1994, 88, 339-344.

11   K. W. Lee, N. Meyer and B. J. Ortwerth, Chromatographic comparison of the UVA sensitizers present in brunescent cataracts and in calf lens proteins ascorbylated in vitro, *Exp. Eye. Res.*, 1999, 69, 375-384.

12   H. R. Taylor, Epidemiology of age-related cataract, *Eye*, 1999, 13, 445-448.

13   L. C. Hayashi, N. Tamiya and E. Yano, Correlation between UVB irradiation and the proportion of cataract--an epidemiological study based on a nationwide patient survey in Japan, *Ind. Health*, 1998, 36, 354-360.

14   H. R. Taylor, S. K. West, F. S. Rosenthal, B. Munoz, H. S. Newland, H. Abbey and E. A. Emmett, Effect of ultraviolet radiation on cataract formation, *N. Engl. J. Med.*, 1988, 319, 1429-1433.

15   F. Hollows and D. Moran, Cataract - the ultraviolet risk factor, *Lancet*, 1981, 2, 1249-1250.

16   R. Hiller, R. D. Sperduto and F. Ederer, Epidemiologic associations with cataract in the 1971-1972 National Health and Nutrition Examination Survey, *Am. J. Epidemiol.*, 1983, 118, 239-249.

17   C. A. McCarty, B. N. Mukesh, C. L. Fu and H. R. Taylor, The epidemiology of cataract in Australia, *Am. J. Opthalmol.*, 1999, 128, 446-465.

18   K. Sasaki, H. Sasaki, M. Kojima, Y. B. Shui, O. Hockwin, F. Jonasson, H. M. Cheng, M. Ono and N. Katoh, Epidemiological studies on UV-related cataract in climatically different countries, *J. Epidemiol.*, 1999, 9, S33-38.

19   S. K. West, D. D. Duncan, B. Munoz, G. S. Rubin, L. P. Fried, K. Bandeen-Roche and O. D. Schein, Sunlight exposure and risk of lens opacities in a population-based study: the Salisbury Eye Evaluation project, *JAMA*, 1998, 280, 714-718.

20   N. Katoh, F. Jonasson, H. Sasaki, M. Kojima, M. Ono, N. Takahashi and K. Sasaki, Cortical lens opacification in Iceland. Risk factor analysis -- Reykjavik Eye Study, *Acta Ophthalmol. Scand.*, 2001, 79, 154-159.

21   S. K. West, Ocular ultraviolet B exposure and lens opacities; a review, *J. Epidemiol.*, 1999, 9, S97-101.

22   O. Hockwin, M. Kojima, Y. Sakamoto, A. Wegener, Y. B. Shui and K. Sasaki, UV damage to the eye lens: further results from animal model studies: a review, *J. Epidemiol.*, 1999, 9, S39-47.

23   D. G. Pitts, A. P. Cullen and P. D. Hacker, Ocular effects of ultraviolet radiation from 295 to 365 nm, *Invest. Ophthalmol. Vis. Sci.*, 1977, 16, 932-939.

24   J. C. Merriam, S. Lofgren, R. Michael, P. Soderberg, J. Dillon, L. Zheng and M. Ayala, An action spectrum for UV-B radiation and the rat lens, *Invest. Ophthalmol. Vis. Sci.*, 2000, 41, 2642-2647.

25   O. M. Oriowo, A. P. Cullen, B. R. Chou and J. G. Sivak, Action spectrum and recovery for in vitro UV-induced cataract using whole lenses, *Invest. Ophthalmol. Vis. Sci.*, 2001, 42, 2596-2602.

26   J. F. Abarca, C. C. Casiccia and F. D. Zamorano, Increase in sunburns and photosensitivity disorders at the edge of the Anartic ozone hole, Southern Chile, 1986-2000, *J. Am. Acad. Dermatol.*, 2002, 46, 193-199.

27   A. R. Young, C. A. Chadwick, G. I. Harrison, O. Nikaido, J. Ramsden and C. S. Potten, The similarity of action spectra for thymine dimers in human epidermis and erythema suggests that DNA is the chromophore for erythema, *J. Invest. Dermatol.*, 1998, 111, 982-988.

28   R. J. Berg, H. J. Ruven, A. T. Sands, F. R. de Gruijl and L. H. Mullenders, Defective global genome repair in XPC mice is associated with skin cancer susceptibility but not with sensitivity to UVB induced erythema and edema, *J. Invest. Dermatol.*, 1998, 110, 405-409.

29   C. Kielbassa, L. Roza and B. Epe, Wavelength dependence of oxidative DNA damage induced by UV and visible light, *Carcinogenesis*, 1997, 18, 811-816.

30   F. R. de Gruijl and J. C. van der Leun, Estimate of the wavelength dependency of ultraviolet carcinogenesis in humans and its relevance to the risk assessment of a stratospheric ozone depletion, *Hlth. Phys.*, 1994, 67, 319-325.

31   M. Horiguchi, K. I. Masumura, H. Ikehata, T. Ono, Y. Kanke and T. Nohmi, Molecular nature of ultraviolet B light-induced deletions in the murine epidermis, *Cancer Res.*, 2001, 61, 3913-3918.

32   R. A. Keulers, A. R. de Roon, S. de Roode and A. D. Tates, The induction and analysis of micronuclei and cell killing by ultraviolet-B radiation in human peripheral blood lymphocytes, *Photochem. Photobiol.*, 1998, 67, 426-432.

33   G. Emri, E. Wenczl, P. Van Erp, J. Jans, L. Roza, I. Horkay and A. A. Schothorst, Low doses of UVB or UVA induce chromosomal aberrations in cultured human skin cells, *J. Invest. Dermatol.*, 2000, 115, 435-440.

34   C. Masutani, R. Kusumoto, A. Yamada, N. Dohmae, M. Yokoi, M. Yuasa, M. Araki, S. Iwai, K. Takio and F. Hanaoka, The XPV (xeroderma pigmentosum variant) gene encodes human DNA polymerase eta, *Nature*, 1999, 399, 700-704.

35   C. L. Limoli, E. Giedzinski, W. F. Morgan and J. E. Cleaver, Inaugural article: polymerase eta deficiency in the xeroderma pigmentosum variant uncovers an overlap between the S phase checkpoint and double-strand break repair, *Proc. Natl. Acad. Sci. USA*, 2000, 97, 7939-7946.

36   P. Wolf, H. Maier, R. R. Mullegger, C. A. Chadwick, R. Hofmann-Wellenhof, H. P. Soyer, A. Hofer, J. Smolle, M. Horn, L. Cerroni, D. Yarosh, J. Klein, C. Bucana, K. Dunner, Jr., C. S. Potten, H. Honigsmann, H. Kerl and M. L. Kripke, Topical treatment with liposomes containing T4 endonuclease V protects human skin in vivo from ultraviolet-induced upregulation of interleukin-10 and tumor necrosis factor-alpha, *J. Invest. Dermatol.*, 2000, 114, 149-156.

37   H. Stege, L. Roza, A. A. Vink, M. Grewe, T. Ruzicka, S. Grether-Beck and J. Krutmann, Enzyme plus light therapy to repair DNA damage in ultraviolet-B-irradiated human skin, *Proc. Natl. Acad. Sci. USA*, 2000, 97, 1790-1795.

38   A. Hannuksela-Svahn, E. Pukkala and J. Karvonen, Basal cell skin carcinoma and other nonmelanoma skin cancers in Finland from 1956 through 1995, *Arch. Dermatol.*, 1999, 135, 781-786.

39   M. Staples, R. Marks and G. Giles, Trends in the incidence of non-melanocytic skin cancer (NMSC) treated in Australia 1985-1995: are primary prevention programs starting to have an effect?, *Int. J. Cancer*, 1998, 78, 144-148.

40   IARC, *Solar and ultraviolet radiation,* Vol. 55, International Agency for Research on Cancer, Lyon, 1992.

41   S. A. Holme, K. Malinovszky and D. L. Roberts, Changing trends in non-melanoma skin cancer in South Wales, 1988-98, *Brit. J. Dermatol.*, 2000, 143, 1224-1229.

42   I. Plesko, G. Severi, A. Obsitnikova and P. Boyle, Trends in the incidence of non-melanoma skin cancer in Slovakia, 1978-1995, *Neoplasma*, 2000, 47, 137-142.

43   R. B. Harris, K. Griffith and T. E. Moon, Trends in the incidence of nonmelanoma skin cancers in southeastern Arizona, 1985-1996, *J. Am. Acad. Dermatol.*, 2001, 45, 528-536.

44   J. Scotto, H. Pitcher and J. A. Lee, Indications of future decreasing trends in skin-melanoma mortality among whites in the United States, *Int. J. Cancer*, 1991, 49, 490-497.

45   R. M. MacKie, D. Hole, J. A. Hunter, R. Rankin, A. Evans, K. McLaren, M. Fallowfield, A. Hutcheon and A. Morris, Cutaneous malignant melanoma in Scotland: incidence, survival, and mortality, 1979-94. The Scottish Melanoma Group, *Brit. Med. J.*, 1997, 315, 1117-1121.

46   G. G. Giles, B. K. Armstrong, R. C. Burton, M. P. Staples and V. J. Thursfield, Has mortality from melanoma stopped rising in Australia? Analysis of trends between 1931 and 1994, *Brit. Med. J.*, 1996, 312, 1121-1125.

47   G. Severi, G. G. Giles, C. Robertson, P. Boyle and P. Autier, Mortality from cutaneous melanoma: evidence for contrasting trends between populations, *Brit. J. Cancer.*, 2000, 82, 1887-1891.

48   A. Green, G. Williams, R. Neale, V. Hart, D. Leslie, P. Parsons, G. C. Marks, P. Gaffney, D. Battistutta, C. Frost, C. Lang and A. Russell, Daily sunscreen application and betacarotene supplementation in prevention of basal-cell and squamous-cell carcinomas of the skin: a randomised controlled trial, *Lancet*, 1999, 354, 723-729.

49   D. Yarosh, J. Klein, A. O'Connor, J. Hawk, E. Rafal and P. Wolf, Effect of topically applied T4 endonuclease V in liposomes on skin cancer in xeroderma pigmentosum: a randomised study. Xeroderma Pigmentosum Study Group, *Lancet*, 2001, 357, 926-929.

50   A. S. Jonason, S. Kunala, G. J. Price, R. J. Restifo, H. M. Spinelli, J. A. Persing, D. J. Leffell, R. E. Tarone and D. E. Brash, Frequent clones of p53-mutated keratinocytes in normal human skin, *Proc. Natl. Acad. Sci. USA*, 1996, 93, 14025-14029.

51   Z. P. Ren, F. Ponten, M. Nister and J. Ponten, Two distinct p53 immunohistochemical patterns in human squamous-cell skin cancer, precursors and normal epidermis, *Int. J. Cancer*, 1996, 69, 174-179.

52   H. Rebel, L. O. Mosnier, R. J. Berg, A. Westerman-de Vries, H. van Steeg, H. J. van Kranen and F. R. de Gruijl, Early p53-positive foci as indicators of tumor risk in ultraviolet-exposed hairless mice: kinetics of induction, effects of DNA repair deficiency, and p53 heterozygosity, *Cancer Res.*, 2001, 61, 977-983.

53   H. Hahn, C. Wicking, P. G. Zaphiropoulous, M. R. Gailani, S. Shanley, A. Chidambaram, I. Vorechovsky, E. Holmberg, A. B. Unden, S. Gillies, K. Negus, I. Smyth, C. Pressman, D. J. Leffell, B. Gerrard, A. M. Goldstein, M. Dean, R. Toftgard, G. Chenevix-Trench, B. Wainwright and A. E. Bale, Mutations of the human homolog of Drosophila patched in the nevoid basal cell carcinoma syndrome, *Cell*, 1996, 85, 841-851.

54   A. Kamb, N. A. Gruis, J. Weaver-Feldhaus, Q. Liu, K. Harshman, S. V. Tavtigian, E. Stockert, R. S. Day, 3rd, B. E. Johnson and M. H. Skolnick, A cell cycle regulator potentially involved in genesis of many tumor types, *Science*, 1994, 264, 436-440.

55   N. Dahmane, J. Lee, P. Robins, P. Heller and A. Ruiz i Altaba, Activation of the transcription factor Gli1 and the Sonic hedgehog signalling pathway in skin tumours, *Nature*, 1997, 389, 876-881.

56   M. R. Gailani, M. Stahle-Backdahl, D. J. Leffell, M. Glynn, P. G. Zaphiropoulos, C. Pressman, A. B. Unden, M. Dean, D. E. Brash, A. E. Bale and R. Toftgard, The role of the human homologue of Drosophila patched in sporadic basal cell carcinomas, *Nat. Genet.*, 1996, 14, 78-81.

57   M. Aszterbaum, J. Epstein, A. Oro, V. Douglas, P. E. LeBoit, M. P. Scott and E. H. Epstein, Jr., Ultraviolet and ionizing radiation enhance the growth of BCCs and trichoblastomas in patched heterozygous knockout mice, *Nat. Med.*, 1999, 5, 1285-1291.

58   M. Ruas and G. Peters, The p16INK4a/CDKN2A tumor suppressor and its relatives, *Biochim. Biophys. Acta*, 1998, 1378, F115-177.

59   J. O. Funk, P. I. Schiller, M. T. Barrett, D. J. Wong, P. Kind and C. A. Sander, p16INK4a expression is frequently decreased and associated with 9p21 loss of heterozygosity in sporadic melanoma, *J. Cutan. Pathol.*, 1998, 25, 291-296.

60   M. Serrano, H. Lee, L. Chin, C. Cordon-Cardo, D. Beach and R. A. DePinho, Role of the INK4a locus in tumor suppression and cell mortality, *Cell*, 1996, 85, 27-37.

61   P. Krimpenfort, K. C. Quon, W. J. Mooi, A. Loonstra and A. Berns, Loss of p16Ink4a confers susceptibility to metastatic melanoma in mice, *Nature*, 2001, 413, 83-86.

62   N. E. Sharpless, N. Bardeesy, K. H. Lee, D. Carrasco, D. H. Castrillon, A. J. Aguirre, E. A. Wu, J. W. Horner and R. A. DePinho, Loss of p16Ink4a with retention of p19Arf predisposes mice to tumorigenesis, *Nature*, 2001, 413, 86-91.

63   A. van Elsas, S. F. Zerp, S. van der Flier, K. M. Kruse, C. Aarnoudse, N. K. Hayward, D. J. Ruiter and P. I. Schrier, Relevance of ultraviolet-induced N-ras oncogene point mutations in development of primary human cutaneous melanoma, *Am. J. Pathol.*, 1996, 149, 883-893.

64   H. Davies, G. R. Bignell, C. Cox, P. Stephens, S. Edkins, S. Clegg, J. Teague, H. Woffendin, M. J. Garnett, W. Bottomley, N. Davis, E. Dicks, R. Ewing, Y. Floyd, K. Gray, S. Hall, R. Hawes, J. Hughes, V. Kosmidou, A. Menzies, C. Mould, A. Parker, C. Stevens, S. Watt, S. Hooper, R. Wilson, H. Jayatilake, B. A. Gusterson, C. Cooper, J. Shipley, D. Hargrave, K. Pritchard-Jones, N. Maitland, G. Chenevix-Trench, G. J. Riggins, D. D. Bigner, G. Palmieri, A. Cossu, A. Flanagan, A. Nicholson, J. W. Ho, S. Y. Leung, S. T. Yuen, B. L. Weber, H. F. Seigler, T. L. Darrow, H. Paterson, R. Marais, C. J. Marshall, R. Wooster, M. R. Stratton and P. A. Futreal, Mutations of the BRAF gene in human cancer, *Nature*, 2002, 417, 949-954.

65   F. P. Noonan, J. A. Recio, H. Takayama, P. Duray, M. R. Anver, W. L. Rush, E. C. De Fabo and G. Merlino, Neonatal sunburn and melanoma in mice, *Nature*, 2001, 413, 271-272.

66   F. P. Noonan, T. Otsuka, S. Bang, M. R. Anver and G. Merlino, Accelerated ultraviolet radiation-induced carcinogenesis in hepatocyte growth factor/scatter factor transgenic mice, *Cancer Res.*, 2000, 60, 3738-3743.

67   E. S. Robinson, G. B. Hubbard, G. Colon and J. L. Vandeberg, Low-dose ultraviolet exposure early in development can lead to widespread melanoma in the opossum model, *Int. J. Exp. Pathol.*, 1998, 79, 235-244.

68   J. Chan, E. S. Robinson, J. Atencio, Z. Wang, S. Kazianis, L. D. Coletta, R. S. Nairn and J. R. McCarrey, Characterization of the CDKN2A and ARF genes in UV-induced melanocytic hyperplasias and melanomas of an opossum (Monodelphis domestica), *Mol. Carcinog.*, 2001, 31, 16-26.

69   E. S. Robinson, R. H. Hill, Jr., M. L. Kripke and R. B. Setlow, The Monodelphis melanoma model: initial report on large ultraviolet A exposures of suckling young, *Photochem. Photobiol.*, 2000, 71, 743-746.

70   S. Q. Wang, R. Setlow, M. Berwick, D. Polsky, A. A. Marghoob, A. W. Kopf and R. S. Bart, Ultraviolet A and melanoma: a review, *J. Am. Acad. Dermatol.*, 2001, 44, 837-846.

71   G. J. Clydesdale, G. W. Dandie and H. K. Muller, Ultraviolet light induced injury: immunological and inflammatory effects, *Immunol. Cell Biol.*, 2001, 79, 547-568.

72   A. M. Moodycliffe, D. Nghiem, G. Clydesdale and S. E. Ullrich, Immune suppression and skin cancer development: regulation by NKT cells, *Nat. Immunol.*, 2000, 1, 521-525.

73   A. Schwarz, S. Beissert, K. Grosse-Heitmeyer, M. Gunzer, J. A. Bluestone, S. Grabbe and T. Schwarz, Evidence for functional relevance of CTLA-4 in ultraviolet-radiation-induced tolerance, *J. Immunol.*, 2000, 165, 1824-1831.

74   J. F. Rooney, Y. Bryson, M. L. Mannix, M. Dillon, C. R. Wohlenberg, S. Banks, C. J. Wallington, A. L. Notkins and S. E. Straus, Prevention of ultraviolet-light-induced herpes labialis by sunscreen, *Lancet*, 1991, 338, 1419-1422.

75   M. Gallerani and R. Manfredini, Seasonal variation in herpes zoster infection, *Brit. J. Dermatol.*, 2000, 142, 588-589.

76   M. Zak-Prelich, J. L. Borkowski, F. Alexander and M. Norval, The role of solar ultraviolet irradiation in zoster., *Epidemiol. Inf.*, 2002, 129, 1 - 5.

77   J. Breuer-McHam, E. Simpson, I. Dougherty, M. Bonkobara, K. Ariizumi, D. E. Lewis, D. B. Dawson, M. Duvic and P. D. Cruz, Jr., Activation of HIV in human skin by ultraviolet B radiation and its inhibition by NFkappaB blocking agents, *Photochem. Photobiol.*, 2001, 74, 805-810.

78   F. Termorshuizen, R. B. Geskus, M. T. Roos, R. A. Coutinho and H. Van Loveren, Seasonal influences on immunological parameters in HIV-infected homosexual men: searching for the immunomodulating effects of sunlight, *Int. J. Hyg. Environ. Health*, 2002, 205, 379-384.

79   R. Akaraphanth and H. W. Lim, HIV, UV and immunosuppression, *Photodermatol. Photoimmunol. Photomed.*, 1999, 15, 28-31.

80   T. A. Swartz, P. Skalska, C. G. Gerichter and W. C. Cockburn, Routine administration of oral polio vaccine in a subtropical area. Factors possibly influencing sero-conversion rates, *J. Hyg. (Lond)*, 1972, 70, 719-726.

81   M. P. Zykov and A. V. Sosunov, Vaccination activity of live influenza vaccine in different seasons of the year, *J. Hyg .Epidemiol. Microbiol. Immunol.*, 1987, 31, 453-459.

82   A. Sleijffers, J. Garssen, F. R. de Gruijl, G. J. Boland, J. van Hattum, W. A. van Vloten and H. van Loveren, Influence of ultraviolet B exposure on immune responses following hepatitis B vaccination in human volunteers, *J. Invest. Dermatol.*, 2001, 117, 1144-1150.

83   D. L. Damian, G. M. Halliday, C. A. Taylor and R. S. Barnetson, Ultraviolet radiation induced suppression of Mantoux reactions in humans, *J. Invest. Dermatol.*, 1998, 110, 824-827.

84   A. J. McMichael and A. J. Hall, Does immunosuppressive ultraviolet radiation explain the latitude gradient for multiple sclerosis?, *Epidemiology*, 1997, 8, 642-645.

85   D. M. Freedman, M. Dosemeci and M. C. Alavanja, Mortality from multiple sclerosis and exposure to residential and occupational solar radiation: a case-control study based on death certificates, *Occup. Environ. Med.*, 2000, 57, 418-421.

86   L. Nystrom, G. Dahlquist, J. Ostman, S. Wall, H. Arnqvist, G. Blohme, F. Lithner, B. Littorin, B. Schersten and L. Wibell, Risk of developing insulin-dependent diabetes mellitus (IDDM) before 35 years of age: indications of climatological determinants for age at onset, *Int. J. Epidemiol*, 1992, 21, 352-358.

87   M. Rihner and H. McGrath, Jr., Fluorescent light photosensitivity in patients with systemic lupus erythematosus, *Arthritis Rheum.*, 1992, 35, 949-952.

88   L. M. Vila, A. M. Mayor, A. H. Valentin, S. I. Rodriguez, M. L. Reyes, E. Acosta and S. Vila, Association of sunlight exposure and photoprotection measures with clinical outcome in systemic lupus erythematosus, *P. R. Health Sci. J.*, 1999, 18, 89-94.

89   H. Van Loveren, A. Boonstra, M. Van Dijk, A. Fluitman, H. F. Savelkoul and J. Garssen, UV exposure alters respiratory allergic responses in mice, *Photochem. Photobiol.*, 2000, 72, 253-259.

90   M. Norval, J. Garssen, H. Van Loveren and A. A. el-Ghorr, UV-induced changes in the immune response to microbial infections in human subjects and animal models, *J. Epidemiol.*, 1999, 9, S84-92.

91   K. Yamamoto, R. Ito, M. Koura and T. Kamiyama, UV-B irradiation increases susceptibility of mice to malarial infection, *Infect. Immun.*, 2000, 68, 2353-2355.

92   J. C. van der Leun, Y. Takizawa and J. Longstreth, in *Environmental Effects Panel Report* eds.: J. C. van der Leun and M. Tevini, United Nations Environmental Programme, Nairobi, 1989, pp. 11-24.

93   L. K. Ryan, D. L. Neldon, L. R. Bishop, M. I. Gilmour, M. J. Daniels, D. M. Sailstad and M. J. Selgrade, Exposure to ultraviolet radiation enhances mortality and pathology associated with influenza virus infection in mice, *Photochem. Photobiol.*, 2000, 72, 497-507.

94   J. Garssen, R. van der Molen, A. de Klerk, M. Norval and H. van Loveren, Effects of UV irradiation on skin and nonskin-associated herpes simplex virus infections in rats, *Photochem. Photobiol.*, 2000, 72, 645-651.

95   E. L. Brown, S. E. Ullrich, M. Pride and M. L. Kripke, The effect of UV irradiation on infection of mice with Borrelia burgdorferi, *Photochem. Photobiol.*, 2001, 73, 537-544.

96   E. C. De Fabo, F. P. Noonan and J. E. Frederick, Biologically effective doses of sunlight for immune suppression at various latitudes and their relationship to changes in stratospheric ozone, *Photochem. Photobiol.*, 1990, 52, 811-817.

97   J. Garssen, W. Goettsch, F. de Gruijl, W. Slob and H. van Loveren, Risk assessment of UVB effects on resistance to infectious diseases, *Photochem. Photobiol.*, 1996, 64, 269-274.

98   D. A. Kelly, S. L. Walker, J. M. McGregor and A. R. Young, A single exposure of solar simulated radiation suppresses contact hypersensitivity responses both locally and systemically in humans: quantitative studies with high-frequency ultrasound, *J. Photochem. Photobiol. B*, 1998, 44, 130-142.

99   T. Yoshikawa, V. Rae, W. Bruins-Slot, J. W. Van den Berg, J. R. Taylor and J. W. Streilein, Susceptibility to effects of UVB radiation on induction of contact hypersensitivity as a risk factor for skin cancer in humans, *J. Invest. Dermatol.*, 1990, 95, 530-536.

100   D. A. Kelly, A. R. Young, J. M. McGregor, P. T. Seed, C. S. Potten and S. L. Walker, Sensitivity to sunburn is associated with susceptibility to ultraviolet radiation-induced suppression of cutaneous cell-mediated immunity, *J. Exp. Med.*, 2000, 191, 561-566.

101   P. H. Hart, M. A. Grimbaldeston, G. J. Swift, A. Jaksic, F. P. Noonan and J. J. Finlay-Jones, Dermal mast cells determine susceptibility to ultraviolet B-induced systemic suppression of contact hypersensitivity responses in mice, *J. Exp. Med.*, 1998, 187, 2045-2053.

102   M. A. Grimbaldeston, L. Skov, O. Baadsgaard, B. G. Skov, G. Marshman, J. J. Finlay-Jones and P. H. Hart, Communications: high dermal mast cell prevalence is a predisposing factor for basal cell carcinoma in humans, *J. Invest. Dermatol.*, 2000, 115, 317-320.

103   P. H. Hart, M. A. Grimbaldeston, G. J. Swift, E. K. Hosszu and J. J. Finlay-Jones, A critical role for dermal mast cells in cis-urocanic acid-induced systemic suppression of contact hypersensitivity responses in mice, *Photochem. Photobiol.*, 1999, 70, 807-812.

104   F. De Fine Olivarius, J. Lock-Andersen, F. G. Larsen, H. C. Wulf, J. Crosby and M. Norval, Urocanic acid isomers in patients with basal cell carcinoma and cutaneous malignant melanoma, *Brit. J. Dermatol.*, 1998, 138, 986-992.

105   E. Snellman, C. T. Jansen, T. Rantanen and P. Pasanen, Epidermal urocanic acid concentration and photoisomerization reactivity in patients with cutaneous malignant melanoma or basal cell carcinoma, *Acta Derm. Venereol.*, 1999, 79, 200-203.

106   S. Beissert, D. Ruhlemann, T. Mohammad, S. Grabbe, A. El-Ghorr, M. Norval, H. Morrison, R. D. Granstein and T. Schwarz, IL-12 prevents the inhibitory effects of cis-urocanic acid on tumor antigen presentation by Langerhans cells: implications for photocarcinogenesis, *J. Immunol.*, 2001, 167, 6232-6238.

107   F. Levi, L. Randimbison, C. La Vecchia, G. Erler and V. C. Te, Incidence of invasive cancers following squamous cell skin cancer, *Am. J. Epidemiol.*, 1997, 146, 734-739.

108 F. Levi, L. Randimbison, V. C. Te and C. La Vecchia, Non-Hodgkin's lymphomas, chronic lymphocytic leukaemias and skin cancers, *Brit. J. Cancer.*, 1996, 74, 1847-1850.

109 M. Frisch, H. Hjalgrim, J. H. Olsen and M. Melbye, Risk for subsequent cancer after diagnosis of basal-cell carcinoma. A population-based, epidemiologic study, *Ann. Intern. Med.*, 1996, 125, 815-821.

110 L. H. Goldberg, Basal-cell carcinoma as predictor for other cancers, *Lancet*, 1997, 349, 664-665.

111 G. Bentham, Association between incidence of non-Hodgkin's lymphoma and solar ultraviolet radiation in England and Wales, *Brit. Med. J.*, 1996, 312, 1128-1131.

112 A. J. McMichael and G. G. Giles, Have increases in solar ultraviolet exposure contributed to the rise in incidence of non-Hodgkin's lymphoma?, *Brit. J. Cancer.*, 1996, 73, 945-950.

113 I. H. Langford, G. Bentham and A. L. McDonald, Mortality from non-Hodgkin lymphoma and UV exposure in the European Community, *Health Place*, 1998, 4, 355-364.

114 J. Adami, G. Gridley, O. Nyren, M. Dosemeci, M. Linet, B. Glimelius, A. Ekbom and S. H. Zahm, Sunlight and non-Hodgkin's lymphoma: a population-based cohort study in Sweden, *Int. J. Cancer*, 1999, 80, 641-645.

115 P. Hartge, S. S. Devesa, D. Grauman, T. R. Fears and J. F. Fraumeni, Jr., Non-Hodgkin's lymphoma and sunlight, *J. Natl. Cancer. Inst.*, 1996, 88, 298-300.

116 L. J. Schouten, H. Meijer, J. A. Huveneers and L. A. Kiemeney, Urban-rural differences in cancer incidence in The Netherlands 1989-1991, *Int. J. Epidemiol.*, 1996, 25, 729-736.

117 N. Hakansson, B. Floderus, P. Gustavsson, M. Feychting and N. Hallin, Occupational sunlight exposure and cancer incidence among Swedish construction workers, *Epidemiology*, 2001, 12, 552-557.

118 M. Nordstrom, L. Hardell, A. Magnusson, H. Hagberg and A. Rask-Andersen, Occupation and occupational exposure to UV light as risk factors for hairy cell leukaemia evaluated in a case-control study, *Eur. J. Cancer. Prev.*, 1997, 6, 467-472.

119 G. Bentham, A. M. Wolfreys, Y. Liu, G. Cortopassi, M. H. Green, C. F. Arlett and J. Cole, Frequencies of hprt(-) mutations and bcl-2 translocations in circulating human lymphocytes are correlated with United Kingdom sunlight records, *Mutagenesis*, 1999, 14, 527-532.

120 W. Jiang, H. N. Ananthaswamy, H. K. Muller, A. Ouhtit, S. Bolshakov, S. E. Ullrich, A. K. El-Naggar and M. L. Kripke, UV irradiation augments lymphoid malignancies in mice with one functional copy of wild-type p53, *Proc. Natl. Acad. Sci. USA*, 2001, 98, 9790-9795.

121 G. P. Studzinski and D. C. Moore, Sunlight--can it prevent as well as cause cancer?, *Cancer Res.*, 1995, 55, 4014-4022.

122 C. L. Hanchette and G. G. Schwartz, Geographic patterns of prostate cancer mortality. Evidence for a protective effect of ultraviolet radiation, *Cancer*, 1992, 70, 2861-2869.

123 C. J. Luscombe, A. A. Fryer, M. E. French, S. Liu, M. F. Saxby, P. W. Jones and R. C. Strange, Exposure to ultraviolet radiation: association with susceptibility and age at presentation with prostate cancer, *Lancet*, 2001, 358, 641-642.

124 J. M. Norris, Can the sunshine vitamin shed light on type 1 diabetes?, *Lancet*, 2001, 358, 1476-1478.

125   TEAP, UNEP Report of Technology and Economic Assessment Panel, United Nations Environmental Programme Report No. Nairobi.

126   M. Kojima, T. Okuno, M. Miyakoshi, K. Sasaki and N. Takahashi, in *Progress in Lens and Cataract Research*, Vol. 35 eds.: O. Hockwin, M. Kojima, N. Takahashi and D. H. Sliney, Karger, Basel, 2002, pp. 125-134.

127   D. T. Shindell, D. Rind and P. Lonergan, Increased polar stratospheric ozone losses and delayed eventual recovery owing to increased greenhouse-gas concentrations, *Nature*, 1998, 392, 589-592.

128   H. Slaper, G. J. Velders, J. S. Daniel, F. R. de Gruijl and J. C. van der Leun, Estimates of ozone depletion and skin cancer incidence to examine the Vienna Convention achievements, *Nature*, 1996, 384, 256-258.

129   G. Kelfkens, A. Bergman, F. R. de Gruijl, J. C. Van der Leun, A. Piquet, T. van Oijen, W. W. C. Gieskens, H. van Loveren, G. J. M. Velders, P. Martens and H. Slaper, Ozone and climate change interactions; Influence on UV levels and UV-related effects, National Programme on Global Air Pollution and Climate Change Report No. Bilthoven, Netherlands.

130   J. A. Bain, H. P. Rusch and B. E. Kline, The effect of temperature upon ultraviolet carcinogenesis with wave lengths 2,800-3,400 A, *Cancer Res.*, 1943, 3, 610-612.

131   R. G. Freeman and J. M. Knox, Influence of temperature on ultraviolet injury, *Arch. Dermatol.*, 1964, 89, 858-864.

132   J. C. van der Leun and F. R. de Gruijl, Climate change and skin cancer, *Photochem. Photobiol. Sci.*, 2002, 1, 324-326.

133   J. Longstreth, Anticipated public health consequences of global climate change, *Environ. Health Perspect.*, 1991, 96, 139-144.

134   A. Leaf, Potential health effects of global climatic and environmental changes, *N. Engl. J. Med.*, 1989, 321, 1577-1583.

135   P. R. Epstein, Global warming and vector-borne disease, *Lancet*, 1998, 351, 1737; discussion 1738.

136   J. Longstreth, Public health consequences of global climate change in the United States--some regions may suffer disproportionately, *Environ. Health Perspect.*, 1999, 107 Suppl 1, 169-179

CHAPTER 3. TERRESTRIAL ECOSYSTEMS, INCREASED SOLAR ULTRAVIOLET RADIATION AND INTERACTIONS WITH OTHER CLIMATIC CHANGE FACTORS

M. M. Caldwell[a], C. L. Ballaré[b], J. F. Bornman[c], S. D. Flint[a], L. O. Björn[d], A. H. Teramura[e], G. Kulandaivelu[f] And M. Tevini[g]

[a] Ecology Center, Utah State University, Logan, Utah 84322-5230, USA

[b] IFEVA, Facultad de Agronomia, CONICET and Universidad de Buenos Aires, Avda. San Martin 4453, C1417DSE Buenos Aires, Argentina

[c] Department of Plant Biology, Research Centre Flakkebjerg, Flakkebjerg, DK-4200 Slagelse, Denmark

[d] Department of Cell and Organism Biology, Lund University, Sölvegatan 35, SE- 223 62 Lund, Sweden

[e] University of Hawaii, 3860 Manoa Road, Honolulu, Hawaii 96822-1180, USA

[f] School of Biological Sciences, Madurai Kamaraj University, Madurai 625021, India

[g] Botanisches Institut II, Universität Karlsruhe, Kaiserstrasse 12, DE-76128 Karlsruhe, Germany

Summary

Based on research to date, we can state some expectations about terrestrial ecosystem response as several elements of global climate change develop in coming decades. Higher plant species will vary considerably in their response to elevated UV-B radiation, but the most common general effects are reductions in height of plants, decreased shoot mass if ozone reduction is severe, increased quantities of some phenolics in plant tissues and, perhaps, reductions in foliage area. In some cases, the common growth responses may be lessened by increasing CO_2 concentrations. However, changes in chemistry of plant tissues will generally not be reversed by elevated CO_2. Among other things, changes in plant tissue chemistry induced by enhanced UV-B may reduce consumption of plant tissues by insects and other herbivores, although occasionally consumption may be increased. Pathogen attack on plants may be increased or decreased as a consequence of elevated UV-B, in combination with other climatic changes. This may be affected both by alterations in plant chemistry and direct damage to some pathogens. Water limitation may decrease the sensitivity of some agricultural plants to UV-B, but for vegetation in other habitats, this may not apply. With global warming, the repair of some types of UV damage may be improved, but several other interactions between warming and enhanced UV-B may occur. For example, even though warming may lead to fewer killing frosts, with enhanced UV-B and elevated CO_2 levels, some plant species may have increased sensitivity to frost damage.

Introduction

Several environmental changes are being imposed on terrestrial ecosystems, including increased solar ultraviolet-B radiation and warming at higher latitudes, increasing carbon dioxide levels globally, and regional tropospheric air pollution and atmospheric nitrogen deposition. Potentially significant changes in the frequency and nature of precipitation and storms are also predicted as the Earth warms. Depending on location, many of these factors will exert their influence on ecosystems more or less concurrently. Terrestrial ecosystems include agricultural lands (agroecosystems), less intensively managed lands such as forests, grasslands, and savannahs, and unmanaged lands such as deserts, tundra, etc. This overview addresses how increased UV-B radiation, interacting with other global change factors, may affect many of the important ecosystem processes and attributes, such as plant biomass production, plant consumption by herbivores including insects, disease incidence of plants and animals, changes in species abundance and composition, and mineral nutrient cycling. Some aspects of ecosystem function, e.g., nutrient cycling, are treated in more detail in Chapter 1[1]

The present report consists of a brief update of our understanding of UV radiation effects, followed by coverage of factor interactions as much as they have been researched to date (Figure 3-1). Ideally, these interactions should be considered across, as well as within, trophic levels. Trophic level refers to groups of organisms constituting different stages of the food chain in an ecosystem, e.g., primary producers (plants), various levels of consumers (herbivores, carnivores, etc.), and decomposer organisms.

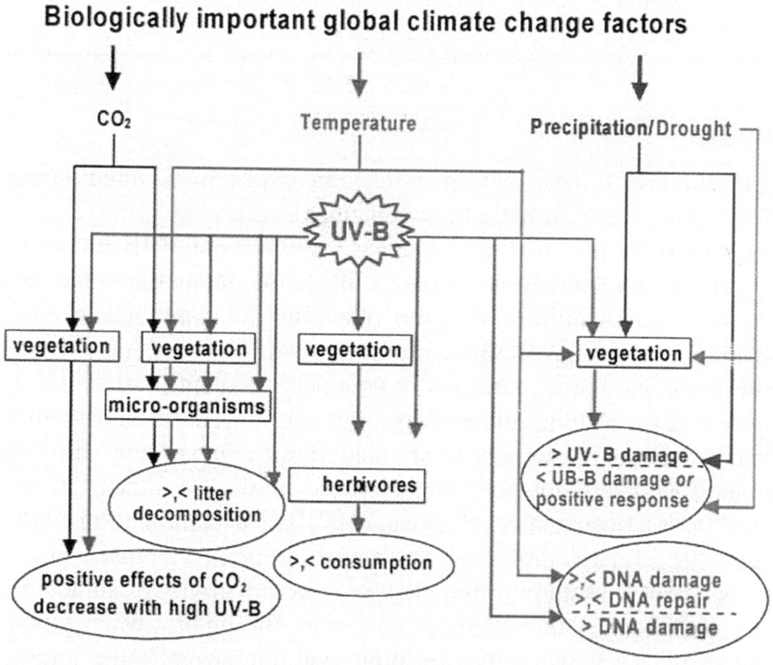

It is now some 30 years since the first suggestions of stratospheric ozone reduction appeared (e.g. [2,3]). Within a few years of these early concerns about the atmosphere, several studies of UV-B effects on higher plants appeared and these continue to represent the emphasis of research in this area. Direct effects of UV-B on insects and other terrestrial animal life have traditionally received comparatively little attention as they are often assumed to be protected from damaging effects of solar UV either by their behavioral patterns or

Figure 3-1 Major interactions of elevated UV-B with other climate change factors in terrestrial ecosystems. Lines indicate influence of climate change factors on different trophic levels (in rectangles) that affect processes (in ovals). Colors of lines: black, elevated CO_2; red, elevated temperature; violet, enhanced UV-B; blue and brown, abundance and deficit of moisture, respectively. The symbols > and < refer to more and less, respectively

by largely UV-opaque body coverings (e.g., fur, feathers, exoskeletons of insects, etc.). Terrestrial microbes have also received little attention though they are usually poorly shielded from penetrating solar UV. In recent years, more attention has been paid to UV-B influence on species interactions in an ecosystem context.

Biologically Effective UV Radiation for Plants

The concept of biologically effective UV radiation has been discussed (Chapter 5).[4] This involves weighting the radiation at different wavelengths with a factor to indicate its relative biological effectiveness. An example of erythemal (human sunburn) effectiveness is given in this volume.[4] For other biological effects, different weighting functions appear to be more appropriate. Earlier reports of this panel (e.g., [5, 6]) have portrayed the importance of different assumptions of the wavelength dependency of UV effects on plants and other organisms. These dependencies involve different degrees to which longer wavelength UV (UV-A) participates in various UV effects on plants. There are also important implications of this in calculating biologically effective UV based on different degrees of ozone reduction (see radiation amplification factors this volume[4] and in evaluating experiments with lamps to supplement the UV. A radiation amplification factor (RAF) refers to the relative increase of biologically effective UV radiation for each increment of ozone column change (Chapter 5).[4] The greater the degree to which longer wavelengths in the UV-B and UV-A are effective in biological reactions, the smaller is the RAF, i.e., less of an increase in biologically effective radiation for a given level of ozone reduction.[7, 8] Biological weighting functions are also used to compare the biologically effective UV radiation from lamp systems with that from the Sun due to ozone reduction, since these UV lamps do not accurately simulate solar radiation.[7]

A new action spectrum for characteristics of higher plant growth and morphology indicates that UV-A participates in these effects more than originally assumed in earlier action spectra.[9] The new spectrum resembles the commonly used generalized plant response function[10] except that it indicates appreciable sensitivity into the UV-A. This spectrum was also tested by exposing plants in the field to different combinations of solar and artificial radiation and indicated that the new spectrum is relevant under field conditions.[11] When used for the ozone reduction problem, this new spectrum predicts less of an increase of biologically effective radiation for a given decrease in ozone thickness (lower RAF) than the generalized plant spectrum. However, it also suggests that the levels of ozone reduction simulated in lamp experiments, often adjusted according to the generalized plant spectrum, results in less simulated ozone reduction than if computed using the new spectrum. For example, if one used the generalized plant spectrum to adjust lamps to result in a 30% simulated ozone reduction, this would only be an 8% ozone reduction if the resulting supplemental radiation is calculated according to the new plant growth spectrum.[11]

Plant growth is a complex response that integrates the influences of many environmental factors, including UV-B, on several physiological processes. It is worth pointing out that the new spectrum that describes the wavelength dependency of growth inhibition may not be appropriate to describe the spectral response of individual physiological processes. The shape of the spectra for individual processes will depend on the particular chromophores involved and, among other factors, the optical shielding imposed on these chromophores by surrounding molecules and cellular structures. Little work has been carried out to define appropriate weighting functions for individual responses under physiologically meaningful conditions. For DNA damage, various action spectra were tested in the field in southern Argentina as the Antarctic "ozone hole" passed over the experimental site and altered the wavelength composition of the solar radiation. The comparisons of plant DNA damage responses with different action spectra indicated an action spectrum with little participation of UV-A as the most appropriate[12] Similarly, Mazza et al.[13] found that the accumulation of phenolic sunscreens in field-grown soybeans was significantly enhanced by solar UV-B, whereas the UV-A component of sunlight had little effect. Therefore, for this particular response, a steep action spectrum also appeared to provide a good description of wavelength dependency.

A Recent View of Enhanced UV-B Effects on Plants: A Synthesis Using Meta-Analysis

Most UV-B research on terrestrial ecosystems continues to be focused on plants and emphasizes experiments addressing the sequence of events upon exposure to levels of UV-B radiation corresponding to stratospheric ozone reduction under outdoor conditions. It was recognized long ago, that if such experiments were conducted in glasshouse or growth-cabinet conditions, the effects of the added UV-B radiation were greatly exaggerated. Thus, over 20 years ago investigators began to conduct such experiments outdoors using special UV lamp systems. There are now well over 100 such studies on different species of plants. Meta-analysis is a technique to use quantitative and statistical information provided in a collection of individual studies in a combined analysis to assess how well the overall research predicts common trends and results. Of the ca. 100 studies reviewed, 62 provided enough quantitative information suitable for a meta-analysis[14] for several types of managed and unmanaged ecosystems (Figure 3-2).

Range of ecosystems and growth forms examined in the meta-analysis

Ecosystem	Growth Form		
	Monocot	Dicot	Gymnosperms
Managed	14	22	6
Unmanaged	1	21	0

Figure 3-2 Types of vegetation examined in the meta-analysis. The numbers refer to studies for individual species. Photographs of three different systems are also shown (a. Wheat and wild oat experiments in Logan, Utah, USA, W. Beyschlag; b. Loblolly pine in Maryland, USA, A. Teramura; c. Subarctic heath in Sweden, from[5]).

Of the 10 physiological and morphological traits examined, overall significance of elevated UV-B in the meta-analysis could only be concluded for shoot mass, plant height and leaf area and increased UV-B absorbing pigments (including flavonoids and other phenolic compounds). The other traits, including changes in chlorophyll and carotenoid pigments, reproductive yield, leaf mass per unit leaf area, net photosynthesis, and photosystem II activity of the photosynthetic system, might have been affected in some individual studies, but the overall effect was not sufficiently robust to be significant in the meta-analysis. For the four characteristics that were found to be significant, Figure 3-3 shows the array of responses in individual studies to elevated UV-B relative to controls. For leaf area, the significant reduction was caused by the manner in which the experimental replicate was selected. When authors selected the individual plant as the replicate, the average response was significant. (These data are included in Figure 3-3) When they selected the plot as the replicate, the response was not significant.[14] For shoot biomass, there are two arrays of studies shown in Figure 3-3 corresponding to the level of ozone reduction being simulated, 10 – 20% and > 20%. Only the group of studies simulating >20% ozone reduction yielded a significant average response in the meta-analysis for shoot mass. (In these studies, the level of simulated ozone reduction was usually effected by adjusting the output of the UV lamps with the old generalized plant spectrum.[10] Had the new plant growth spectrum[9] been used, the levels of simulated ozone reduction would have been much smaller, as explained in the foregoing section.)

Although all these studies in the meta-analysis involved lamp systems under outdoor conditions in natural sunlight, the methods included different degrees of replication and control of the lamp intensities. Most of these studies employed an "on-off" system of lamp control, sometimes called "square-wave", while others used more elaborate control that gradually changed lamp output according to ambient solar UV-B, sometimes called "modulated" control. Thus, all studies are not of equivalent quality; they also do not have equal capability to discriminate plant responses. While this should be borne in mind, there is increased value in comparing a large number of such experiments through meta-analysis since it affords a quantitative comparison.

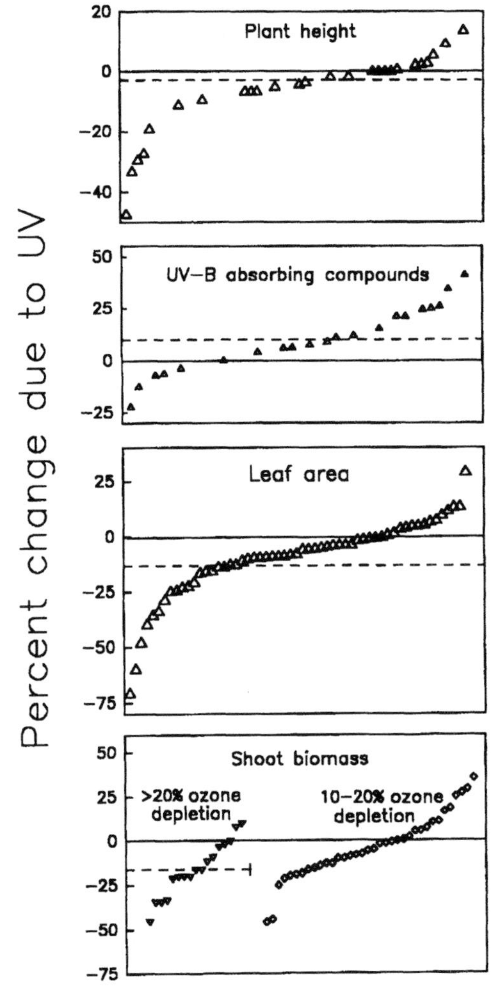

Apart from experiments with UV-emitting lamps, there is a lesser number of experiments using special filters that remove, or attenuate, the UV-B in normal sunlight (along with appropriate control filters that are largely transparent to UV-B). In the majority of cases, when sunlight UV-B was attenuated, plants exhibited better growth which indicates that normal sunlight UV-B reduces growth to some extent.[15-17] Attenuation experiments have been carried out in areas that are currently exposed to enhanced solar UV-B levels, such as the southern tip of South America (Tierra del Fuego, Argentina) and on the Antarctic Peninsula.[18, 19] Herbaceous plants native to both regions were negatively affected by the ambient solar UV-B levels. A comparison between the growth inhibition data collected in these UV-B attenuation experiments carried out in Tierra del Fuego and the Antarctic Peninsula showed that

Figure 3-3 The response of four plant characteristics in field studies in the order of increasing positive effects. These experiments all employed supplemental UV-B from lamp systems. Each symbol represents a different study. The dashed line in each represents the average response calculated by the meta-analysis over all studies shown. The average responses shown were significant at *P*<0.05. For shoot mass, the studies are grouped into two arrays corresponding to studies in which the level of simulated stratospheric ozone reduction is between 10 and 20%, and those in which the simulated ozone reduction was greater

a similar fractional level of UV-B attenuation by filters (approximately 80 %) had effects on plant growth that increased with the level of ozone depletion (i.e., from Tierra del Fuego to Antarctica).[18]

As can be seen in Figure 3-3, some UV-B lamp studies reported enhancement in some plant characteristics (plant height, leaf area, and shoot mass) although most studies reported decreases in these characteristics. There are also a few recent reports of filter studies where solar UV-B promoted plant growth.[20, 21] Mechanisms mediating this apparent enhancement of growth are not known and it is not clear that this would occur over the long term in a natural setting.

Apart from higher plant responses, other effects of enhanced UV-B radiation on terrestrial ecosystems are represented by too few studies to allow for meta-analysis.

Do Small Effects of UV-B Accumulate Through the Years?

An intriguing, and potentially important, phenomenon suggested by some earlier research is that even small effects of UV-B radiation might accumulate to produce larger effects in subsequent years in perennial plants. The first suggestions of this were in seedlings of one of four seed sources of a conifer. In these plants, the effect of exposing the plants to elevated UV-B from lamps became progressively more expressed in subsequent years.[22] However, this did not appear to be significant in young trees tested from the other three seed sources. Indications of cumulative effects of elevated UV-B in Subarctic heath perennials were apparent for some traits of some species, but not for others (e.g. [23]). Also, early indications of cumulative effects disappeared over a longer period of time.[24] Thus, while there may be some indications of this accumulation phenomenon in certain specific instances, there is no convincing evidence for it as a general trend. However, its potential significance should not be dismissed, since it might affect competitive persistence of some species through time.

Analogous to these putative cumulative effects, an apparent carry-over and accumulation of elevated UV-B effects on plant growth form, from generation to generation, has been reported for a desert annual plant species.[25, 26] If this is a widespread phenomenon among species, an amplification of sorts might be effected. The mechanism for this is not understood.

Although suspected for some time, there are now a few new reports indicating that enhanced UV-B may affect the genetic stability of plants causing long-term heritable effects, with a high frequency of mutations which are generally considered to be deleterious to organisms. High UV-B exposure can activate what is known as "mutator transposons" in maize that amplify the mutation effect of the UV-B beyond the immediate DNA damage.[27] In *Arabidopsis*, increased UV-B was found not only to cause direct DNA damage; but also, errors in DNA repair leading to an increased tendency for mutations in subsequent generations.[28, 29] In cyanobacteria, considerable genetic polymorphism was found in highly stressful environments, and was presumed to be caused by UV-B-induced genome instability and replication errors.[30] These instabilities could affect future generations, and result in an increased mutation rate even after the ozone layer has recovered.

Recent reports of UV-B effects on soil and soil surface processes such as nitrogen fixation and litter decomposition suggest that these changes are not transient phenomena. Elevated UV-B treatments applied over several years may become apparent years after the treatments were begun. This was the case for depression of nitrogen fixation in some species of cyanobacteria [31] that had been exposed to elevated UV-B for several years in both high Arctic and Subarctic locations. A one-year exposure to elevated UV-B became apparent four years later as accelerated decomposition of oak leaf litter.[32] Both nitrogen fixation and litter decomposition are nutrient cycling processes that are important in ecosystem function.

Insect Herbivory of Plants

Insects have enormous potential to consume vegetation, but the degree to which they feed on different species is dependent not only on the species of plants, but also on a suite of other environmental factors, including UV-B radiation. There are now over 20 reports of various insect-plant species combinations that have been studied with respect to the influence of UV-B radiation (Table 3-1).

Generally, when there was an effect, a higher level of UV-B led to less insect herbivory and/or reduced insect growth compared to lower levels of UV-B. (Most of these experiments were conducted by filtering ambient solar radiation.) The magnitude of the effects can be sizeable, with potential ecosystem-level consequences for species composition, organic matter decomposition and nutrient cycling. In several cases, it was possible to show, using feeding bioassays, that the effects of the UV-B radiation were mediated through the host plant, i.e., they were the result of UV-induced changes in the characteristics of the plant tissues. Two types of bioassays have been used: In the "no choice" bioassays (NC, in Table 3-1) insects were given either UV-B-exposed or control plant material (exposed to less, or no UV-B), whereas in the "choice" (C) bioassays the insects received both types of pretreated plant materials in the same feeding area. Of course, the interpretation of the response (altered herbivory or insect performance) in the context of projecting ecosystem-level consequences requires consideration of the type of experiment that was used to detect UV-B effects on plant-insect interactions. It is also important to point out that the nature of the UV-B-induced changes in plant characteristics that cause herbivory responses is not known for any system; the possible mechanisms listed in Table 3-1 are based on correlative, circumstantial evidence. Insects are generally thought to be blind to variations in the UV-B component of sunlight, since their visual systems are primarily sensitive to UV-A radiation. However, one field study showed that a species of thrips can perceive and avoid solar UV-B under natural daylight conditions[34], and laboratory study showed behavioral responses to artificial UV-B in a moth caterpillar.[39]

Table 3-1. Effects of UV-B radiation on insect herbivory

Insect	Type of expt [a]	Plant species	UV-B effect on herbivory/insects	Possible mechanism [e]	Study
Caliothrips phaseoli (thrips)	E	*Glycine max* (soybean)	Less herbivory [33]	Direct response of insects to solar UV-B	[34]
Diabrotica speciosa (leaf beetle), lepidopteran larvae, grasshoppers	E	*Glycine max* (soybean)	Less herbivory		[35]
Anticarsia gemmatilis (moth larva)	E [b]	*Glycine max* (soybean)	Slower growth, higher mortality	Indirect effect. (NC) [e] Increased phenolics but decreased lignin	
Schistocera gregaria (desert locust)	F [b]	*Lolium perenne, Festuca rubra, F. arundinaceae, F. pratensis*	No response in 3 species; in *Festuca pratensis*, preference for endophyte-infected plants changed	Indirect effect. (C) [e] Loline content changed, but this did not influence herbivory	[36]
Various chewing insects (not identified)	E	*Gunnera magellanica* (devil's strawberry)	Less herbivory	Not known	[37]
Spodoptera litura, Graphania mutans (moth larva)	C	*Trifolium repens* (white clover)	Tendency toward slight reduction in herbivory	Indirect effect. (NC) Slight N increase, larger carbohydrate decrease, population-specific changes in cyanogenesis	[38]
Epirrita antumnata (moth larva)	F	*Betula pubescens* (mountain birch)	More herbivory	Mechanism not known. (NC). Laboratory study indicated direct UV-B preference	[39]
Precis coenia, Trichoplusia ni (both lepidopteran larvae)	G	*Plantago lanceolata* (English plantain)	*Precis* - no effect *Trichoplusia* - more growth from eating treated material but direct UV-B growth inhibition	Direct inhibitory effect of UV-B on insect growth; indirect effects. (NC) Reduced crown and reproductive growth; some increase in leaf N and verbascosides	[40]
Various chewing insects (not identified)	F	*Quercus robur* (pedunculate oak)	No UV-B effect [c]		[41]

Insect	Type of expt [a]	Plant species	UV-B effect on herbivory/insects	Possible mechanism [e]	Study
Caliothrips phaseoli (thrips)	E	*Glycine max* (soybean)	Less herbivory	Indirect effect (C) and direct UV-B avoidance	[33, 34]
Lepidoptera: Noctuidae (moth larva)	E	*Gunnera magellanica* (devil's strawberry)	Less herbivory	Indirect effect. (C) Increase in leaf N	[42]
Strophingia ericae (psyllid)	F	*Calluna vulgaris* (heather)	Reduced insect populations	Not known. Reduced amino acid isoleucine	[43]
Operophtera brumata (moth larva)	G	*Betula pendula* (silver birch)	More herbivory	Indirect effect. (C) Leaf flavonoids increased, but flavonoids added to an artificial diet did not increase feeding.	[44]
Insects not identified	F	*Vaccinium myrtillus, V. uliginosum, V. vitis-idaea* (heathland shrubs)	More herbivory in *V. myrtillus*, less in *V. uliginosum*, no effect in *V. vitis-idaea*	Mechanism not known	[45, 46]
Pieris rapae, (butterfly larva) *Trichoplusia ni* (moth larva)	C	*Arabidopsis thaliana*	*Pieris*: less herbivory and less insect weight gain	Indirect effect. (NC) Leaf flavonoids increased	[47]
Coleoptera (leaf beetles)	E	*Datura ferox* (summer annual)	Less herbivory	Indirect effect. (C) Mechanism not known	[48]
Acronicta, Nycteola, Orthosia, Ptiloden (moth larva)	F	*Quercus robur* (pedunculate oak)	No specific UV-B effect [c]		[49]
Autographa gamma (moth larva)	C	*Pisum sativum* (pea)	Less herbivory, but greater insect growth	Indirect effect. (NC) Higher phenolic and N contents	[50]
Ostrinia nubilalis (European corn borer)	E [d]	*Zea mays* (corn)	Less herbivory	Indirect effect. (NC) More cell-wall-bound truxillic and truxinic acids	[51, b]
Trichoplusia ni (moth larva)	G	*Citrus jambhiri* (rough lemon)	Decrease in survivorship and growth	UV-B increased furanocoumarin levels	[52]

[a] C = controlled environment chamber, G = greenhouse, F = field UV-B supplement from lamps, E = field UV-B exclusion

[b] Field-treated material used in laboratory feeding trials.

[c] More herbivory under UV-A and UV-B lamps compared to controls, but no specific UV-B effect.

[d] UV-A and UV-B responses cannot be separated

[e] "Indirect effect" implies that an UV-B effect mediated by changes in the plant was demonstrated in a bioassay, even if the nature of the changes was not identified. (C), "choice" bioassay, (NC) "no choice" bioassay.

Bacteria and Fungi

Fungi and bacteria play crucial roles in ecosystem function including decomposition of dead biological material, mineral nutrient cycling and as pathogens of plants and animals. In the last few years, more attention has been paid to direct UV-B effects on these microbes if they are exposed to sunlight (such as on foliage surfaces or litter). Changes in species composition and biodiversity of these microbes in response to UV-B have been documented and many of these changes appear to be related to how well species and strains of these fungi and bacteria tolerate UV.[53-56] Beneficial fungi that infect plant roots and assist in absorption of nutrients (termed mycorrhizae), although not exposed to solar radiation, might be indirectly affected by UV-B exposure of the host plant shoots.[57, 58] This would need to be mediated by systemic tissue changes in the roots caused by UV-B exposure of the shoots.

Bacteria and fungi can also be pathogenic for both plants and animals, although plant pathogens have received more attention than animal pathogens with respect to UV-B radiation. As compiled by Paul[59], plant disease incidence can be increased or reduced by UV-B radiation. Increasing disease severity is thought to primarily involve modifications in the host plant tissues, while decreased severity appears due either to host plant changes or direct UV-B damage to the pathogen (Table 3-2).

Table 3-2. Effects of UV-B radiation on plant-microbe interactions for living plants and plant litter.

Microbe genus	Type of expt. [a]	Plant Species	Fungal response to UV-B	Plant response to UV-B	Study
A. Experiments on live plants					
Aureobasidium (phylloplane yeast)	E	*Nothofagus antarctica (southern beech)*	Proportionately less on upper leaf surface, several other plant-microbe systems not affected	none	[53]
bacteria (e.g. *Clavibacter*)	E	*Arachis hypogene* (peanut)	altered species composition	none	[55]
Microsphaera (powdery mildew pathogen)	F	*Quercus robur* (pedunculate oak)	increased infection	photosynthesis decreased due to increased mildew	[60]
Neotyphodium (leaf endophyte)	F	*Lolium perenne* (rye grass)	no effect	reduced yield in the presence of the leaf endophyte	[61]
Septoria (leaf blotch pathogen)	C	*Triticum aestivum* (wheat)	fewer lesions on plant (a direct response to UV-B) or no effect depending on time of year	not assessed. If changes occurred, they did not affect the pathogen	[62]
Exobasidium (blister blight pathogen)	E	*Camellia sinensis* (tea)	reduced infection sites; no effect on sporulation	not assessed	[63]

Microbe genus	Type of expt. [a]	Plant Species	Fungal response to UV-B	Plant response to UV-B	Study
Aureobasidium, Sporo-bolomyces (phylloplane yeasts)	F	*Quercus robur* (pedunculate oak)	abundance on the upper; but not lower leaf surface affected for some sampling dates. Several other fungi not affected	not assessed	64
Fusarium (damping-off pathogen)	C	*Spinacia oleracea* (spinach)	more damping off evident	decreased shoot growth	65
Bullera (phylloplane yeasts)	E	*Vicia faba* (faba bean), *Malus domestica* (apple), *Quercus robur* (pedunculate oak), *Pisum sativum* (pea)	less colony forming units isolated from leaves	not assessed	66
Pyricularia (also known as *Magnaporthe*) (rice blast pathogen)	G	*Oryza sativa* (rice)	greater lesions on plant in a few cases (an indirect UV-B effect mediated through the plant)	reduced plant height, leaf area, dry weight in a few cases	67
Cercospora (leaf spot pathogen)	C	*Beta vulgaris* (sugar beet)	not assessed	reduced dry weight of leaf laminae and other plant parts in the presence of the pathogen	68
Colletotrichum, Cladosporium (anthracnose and scab pathogens)	G	*Cucumis sativus* (cucumber)	increased infection in some cases (an indirect UV-B effect mediated through the plant)	reduced plant height, leaf area, dry weight; increased leaf mass per area	69
Puccinia (leaf rust pathogen)	F	*Triticum aestivum* (wheat)	increased infection with results varying some by wheat cultivar	little; if any, reduction in dry weight and seed yield	70
Diplocarpon (blackspot pathogen)	G	*Rosa* (rose)	inhibition only when conidia were germinating	no response	71
potato virus S	G	*Chenopodium quinoa*	fewer lesions	no response	72
B. Experiments on plant litter					
Cladosporium, Cystodendron, Phoma	F	*Betula pubescens* (mountain birch)	changes in fungal community structure	live plants received no treatments	73
Aspergillus, Cladosporium, Epicoccum	F [b]	*Brassica napus* (oil seed rape)	direct and indirect effects on fungal competitive ability	increased flavonoids	74

Microbe genus	Type of expt. [a]	Plant Species	Fungal response to UV-B	Plant response to UV-B	Study
Cladosporium, Acremonium, and others (saprotrophs)	F	*Quercus robur* (pedunculate oak)	reduced fungal colonization of decomposing leaves; change in fungal species composition	some transitory UV-B effect on mass loss of decomposing litter	[75]
Mucor, Truncatella, Penicillium (saprotrophs)	F [b]	*Vaccinium uliginosum* (a heathland shrub)	reduced fungal colonization of decomposing leaves; change in fungal species composition	altered leaf litter quality	[76]

[a] C = controlled environment chamber, G = greenhouse, F = field UV-B supplement from lamps, E = field UV-B exclusion.

[b] All or some decomposition conducted in laboratory.

Pathogens of insects and other animals may also be influenced by solar UV radiation. Studies involving biological control of insect pests using pathogens provide some indication of how solar UV may influence insect pathogens. For example, Braga *et al.*[77, 78] showed that fungal strains of an insect pathogen were sensitive to solar UV-B radiation and to lamp UV-B in a range corresponding to that in sunlight. These particular fungi commonly used in biological control of insects such as grasshoppers were isolated from soil fungi that would not normally be exposed to sunlight. However, if strains isolated from locations at different latitudes were exposed to UV-B, their relative UV-B sensitivity corresponded to the respective latitudinal differences in solar UV-B at their sites of origin. Viral pathogens of insects are also inhibited by UV-B radiation[79] Thus, as used for biological control, attention to UV-B sensitivity is necessary and enhanced UV-B stemming from ozone reduction would further limit their usefulness.

Global Environmental Changes

The changing environment we are now witnessing and will likely experience in the coming decades involves both global climate change and broad regional changes. Both the predictability and the rate of these environmental changes vary widely. Solar UV-B has increased at higher latitudes, and CO_2 and temperature are continuing to increase globally. Regionally, nitrogen deposition and tropospheric ozone have increased. Changes in regional precipitation frequency and weather systems are driven by global climate change and are highly important, but less well understood and predicted.

Thus, all the foregoing changes need to be considered as acting in concert with stratospheric ozone reduction. Experimental work is progressing, usually with two-factor interactions, e.g., elevated CO_2 and UV-B. However, the complications and costs of two- or multi-factor experiments clearly limit how representative and comprehensive such experiments can be.

Drawing on the existing experimental data base, we attempt to generalize how elevated UV-B might interact with each of the other factors with respect to vegetation and ecosystem responses. For example, some combinations of factors appear to have largely additive effects, although these can operate in opposite directions. There can also be significant interactions, i.e., at different levels of one factor there is a non-additive response to a second factor (synergistic). The following sections contain such generalizations.

Elevated CO_2 and UV-B

Several studies are now available in which plants, and sometimes combinations of plants and insect herbivores, were subjected to combinations of two or more levels of CO_2 and UV-B. Typically, elevated CO_2 treatments involved a doubling of CO_2 and elevated UV-B treatments corresponded to a simulated 15 to 30% ozone depletion (assuming the generalized plant spectrum[10] as explained earlier). Generally, if either elevated CO_2 or UV-B exerted effects, the CO_2 influence was more pronounced than that of the enhanced UV-B. Also, the effects of elevated CO_2 and enhanced UV-B caused responses in opposite directions, e.g., additional CO_2 stimulated plant growth and enhanced UV-B tended to depress growth.[46, 69, 80-89] In all these studies, the effects of the two factors were usually counteractive, as just described. Synergistic effects were rare.

Combined application of UV-B and elevated CO_2 followed by short exposures to ozone, as would be experienced from regional air pollution, resulted in interesting interactions. The stimulating effect of elevated CO_2 on plant growth was apparent when plants were exposed to ambient (normal) UV-B. If given both elevated UV-B and high CO_2, the stimulating effect of the high CO_2 was reduced. These patterns are typical of the combined effects of elevated UV-B and high CO_2. Application of a high ozone exposure following growth in the combinations of UV-B and CO_2 eliminated the stimulating effect of high CO_2 if the plants had been exposed to low UV-B, but did not if the plants had been given elevated UV-B along with the elevated CO_2.[86]

Apart from plant growth and related processes like photosynthesis, the attractiveness of plant foliage to insect herbivores may vary under a combination of elevated CO_2 and enhanced UV-B. Lavola et al.[90] found that insects preferred plants grown with enhanced UV-B, contrary to the general trend described above, and the combination of high CO_2 and enhanced UV-B led to even further tendency of the insects to consume foliage. In another study of this nature, enhanced UV-B either increased or reduced herbivory, depending on the plant species, but if the enhanced UV-B were combined with high CO_2, or if the plants were given just high CO_2 by itself, there was no effect on herbivory relative to controls (low UV-B and normal CO_2).[46]

UV-B, Water and Nitrogen Supply

Climate change will likely result in modifications in the timing and amount of precipitation on a regional scale, although predicting these changes is difficult. Experiments to date largely suggest that if enhanced UV-B is applied to plants undergoing drought stress, the UV-B response seen with adequately watered plants is usually dampened (e.g.[91-93]), at least where cultivated plants are concerned. However, some species native to the Mediterranean seemed to thrive during periods of water limitation if exposed to elevated UV-B.[94]

Atmospheric nitrogen (N) deposition in many regions leads to N fertilization of vegetation. Nitrogen supply to vegetation has received relatively little attention in relation to UV-B radiation. One study involving a combination of different levels of N supply and two levels of UV-B showed that as cucumber plants received more N, their growth was depressed to a greater degree by elevated UV-B.[95] If N deficient, these plants were not responsive to UV-B in that study.

Warming and UV-B

The Earth is warming and this is especially apparent in many regions at higher latitudes. These are also the latitudes where ozone depletion is more pronounced. Some responses to the combination of these factors might be rather predictable, such as increased repair (an enzymatic process) of DNA damage at higher temperatures. This has been experimentally demonstrated in terrestrial plants for DNA damage (manifest as DNA dimers). There was little repair of DNA damage at low temperatures and very adequate repair in a temperature range of 24 - 30°C.[96, 97] The effectiveness of DNA repair was low at relatively high temperature.[97, 98]

Of course, temperatures that are above or below the optimum for a particular organism can limit performance and, in the extreme, cause direct damage. Interactions among factors can occur such that the limits of temperature tolerance are altered. A study on Subarctic heath species showed that enhanced UV-B considerably increased the frost sensitivity in three of four species tested.[99] In one species, this meant that the lower temperature limit of frost tolerance for some plants was 5°C higher than for plants not given elevated UV-B. Furthermore, elevated CO_2 led to an increase in frost sensitivity of these species and if both elevated CO_2 and enhanced UV-B were applied, there was a further increase in frost sensitivity. Thus, even with warming at high latitudes, the frost damage to some of the plant species may be increased at higher CO_2 and UV-B.[99]

When low temperatures are generally limiting growth or other processes, but not causing damage, warming should render a benefit to growth, but the degree to which this interacts with different levels of UV-B is not well understood. As appears to be the case with combinations of elevated CO_2 and enhanced UV-B, the effects of warming and UV-B usually exhibit few synergistic effects, based on the available experiments. This is the case for the response of Antarctic plants to combinations of warming and UV-B manipulations.[100, 101] However, at high temperatures, some synergistic effects of enhanced UV-B and the elevated temperatures have been reported. In some tropical legumes, enhanced UV-B reduced growth of the plants at moderate temperatures (20° to 30°C), but at 40°C, chloroplasts in the leaves were modified and this masked UV-B depressions of growth (e.g., [102, 103]).

Interaction of Global Climate Change Factors Across Trophic Levels

The interactions addressed above largely involve the effects of factor combinations on a single trophic level, usually higher plants. However, environmental factors may also interact by affecting different components of the same trophic chain (Figure 3-1). For example, plant-insect interactions may be affected by the responses of both plants and insects to changes in UV-B, temperature, and precipitation patterns. Enhanced UV-B can affect the quality of plant foliage as a food source for insect herbivores and this has been shown in several studies (see earlier section). Of the climatic change factors, insects themselves are primarily affected by temperature[104] and changes in the frequency and patterns of precipitation.[105] These factors may exert a direct influence on the insect, and also indirect effects mediated through changes and seasonal timing of the vegetation. Thus, factor interactions across trophic levels might involve warming, altering plant and insect seasonal timing[104], and enhanced UV-B affecting the quality of plant tissue for insect consumption. The micro-organisms that are responsible for decomposing dead plant and animal materials constitute another trophic level. Warming may accelerate decomposition, given sufficient moisture, although UV-B exposure of vegetation when alive can change the decomposability of the plant material after senescence and death.[76] Furthermore, UV-B can also directly affect the microbes decomposing the plant litter if they are exposed to sunlight.[76, 106] Thus, climatic change factors may affect or operate at different trophic levels, thereby complicating the analysis resulting from single trophic level studies.

Climate change over a longer span of time will also affect the geographic distribution of vegetation and animal populations.[107] Migration of different species in response to warming can involve shifts to higher latitudes and altitudes[108-110], which in turn would change their exposure to prevailing solar UV-B in these new locations.

Concluding Remarks

This assessment emphasizes generalizations that can be made about the effects of enhanced UV-B on terrestrial ecosystems and those of UV-B when interacting with other climatic factors. Clearly, as with any generalization, exceptions are to be found and the generalizations necessarily involve simplifications. Also, when moving from effects of UV radiation and other factors at single trophic levels (such as higher plants) to whole-system function, numerous complications arise and experimentation becomes more difficult and costly. Nevertheless, progress is being made and we feel the conclusions drawn here are realistic.

References

1   R. G. Zepp, T. V. Callaghan and D. J. Erickson, Interactive effects of ozone depletion and climate change on biogeochemical cycles, *Photochem. Photobiol. Sci.*, 2003, In press.

2   H. Johnston, Reduction of stratospheric ozone by nitrogen oxide catalysts from supersonic transport exhaust, *Science*, 1971, **173**, 517-522.

3   P. J. Crutzen, SSTs--a threat to the Earth's ozone shield, *Ambio*, 1972, **1**, 41-51.

4   R. L. McKenzie, L. O. Björn, A. Bais and M. Ilyas, Changes in biologically active ultraviolet radiation reaching the Earth's surface, *Photochem. Photobiol. Sci.*, 2003, In press.

5   M. M. Caldwell, A. H. Teramura, M. Tevini, J. F. Bornman, L. O. Björn and G. Kulandaivelu, Effects of increased solar ultraviolet radiation on terrestrial plants, *Ambio*, 1995, **24**, 166-173.

6   M. M. Caldwell, L. O. Björn, J. F. Bornman, S. D.Flint, G. Kulandaivelu, A. H. Teramura and M. Tevini, Effects of increased solar ultraviolet radiation on terrestrial ecosystems, *J. Photochem. Photobiol. B*, 1998, **46**, 40-52.

7   M. M. Caldwell, L. B. Camp, C. W. Warner and S. D. Flint, in *Stratospheric ozone reduction, solar ultraviolet radiation and plant life* ed.: M. M. Caldwell, Springer, Berlin, 1986, pp. 87-111.

8   S. Madronich, R. L. McKenzie, M. M. Caldwell and L. O. Björn, Changes in ultraviolet radiation reaching the Earth's surface, *Ambio*, 1995, **24**, 143-152.

9   S. D. Flint and M. M. Caldwell, A biological spectral weighting function for ozone depletion research with higher plants, *Physiologia Plantarum*, 2003, **117**, In press.

10   M. M. Caldwell, in *Photophysiology,* **Vol. 6** ed.: A. C. Giese, Academic Press, New York, 1971, pp. 131-177.

11   S. D. Flint and M. M. Caldwell, Field testing of UV biological spectral weighting functions for higher plants, *Physiologia Plantarum*, 2003, **117**, In press.

12   M. C. Rousseaux, C. L. Ballaré, C. V. Giordano, A. L. Scopel, A. M. Zima, M. Szwarcberg-Bracchitta, P. S. Searles, M. M. Caldwell and S. B. Diaz, Ozone depletion and UVB radiation: Impact on plant DNA damage in southern South America, *Proc. Nat. Acad. Sci.*, 1999, **96**, 15310-15315.

13   C. A. Mazza, H. E. Boccalandro, C. V. Giordano, D. Battista, A. L. Scopel and C. L. Ballaré, Functional significance and induction by solar radiation of ultraviolet-absorbing sunscreens in field-grown soybean crops., *Plant Physiol.*, 2000, **122**, 117-126.

14   P. S. Searles, S. D. Flint and M. M. Caldwell, A meta-analysis of plant field studies simulating stratospheric ozone depletion, *Oecologia*, 2001, **127**, 1-10.

15   J. E. Hunt and D. L. McNeil, The influence of present-day levels of ultraviolet-B radiation on seedlings of two southern hemisphere temperate tree species, *Plant Ecol.*, 1999, **143**, 39-50.

16   K. Lingakumar, P. Amudha and G. Kulandaivelu, Exclusion of solar UV-B (280-315 nm) radiation on vegetative growth and photosynthetic activities in *Vigna unguiculata* L., *Plant Sci.*, 1999, **148**, 97-103.

17   C. A. Mazza, D. Battista, A. M. Zima, M. Szwarcberg-Bracchitta, C. V. Giordano, A. Acevedo, A. L. Scopel and C. L. Ballaré, The effects of solar ultraviolet-B radiation on the growth and yield of barley are accompanied by increased DNA damage and antioxidant responses, *Plant Cell Environ.*, 1999, **22**, 61-70.

18   C. L. Ballaré, M. C. Rousseaux, P. S. Searles, J. G. Zaller, C. V. Giordano, T. M. Robson, M. M. Caldwell, O. E. Sala and A. L. Scopel, Impacts of solar ultraviolet-B radiation on terrestrial ecosystems of Tierra del Fuego (Southern Argentina). An overview of recent progress, *J. Photochem. Photobiol. B*, 2001, **62**, 67-77.

19   T. A. Day, C. T. Ruhland and F. S. Xiong, Influence of solar ultraviolet-B radiation on Antarctic terrestrial plants: results from a four year field study, *Journal of Photochemistry and Photobiology B: Biology*, 2001, **62**, 78-87.

20   W. J. I. Cybulski and W. T. Peterjohn, Effects of ambient UV-B radiation on the above-ground biomass of seven temperate-zone plant species, *Plant Ecol.*, 1999, **145**, 175-181.

21   J. A. Zavala and J. F. Botto, Impact of solar UV-B radiation on seedling emergence, chlorophyll fluorescence, and growth and yield of radish (*Raphanus sativus*), *Funct. Plant Biol.*, 2002, **29**, 797-804.

22   J. H. Sullivan and A. H. Teramura, The effects of ultraviolet-B radiation on loblolly pine. 2. Growth of field-grown seedlings, *Trees*, 1992, **6**, 115-120.

23   L. O. Björn, T. V. Callaghan, I. Johnsen, J. A. Lee, Y. Manetas, N. D. Paul, M. Sonesson, A. R. Wellburn, D. J. S. Coop, H. S. Heide-Jorgensen, C. Gehrke, D. Gwynn-Jones, U. Johanson, A. Kyparissis, E. Levizou, D. Nikolopoulos, Y. Petropoulou and M. Stephanou, The effects of UV-B radiation on European heathland species, *Plant Ecol.*, 1997, **128**, 252-264.

24   G. K. Phoenix, D. Gwynn-Jones, T. V. Callaghan, D. Sleep and J. A. Lee, Effects of global change on a sub-Arctic heath: effects of enhanced UV-B radiation and increased summer precipitation, *J. Ecol.*, 2001, **89**, 256-267.

25   C. F. Musil, Accumulated effect of elevated ultraviolet-B radiation over multiple generations of the arid-environment annual *Dimorphotheca sinuata* DC. (Asteraceae), *Plant Cell Environ.*, 1996, **19**, 1017-1027.

26   C. F. Musil, G. F. Midgley and S. J. E. Wand, Carry-over of enhanced ultraviolet-B exposure effects to successive generations of a desert annual: interaction with atmospheric CO_2 and nutrient supply, *Global Change Biology*, 1999, **5**, 311-329.

27   V. Walbot, UV-B damage amplified by transposons in maize, *Nature*, 1999, **397**, 398-399.

28   G. Ries, G. Buchholz, H. Frohnmeyer and B. Hohn, UV-damage-mediated induction of homologous recombination in *Arabidopsis* is dependent on photosynthetically active radiation, *Proc. Nat. Acad. Sci.*, 2000, **97**, 13425-13429.

29   G. Ries, W. Heller, H. Puchta, H. Sandermann, H. K. Seidlitz and B. Hohn, Elevated UV-B radiation reduces genome stability in plants, *Nature*, 2000, **406**, 98-101.

30   V. Dvornyk, O. Vinogradova and E. Nevo, Long-term microclimate stress causes rapid adaptive radiation of kaiABC clock gene family in a cyanobacterium, *Nostoc linckia*, from "Evolution Canyons" I and II, Israel, *Proc. Nat. Acad. Sci.*, 2002, **99**, 2082-2087.

31   B. Solheim, U. Johanson, T. V. Callaghan, J. A. Lee, D. Gwynn-Jones and L. O. Björn, The nitrogen fixation potential of arctic cryptogam species is influenced by enhanced UV-B radiation, *Oecologia*, 2002, **133**, 90-93.

32   K. K. Newsham, J. M. Anderson, T. H. Sparks, P. Splatt, C. Woods and A. R. McLeod, UV-B effect on *Quercus robur* leaf litter decomposition persists over four years, *Global Change Biology*, 2001, **7**, 479-483.

33   C. A. Mazza, J. Zavala, A. L. Scopel and C. L. Ballaré, Perception of solar UVB radiation by phytophagous insects: Behavioral responses and ecosystem implications., *Proc. Nat. Acad. Sci.*, 1999, **96**, 980-985.

34   C. A. Mazza, M. M. Izaguirre, J. Zavala, A. L. Scopel and C. L. Ballaré, Insect perception of ambient ultraviolet-B radiation, *Ecol. Lett.*, 2003, **6**, In press.

35   J. A. Zavala, A. L. Scopel and C. L. Ballaré, Effects of ambient UV-B radiation on soybean crops: Impact on leaf herbivory by *Anticarsia gemmatalis*, *Plant Ecol.*, 2001, **156**, 121-130.

36   A. R. McLeod, A. Rey, K. K. Newsham, G. C. Lewis and P. Wolferstan, Effects of elevated ultraviolet radiation and endophytic fungi on plant growth and insect feeding in *Lolium perenne*, *Festuca rubra*, *F. arundinacea* and *F. pratensis*, *J. Photochem. Photobiol. B*, 2001, **62**, 97-107.

37   M. C. Rousseaux, A. L. Scopel, P. S. Searles, M. M. Caldwell, O. E. Sala and C. L. Ballaré, Responses to solar ultraviolet-B radiation in a shrub-dominated natural ecosystem of Tierra del Fuego (southern Argentina), *Global Change Biology*, 2001, **7**, 467-478.

38   R. L. Lindroth, R. W. Hofmann, B. D. Campbell, W. C. McNabb and D. Y. Hunt, Population differences in *Trifolium repens* L. response to ultraviolet-B radiation: foliar chemistry and consequences for two lepidopteran herbivores, *Oecologia*, 2000, **122**, 20-28.

39   N. Buck and T. V. Callaghan, The direct and indirect effects of enhanced UV-B on the moth caterpillar *Epirrita autumnata*, *Ecol. Bulls.*, 1999, **47**, 68-76.

40   E. S. McCloud and M. R. Berenbaum, Effects of enhanced UV-B radiation on a weedy forb (*Plantago lanceolata*) and its interactions with a generalist and specialist herbivore, *Entomoligia Experimentalis et Applicata*, 1999, **93**, 233-247.

41   K. K. Newsham, P. D. Greenslade and A. R. McLeod, Effects of elevated ultraviolet radiation on *Quercus robur* and its insect and ectomycorrhizal associates, *Global Change Biology*, 1999, **5**, 881-890.

42   M. C. Rousseaux, C. L. Ballaré, A. L. Scopel, P. S. Searles and M. M. Caldwell, Solar ultraviolet-B radiation affects plant-insect interactions in a natural ecosystem of Tierra del Fuego (southern Argentina), *Oecologia*, 1998, **116**, 528-535.

43   D. T. Salt, S. A. Moody, J. B. Whittaker and N. D. Paul, Effects of enhanced UVB on populations of the phloem feeding insect *Strophingia ericae* (Homoptera: Psylloidea) on heather (*Calluna vulgaris*), *Global Change Biology*, 1998, **4**, 91-96.

44   A. Lavola, R. Julkunen-Tiitto, H. Roininen and P. J. Aphalo, Host-plant preference of an insect herbivore mediated by UV-B and CO_2 in relation to plant secondary metabolites, *Biochem. Syst. Ecol.*, 1998, **26**, 1-12.

45   D. Gwynn-Jones, Enhanced UV-B radiation and herbivory, *Ecol. Bulls.*, 1999, **47**, 77-83.

46   D. Gwynn-Jones, J. A. Lee and T. V. Callaghan, Effects of enhanced UV-B radiation and elevated carbon dioxide concentrations on a sub-arctic forest heath ecosystem, *Plant Ecol.*, 1997, **128**, 242-249.

47   J. Grant-Petersson and J. A. A. Renwick, Effects of ultraviolet-B exposure of *Arabidopsis thaliana* on herbivory by two crucifer-feeding insects (Lepidoptera), *Environ. Entomol.*, 1996, **25**, 135-142.

48   C. L. Ballaré, A. L. Scopel, A. E. Stapleton and M. J. Yanovsky, Solar ultraviolet-B radiation affects seeding emergence, DNA integrity, plant morphology, growth rate, and attractiveness to herbivore insects in *Datura ferox*, *Plant Physiol.*, 1996, **112**, 161-170.

49   K. K. Newsham, A. R. McLeod, P. D. Greenslade and B. A. Emmett, Appropriate controls in outdoor UV-B supplementation experiments, *Global Change Biology*, 1996, **2**, 319-324.

50   P. E. Hatcher and N. D. Paul, The effect of elevated UV-B radiation on herbivory of pea by *Autographa gamma*, *Entomol. Exp. Appl.*, 1994, **71**, 227-233.

51   D. J. Bergvinson, J. T. Arnason, R. I. Hamilton, S. Tachibana and G. H. N. Towers, Putative role of photodimerized phenolic acids in maize resistance to *Ostrinia nubilalis* (Lepidoptera: Pyralidae), *Environ. Entomol.*, 1994, **23**, 1516-1523.

52   E. S. McCloud and M. R. Berenbaum, Stratospheric ozone depletion and plant-insect interactions: Effects of UVB radiation on foliage quality of *Citrus jambhiri* for *Trichoplusia ni*, *J. Chem. Ecol.*, 1994, **20**, 525-539.

53   P. S. Searles, B. R. Kropp, S. D. Flint and M. M. Caldwell, Influence of solar UV-B radiation on peatland microbial communities of Southern Argentina, *New. Phytol.*, 2001, **152**, 213-221.

54   S. A. Moody, K. K. Newsham, P. G. Ayres and N. D. Paul, Variation in the responses of litter and phylloplane fungi to UV-B radiation (290-315 nm), *Mycol. Res.*, 1999, **103**, 1469-1477.

55   J. L. Jacobs and G. W. Sundin, Effect of solar UV-B radiation on a phyllosphere bacterial community, *Appl. Environ. Microbiol.*, 2001, **67**, 5488-5496.

56   D. Johnson, C. D. Campbell, D. Gwynn-Jones, J. A. Lee and T. V. Callaghan, Arctic soil microorganisms respond more to long-term ozone depletion than to atmospheric CO2, *Nature*, 2002, **416**, 82-83.

57   J. W. M. van de Staaij, J. Rozema, A. van Beem and R. Aerts, Increased solar UV-B radiation may reduce infection by arbuscular mycorrhizal fungi (AMF) in dune grassland plants: evidence from five years of field exposure, *Plant Ecol.*, 2001, **154**, 171-177.

58   J. G. Zaller, M. M. Caldwell, S. D. Flint, A. L. Scopel, O. E. Sala and C. L. Ballaré, Solar UV-B radiation affects below-ground parameters in a fen ecosystem in Tierra del Fuego, Argentina: implications of stratospheric ozone depletion, *Global Change Biology*, 2002, **8**, 867-871.

59   N. D. Paul, Stratospheric ozone depletion, UV-B radiation and crop disease, *Environ. Poll.*, 2000, **108**, 343-355.

60   K. K. Newsham, K. Oxborough, R. White, P. D. Greenslade and A. R. McLeod, UV-B radiation constrains the photosynthesis of *Quercus robur* through impacts on the abundance of *Microsphaera alphitoides*, *Forest Pathol.*, 2000, **30**, 265-275.

61   K. K. Newsham, G. C. Lewis, P. D. Greenslade and A. R. McLeod, *Neotyphodium lolii*, a fungal leaf endophyte, reduces fertility of *Lolium perenne* exposed to elevated UV-B radiation, *Ann. Bot.*, 1998, **81**, 397-403.

62   N. D. Paul, S. Rasanayagam, S. A. Moody, P. E. Hatcher and P. G. Ayres, The role of interactions between trophic levels in determining the effects of UV-B on terrestrial ecosystems, *Plant Ecol.*, 1997, **128**, 296-308.

63   T. S. Gunasekera, N. D. Paul and P. G. Ayres, The effects of ultraviolet-B (UV-B: 290-320 nm) radiation on blister blight disease of tea (*Camellia sinensis*), *Plant Pathol.*, 1997, **46**, 179-185.

64   K. K. Newsham, M. N. R. Low, A. R. McLeod, P. D. Greenslade and B. A. Emmett, Ultraviolet-B radiation influences the abundance and distribution of phylloplane fungi on pedunculate oak (*Quercus robur*), *New. Phytol.*, 1997, **136**, 287-297.

65   Y. Naito, Y. Honda and T. Kumagai, Effects of supplementary UV-B radiation on development of damping-off in spinach caused by the soil-borne fungus *Fusarium oxysporum*, *Mycosci.*, 1996, **37**, 15-19.

66   P. G. Ayres, T. S. Gunasekera, M. S. Rasanayagam and N. D. Paul, in *Fungi and environmental change* ed.: G. M. Gadd, Cambridge University Press, 1996, pp. 32-50.

67   M. R. Finckh, A. Q. Chavez, Q. Dai and P. S. Teng, Effects of enhanced UV-B radiation on the growth of rice and its susceptibility to rice blast under glasshouse conditions, *Agric. Ecosyt. Eviron.*, 1995, **52**, 223-233.

68   I. Panagopoulos, J. F. Bornman and L. O. Björn, Response of sugar beet plants to ultraviolet-B (280-320 nm) radiation and *Cercospora* leaf spot disease, *Physiologia Plantarum*, 1992, **84**, 140-145.

69   A. B. Orth, A. H. Teramura and H. D. Sisler, Effects of ultraviolet-B radiation on fungal disease development in *Cucumis sativus*, *Am. J. Bot.*, 1990, **77**, 1188-1192.

70   R. H. Biggs and P. G. Webb, in *Stratospheric ozone reduction, solar ultraviolet radiation and plant life* ed.: M. M. Caldwell, Springer-Verlag, Berlin, 1986, pp. 303-311.

71   P. Semeniuk and R. N. Stewart, Effect of ultraviolet (UV-B) irradiation on infection of roses by *Diplocarpon rosae* Wolf, *Environ. Exp. Bot.*, 1981, **21**, 45-50.

72   P. Semeniuk and R. W. Goth, Effects of ultraviolet irradiation on local lesion development of potato virus S on *Chenopodium quinoa* 'Valdivia' leaves, *Environ. Exp. Bot.*, 1980, **20**, 95-98.

73   S. Moody, N. D. Paul, L. O. Björn, T. V. Callaghan, J. A. Lee, Y. Manetas, J. Rozema, D. Gwynn-Jones, U. Johanson, A. Kyparissis and A. Oudejans, The direct effects of UVB radiation on Betula pubescens litter decomposing at four European field sites., *Plant Ecol.*, 2001, **154**, 29-36.

74   K. J. Duguay and J. N. Klironomos, Direct and indirect effects of enhanced UV-B radiation on the decomposing and competitive abilities of saprobic fungi, *Appl. Soil. Ecol.*, 2000, **14**, 157-164.

75   K. K. Newsham, A. R. McLeod, J. D. Roberts, P. D. Greenslade and B. A. Emmet, Direct effects of elevated UV-B radiation on the decomposition of *Quercus robur* leaf litter, *Oikos*, 1997, **79**, 592-602.

76   C. Gehrke, U. Johanson, T. V. Callaghan, D. Chadwick and C. H. Robinson, The impact of enhanced ultraviolet-B radiation on litter quality and decomposition processes in *Vaccinium* leaves from the subarctic, *Oikos*, 1995, **72**, 213-222.

77   G. U. L. Braga, S. D. Flint, C. D. Miller, A. J. Anderson and D. W. Roberts, Variability in response to UV-B among species and strains of *Metarhizium* isolated from sites at latitudes from 61°N to 54°S, *J. Invertebr. Pathol.*, 2001, **78**, 98-108.

78   G. U. L. Braga, S. D. Flint, C. D. Miller, A. J. Anderson and D. W. Roberts, Both solar UVA and UVB radiation impair conidial culturability and delay germination in the entomopathogenic fungus *Metarhizium anisopliae*, *Photochem. Photobiol.*, 2001, **74**, 734-739.

79   M. Shapiro and J. Domek, Relative effects of ultraviolet and visible light on the activities of corn earworm and beet armyworm (Lepidoptera: Noctuidae) nucleopolyhedroviruses, *J. Econ. Entomol.*, 2002, **95**, 261-268.

80   J. Rozema, G. M. Lenssen and J. W. M. van de Staaij, in *The greenhouse effect and primary productivity in European agroecosystems* ed.: H. H. VanLaar, Pudoc, Wageningen, 1990, pp. 68-71.

81   L. H. Ziska and A. H. Teramura, CO_2 enhancement of growth and photosynthesis in rice (*Oryza sativa*). Modification by increased ultraviolet-B radiation, *Plant Physiol.*, 1992, **99**, 473-481.

82   J. H. Sullivan and A. H. Teramura, The effects of UV-B radiation on loblolly pine. 3. Interaction with CO_2 enhancement, *Plant Cell Environ.*, 1994, **17**, 311-317.

83   A. J. Visser, M. Tosserams, M. W. Groen, G. W. H. Magendans and J. Rozema, The combined effects of CO_2 concentration and solar UV-B radiation on faba bean grown in open-top chambers, *Plant Cell Environ.*, 1997, **20**, 189-199.

84   J. Rozema, G. M. Lenssen, J. W. M. van de Staaij, M. Tosserams, A. J. Visser and R. A. Broekman, Effects of UV-B radiation on terrestrial plants and ecosystems: interaction with CO_2 enrichment, *Plant Ecol.*, 1997, **128**, 182-191.

85   J. H. Sullivan, Effects of increasing UV-B radiation and atmospheric CO_2 on photosynthesis and growth: implications for terrestrial ecosystems, *Plant Ecol.*, 1997, **128**, 194-206.

86   X. Hao, B. A. Hale, D. P. Ormrod and A. P. Papadopoulos, Effects of pre-exposure to ultraviolet-B radiation on responses of tomato (*Lycopersicon esculentum* cv. New Yorker) to ozone in ambient and elevated carbon dioxide, *Environ. Poll.*, 2000, **110**, 217-224.

87   S. A. Moody, D. J. S. Coop and N. D. Paul, in *Plants and UV-B. Responses to environmental change* ed.: P. J. Lumsden, Cambridge University Press, 1997, pp. 283-304.

88   A. Lavola, R. Julkunen-Tiitto, T. M. de la Rosa, T. Lehto and P. J. Aphalo, Allocation of carbon to growth and secondary metabolites in birch seedlings under UV-B radiation and CO_2 exposure, *Physiologia Plantarum*, 2000, **109**, 260-267.

89   M. Tosserams, A. J. Visser, M. W. Groen, G. Kalis, E. Magendans and J. Rozema, Combined effects of CO_2 concentration and enhanced UV-B radiation on faba bean, *Plant Ecol.*, 2001, **154**, 197-210.

90   A. Lavola, R. Julkunen-Tiitto, H. Roininen and P. Aphalo, Host-plant preference of an insect herbivore mediated by UV-B and CO_2 in relation to plant secondarv metabolites, *Biochem. Syst. Ecol.*, 1998, **26**.

91   J. H. Sullivan and A. H. Teramura, Field study of the interaction between solar ultraviolet-B radiation and drought on photosynthesis and growth in soybean, *Plant Physiol.*, 1990, **92**, 141-146.

92   T. Balakumar, V. H. B. Vincent and K. Paliwal, On the interaction of UV-B radiation (280-315-nm) with water stress in crop plants, *Physiologia Plantarum*, 1993, **87**, 217-222.

93   B. D. Campbell, R. W. Hofmann and C. L. Hunt, in *Stratospheric ozone depletion: the effects of enhanced UV-B radiation on terrestrial ecosystems* ed.: J. Rozema, Backhuys, Leiden, 1999, pp. 226-249.

94   Y. Manetas, Y. Petropoulou, K. Stamatakis, D. Nikolopoulos, E. Levizou, G. Psaras and G. Karabourniotis, Beneficial effects of enhanced UV-B radiation under field conditions: improvement of needle water relations and survival capacity of *Pinus pinea* L. seedlings during the dry Mediterranean summer., *Plant Ecol.*, 1997, **128**, 100-108.

95   J. E. Hunt and D. L. McNeil, Nitrogen status affects UV-B sensitivity of cucumber, *Aust. J. Plant. Phys.*, 1998, **25**, 79-86.

96   S. Li, M. Paulsson and L. O. Björn, Temperature-dependent formation and photorepair of DNA damage induced by UV-B radiation in suspension-cultured tobacco cells, *J. Photochem. Photobiol. B*, 2002, **66**, 67-72.

97   Y. Takeuchi, M. Murakami, N. Nakajima, N. Kondo and O. Nikaido, Induction and repair of damage to DNA in cucumber cotyledons irradiated with UV-B, *Plant Cell Physiol.*, 1997, **37**, 181-187.

98   Q. Pang and J. B. Hays, UV-B-inducible and temperature-sensitive photoreactivation of cyclobutane pyrimidine dimers in *Arabidopsis thaliana*, *Plant Physiol.*, 1991, **95**, 536-543.

99   D. J. Beerling, A. C. Terry, P. L. Mitchell, T. V. Callaghan, D. Gwynn-Jones and J. A. Lee, Time to chill: Effects of simulated global change on leaf ice nucleation temperatures of subarctic vegetation, *Am. J. Bot.*, 2001, **88**, 628-633.

100   T. A. Day, C. T. Ruhland, C. W. Grobe and F. Xiong, Growth and reproduction of Antarctic vascular plants in response to warming and UV radiation reductions in the field, *Oecologia*, 1999, **119**, 24-35.

101   D. Lud, A. H. L. Huiskes, T. C. W. Moerdijk and J. Rozema, The effects of altered levels of UV-B radiation on an Antarctic grass and lichen, *Plant Ecol.*, 2001, **154**, 87-99.

102   G. Kulandaivelu and N. Nedunchezhian, Synergistic effects of ultraviolet-B enhanced radiation and growth temperature on ribulose 1,5-bisphosphate carboxylase and $^{14}CO_2$ fixation in *Vigna sinensis* L., *Photosynthetica*, 1993, **29**, 377-383.

103   N. Nedunchezhian and G. Kulandaivelu, Effects of ultraviolet-B enhanced radiation and temperature on growth and photochemical activities in *Vigna unguiculata*, *Biol. Plant.*, 1996, **38**, 205-214.

104   J. S. Bale, G. J. Masters, I. D. Hodkinson, C. Awmack, T. M. Bezemer, V. K. Brown, J. Butterfield, A. Buse, J. C. Coulson, J. Farrar, J. E. G. Good, R. Harrington, S. Hartley, T. H. Jones, R. L. Lindroth, M. C. Press, I. Symrnioudis, A. D. Watt and J. B. Whittaker, Herbivory in global climate change research: direct effects of rising temperature on insect herbivores, *Global Change Biology*, 2002, **8**, 1-16.

105   T. C. R. White, Weather, food and plagues of locusts, *Oecologia*, 1976, **22**, 119-134.

106   S. A. Moody, K. K. Newsham, P. G. Ayres and N. D. Paul, Variation in the responses of litter and phylloplane fungi to UV-B radiation (290-315 nm). *Mycol. Res.*, 1999, **103**, 1469-1477.

107   B. Huntley, in *Vegetation History* ed.: T. I. Webb, Kluwer Academic Publishers, Dordrecht, 1988, pp. 341-383.

108   M. T. Sykes, in *Past and future rapid environmental changes: The spatial and evolutionary responses of terrestrial biota* ed.: J. R. M. Allen, Springer-Verlag, Berlin, 1997, pp. 427-440.

109   M. T. Sykes, I. C. Prentice and W. Cramer, A bioclimatic model for the potential distributions of north European tree species under present and future climates., *J. Biogeogr.*, 1996, **23**, 203-233.

110   M. Sturm, C. Racine and K. Tape, Increasing shrub abundance in the Arctic, *Nature*, 2001, **411**, 546-547.

CHAPTER 4. AQUATIC ECOSYSTEMS: EFFECTS OF SOLAR ULTRAVIOLET RADIATION AND INTERACTIONS WITH OTHER CLIMATIC CHANGE FACTORS

D-P. Häder,[A] H. D. Kumar,[B] R. C. Smith[c] And R. C. Worrest[d]

[a] *Institut für Botanik und Pharmazeutische Biologie, Friedrich-Alexander-Universität, Staudtstr. 5, DE-91058 Erlangen, Germany*

[b] *214 Saketnagar Colony, Naria, Varanasi 221005, India*

[c] *Institute for Computational Earth System Science (ICESS) and Department of Geography, University of California, Santa Barbara, California 93106, USA*

[d] US Global Change Research Information Office (GCRIO), CIESIN, Columbia University, 400 Virginia Avenue SW, Suite 750, Washington DC 20024, USA

Summary

Aquatic ecosystems are a key component of the Earth's biosphere. A large number of studies document substantial impact of solar UV radiation on individual species yet considerable uncertainty remains with respect to assessing impacts on ecosystems. Several studies indicate that the impact of increased UV radiation appears relatively low when considering overall ecosystem response, while, in contrast, effects on individual species show considerable responses. Ecosystem response to climate variability incorporates both synergistic and antagonistic processes with respect to UV-related effects, significantly complicating understanding and prediction at the ecosystem level. The impact of climate variability on UV-related effects often becomes manifest via indirect effects such as reduction in sea ice, changes in water column bio-optical characteristics, changes in cloud cover and shifts in oceanographic biogeochemical provinces.

Introduction

Life on Earth has developed in the absence of a stratospheric ozone layer with much higher UV levels than today.[1-3] Surviving populations of organisms likely possessed efficient strategies and physiological mechanisms to prevent and repair UV-induced damage[4, 5] including biosynthesis of UV-absorbing substances, DNA repair mechanisms and enzymes that reduce photooxidative stress.[6, 7] It has been postulated that some of the first screening pigments such as scytonemin may have evolved in cyanobacteria during the Precambrian and allowed colonization of exposed, shallow-water and terrestrial habitats.[8] However, protection is not perfect, and UV-B can cause molecular damage to lipids, proteins and nucleic acids and it may exert indirect effects through oxidative stress due to molecular reactions of UV-B with cellular targets.[9]

Recent results continue to confirm the general consensus that solar UV negatively affects aquatic organisms.[10-13] Reductions in productivity, impaired reproduction and development and increased mutation rate have been shown for phytoplankton,[14, 15] macroalgae,[16, 17] fish eggs and larvae[18, 19] zooplankton[20] and primary and secondary consumers exposed to UV radiation.[21-23] Decreases in biomass productivity due to enhanced UV-B are relayed through all levels of the intricate food web, possibly resulting in reduced food production for humans,[21] reduced sink capacity for atmospheric carbon dioxide,[24] as well as changes in species composition and ecosystem integrity.[25] However, quantitative assessments of UV-related effects in natural waters are complex because species respond differentially to increased solar radiation and other environmental stress factors. This, in turn, affects physiological functions such as growth, reproduction and behavior[26] and the consequent population fitness and species interactions (Figure 4-1). Consequently, community structure and trophic interaction will change with time and this ultimately will also alter biogeochemical cycling.[27, 28]

For many aquatic ecosystems, pre-ozone depletion conditions are not known; consequently effects caused by ozone depletion are difficult to evaluate.[29] Impacts of environmental factors are evaluated mostly on the basis of specific species which should be carefully selected for long-term monitoring of environmental change.[30] Species interactions and ecosystem dynamics are more difficult to evaluate, model and predict. Feedback mechanisms between aquatic ecosystems, physical factors and atmospheric and oceanic circulation have significant impact on primary productivity and ecosystem integrity, but are not well understood and are difficult to predict. Changing environmental conditions may have positive or negative effects on populations and species responses, and interact either positively or negatively with respect to UV-related changes,[28, 31] thus confounding quantitative assessment.[32]

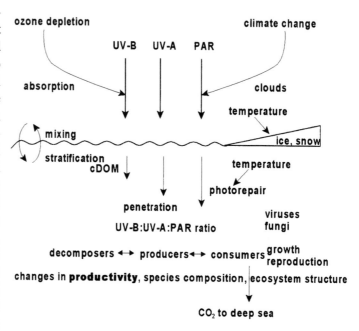

Figure 4-1. Concept of the aquatic food web affected by ozone depletion and climate change. PAR, photosynthetic active radiation (400 – 700 nm); cDOM, colored dissolved organic material

Solar UV Radiation and Penetration in Aquatic Ecosystems

Incident solar UV radiation and the depth of penetration into the water column are key factors in assessing the potential for damage to aquatic organisms. In addition to the Antarctic ozone hole,[33] increasing ozone loss has been observed over the Arctic during spring and early summer months.[34] Areas with reduced ozone concentrations[35] separate from the Arctic ozone hole and pass over Northern and Mid Europe and sometimes even cross the European Alps,[36] which increases the UV stress due to gradual ozone loss over mid latitudes[37] with clearly demonstrated trends of increasing UV-B radiation.[38] Sabziparvar et al.[39] have developed a model to describe the global climatology of the UV irradiation at the Earth's surface to predict future UV trends on a global scale.

Aquatic ecosystems differ tremendously in their transparency and thus the depth of solar UV penetration.[40] Absorbing and scattering substances reduce the transparency of the water, especially in eutrophic freshwater systems and coastal areas of the oceans,[41, 42] while UV penetrates to greater depths in clear oceanic waters. Often there is a pronounced variability and seasonal changes in the transparency.[43, 44] In addition to inorganic particulate matter, dissolved and particulate organic carbon (DOC and POC) and various humic substances contribute considerably to the attenuation of short wavelength radiation.[45] DOC is only slowly degraded in the water column but is broken down by solar UV to smaller subunits,[46] which can be taken up by bacterioplankton, which consequently increases the transparency of the water column leading to a deeper penetration of solar UV.[47] As a consequence, the concentration of DOC and the mechanisms that influence its abundance will have an important impact on the penetration of UV and the subsequent UV-related effects.[48] Another consequence is a shift from autotrophic (photosynthetic) to heterotrophic (consumers) organisms under UV stress. [49] Penetration of solar UV into the water column can be measured with a number of instruments.[50] Recently, the attenuation of biologically effective UV radiation has been measured using biochemical dosimeters based on the formation of cyclobutane dimers in isolated DNA or on the behavior of microorganisms.[51, 52] The impact of solar UV is modified by the depth and rate of the mixing layer.[53]

Bacterioplankton and Picoplankton

Bacterioplankton and picoplankton are major constituents in the production and recycling of energy and nutrients within aquatic ecosystems. Disrupting the function of these critical components would have far-reaching impacts on organisms, including humans, many of which depend on aquatic ecosystems for their food supply.

Bacteria and small planktonic organisms (nano- and picoplankton) usually are too small to effectively protect themselves against solar UV by absorbing substances since there is an upper limit of the concentration of these substances due to osmotic effects. These populations overcome the stress of solar UV (as well as predation and other adverse effects) by fast cell division and growth. In clear oceanic waters with high UV penetration, bacterioplankton are affected in the top layers of the water column. Growth and survival are impaired, and the activity of enzymes is inhibited. Solar UV damages the DNA mainly through the formation of pyrimidine dimers[54] which may cause mutagenesis and cell death.[55] As long as the repair mechanisms keep up with the damage,[56] the population is not at stake; it is only when the dimers accumulate under strong ambient radiation, that the population will decrease.

Solar and artificial UV radiations was found to have little effect on the composition of coastal marine bacterioplankton communities in the North Sea.[57] DNA showed only minor changes under the different radiation regimes. Some of the species were more sensitive than others, but only about 10 % of the species appeared to be affected by UV radiation. The resistance of bacterioplankton to solar UV in these coastal areas is due to high turbidity and indicates the presence of an efficient DNA repair system, which has made bacterial evolution possible.[58]

Cyanobacteria

Cyanobacteria have a cosmopolitan distribution in both aquatic and terrestrial ecosystems ranging from hot springs to the Antarctic and Arctic regions. The significant role of these N_2-fixing microorganisms in improving the fertility of rice paddy fields and other soils is well documented.[59] Cyanobacteria are also prominent constituents of marine ecosystems and account for a significant percentage of oceanic primary productivity.

UV-B radiation is known to impair motility and photoorientation[60] and to affect a number of other physiological and biochemical processes in cyanobacteria,[21, 61] resulting in reduced overall productivity, germination and differentiation.[62] Photosynthetic pigments can be bleached by UV-B and the structure of the light harvesting complexes is affected resulting in impaired photosynthesis.[63]

Proteins and DNA are the main targets of UV-B.[64] Enzymes of nitrogen metabolism show differential sensitivity towards UV-B. In contrast to the inhibition of nitrogenase and glutamine synthetase activity, there was an induction in nitrate reductase activity by artificial UV-B.[62] The primary photosynthetic reactions and CO_2 uptake are affected by UV-B.[65] *Synechococcus* resists UV-B by rapidly exchanging alternate protein forms in the photosynthetic apparatus. This molecular plasticity may be an important element in community-level responses to UV-B, where susceptibility to UV-B inhibition of photosynthesis changes diurnally.[66] However, photosynthesis may be reactivated by UV-A/blue light exposure.[67]

Cyanobacteria have developed protective strategies to counteract the damaging effects of UV-B. These include (a) production of photoprotective compounds such as mycosporine-like amino acids (MAAs) and scytonemin,[68, 69] (b) escape from UV radiation by migration into habitats with reduced light exposure,[21] (c) production of quenching agents such as carotenoids[70] and superoxide dismutase,[71] (d) repair mechanisms such as photoreactivation and light-independent nucleotide excision repair of DNA[72] and (e) activity of a number of antioxidant enzymes.[73] UV-B induces synthesis of MAAs in a number of cyanobacteria.[74] A polychromatic action spectrum for the induction of MAAs in *Anabaena* sp. shows a single prominent peak at 290 nm.[75] In addition to having photo-protective functions, MAAs also play an important role as osmotic regulators and antifreeze compounds.[76] Other UV-A-absorbing compounds were found to be induced by UV-A.[77] A database on photoprotective compounds in cyanobacteria and algae[78] is available (www.biologie.uni-erlangen.de/botanik1/index.html).

Cyanobacteria form large mat communities in e.g. Antarctica. A *Leptolyngbya* mat showed significant photochemical inhibition under supplemental UV-B, while inhibition was less prominent in a *Phormidium* mat.[79] The latter contained 25 times the concentration of UV protecting MAAs and double the concentration of carotenoids compared to the *Leptolyngbya* mat showing the ameliorating action of screening pigments. Rai and coworkers[80] studied the interactive effects of UV-B and heavy metal pollution on nitrogen-fixing cyanobacteria and found synergistic effects of the two stress factors.

Phytoplankton

Phytoplankton are by far the major biomass producers in the oceans and thus represent the base of the food web. Their productivity matches that of all terrestrial ecosystems taken together.[81] A large number of recent studies indicate a considerable sensitivity to solar ambient UV of phytoplankton communities distributed from polar to tropical habitats.[82, 83] Satellite studies over the last decade indicate a significant global decrease in phytoplankton.[84] The reasons for this are not known, but the authors suggest increased stratification. Solar UV impairs photosynthesis, bleaches photosynthetic pigments, nitrogen metabolism and induces DNA damage.[85, 86] However there are efficient protection and repair mechanisms in these organisms, including the xanthophyll cycle in photosynthesis, screening pigment production, synthesis of antioxidants and DNA repair.[87-89] While the effectiveness of screening pigments was postulated but not demonstrated in the past, recent experiments showed that vital physiological functions were protected by the presence of MAAs.[90]

Large-scale quantification and assessment of phytoplankton photochemical characteristics can be determined by pigment analysis[91] or by airborne monitoring using laser pump-and-probe techniques.[92] Systematic monitoring revealed strong daytime declines in photosynthetic quantum yield under ambient light in the near-surface water layer over large aquatic areas.

Blooms of diatoms or *Phaeocystis* are common during Austral spring. *Phaeocystis* has a high UV absorption, but there can be a 10-fold variability in the screening pigment to chlorophyll ratio. Its sensitivity to UV is not clear: several experimental approaches have suggested that it is more sensitive to UV than diatoms, which have a significantly lower UV absorption.[93] In contrast, other studies show changes in species composition favoring *Phaeocystis*.[94] Colonial *Phaeocystis antarctica* produce a number of MAAs which strongly absorb in the UV.[95]

The repair mechanism of the photosynthetic apparatus was studied in UV-B sensitive and tolerant species of several alga groups.[96] Application of an inhibitor of chloroplast protein synthesis aggravated the UV-B induced inhibition of photosynthesis in UV-B tolerant species while it did not in the sensitive species. Thus, UV-B tolerance of photosynthesis is associated with recovery capacity and repair. Phytoplankton are also affected by changing ambient CO_2 concentrations. However, they can acclimate to a wide range of CO_2 concentrations.[97] It should be mentioned that many results are based on short-term studies (days). This is quite appropriate, since the organisms have short generation times on the order of hours or days. However, genetic adaptation to increased UV stress is expected to occur on much longer time scales.

Models have been developed to predict the productivity of phytoplankton communities[98] taking into account the variability in exposure and differences in sensitivity. Another model evaluates the role of 3D currents, vertical mixing and turbulence on the growth and dispersion of marine phytoplankton.[99]

Studies in Patagonia (Argentina), which is occasionally under the influence of the Antarctic ozone hole, showed that photosynthetic inhibition in phytoplankton varies considerably between different environments and it depends on the optical depth of the water column. The contributions to decreased photosynthesis of UV-A and UV-B were approximately equal and maximum inhibition was about 35 % at the surface.[100] Freshwater phytoplankton seem to be more inhibited by solar UV than marine phytoplankton. There was also significant DNA damage (cyclobutane pyrimidine dimers, CPD), which was higher than in tropical seawater.[101] However, in evaluating the impact of solar UV it is necessary to monitor other variables such as changes in cloud cover, species composition including cell size distribution, and depth of the mixed layer.

The importance of cloudiness has been shown by an analysis of solar irradiance measurements from Ushuaia (Argentina) and Palmer (Antarctica). Calculations showed that the biologically effective daily UV doses changed to a larger degree due changing cloud cover than with ozone depletion.[102]

Sensitivity to natural UV radiation varies considerably between dominant phytoplankton species as shown in three Arctic lakes.[103] Growth of small chlorophytes, diatoms and cyanobacteria was impaired mainly by short wavelength UV while the larger colony forming species were stimulated. Since the latter species are not preferred food for daphnia they dominated in the end of the experiment.

Macroalgae and Seagrasses

Macroalgae and seagrasses are important biomass producers along the coastlines and on the continental shelves. They are exploited commercially on a large scale and form habitats for larval stages of fish, shrimp, crustaceans and other ecologically and economically important animals. Both short- and long-tem exposure to solar radiation inhibits growth in adult stages of several species of macroalgae.[104] Photosynthesis is seriously impaired in red, brown and green algae[105-107] resulting in reduced oxygen production.[108] Susceptibility of marine macroalgae to UV is highly variable among species which results in a specific depth distribution of species.[109] Deep-water species are generally more sensitive to UV radiation than intertidal species.[110] This can be easily demonstrated by transplantation experiments of algae from deep to shallow waters.[111] Eulittoral and upper sublittoral species generally tolerate or acclimate to UV.[112]

In King George Island, Antarctica, biomass productivity and species diversity decreased at 20 m, probably due to limited light conditions.[113] Also in the Arctic fjords primary productivity of seaweeds is strongly affected by the availability of solar radiation.[114] Even though the downwelling solar UV-B radiation never exceeded 0.27 W m^{-2}, UV radiation deeply penetrated into the water column and affected primary productivity to a depth of 5-6 m. The harmful effects were ameliorated during summer following the influx of turbid fresh water from snow and glacier ice into the fjord water, increasing the light attenuation in the top water layer.

Many macroalgae produce one or several UV absorbing substances.[115] Most MAA-producing species belong to the red algae, followed by brown algae, and only a few green algae produce MAAs.[78] Three different types of protection by UV screening pigments have been found: one group (sublittoral algae not likely to be exposed to higher doses of solar UV) does not synthesize UV absorbing pigments at all; another group produces high amounts of MAAs, but cannot be further induced by exposure to any radiation.[78] This group includes supralittoral species with high natural exposure to solar UV. In the third group, MAA production can be induced by solar radiation. MAAs are very stable compounds and are not easily modified by heat, UV or extreme pH.[116, 117] A polychromatic action spectrum was determined for the induction of MAAs in the chlorophyte *Prasiola stipitata* showing a clear maximum at 300 nm.[118] In contrast, in the red alga *Chondrus crispus* blue light and UV-A radiation control the synthesis of MAAs, but the induction by UV was not investigated.[119] While most algae use MAAs, a few produce different types of UV-absorbing compounds.[120]

Young developmental stages of algae (zoospores, gametes, zygotes and young germlings) are extremely susceptible to UV radiation stress:[121] Mortality of zoospores of kelp species from southern Spain was induced by UV radiation (more by UV-B than by UV-A).[122] In kelp zoospores there is loss of viability, cellular disintegration and impairment of motility and phototaxis.[123] DNA damage (pyrimidine dimers) increased linearly with UV-B dose.[122] Zoospores of the shallow water species *Chordaria flagelliformis* need higher UV doses than the mid-sublittoral species *Laminaria saccharina* to suffer mortality.[122] Polarity formation, mitosis and cytokinesis during development of brown algae zygotes are affected.

The green alga *Chara* is regarded as a link to higher plants, which makes it interesting for research on UV-related responses. Under elevated UV-B there was an increased vegetative reproduction while generative reproduction was suppressed. UV-B did not induce the synthesis of protective pigments in this alga.[124]

Zooplankton

Zooplankton are primary consumers in the aquatic food web, providing a vital link to populations, including humans, that depend upon aquatic ecosystems for their food supply. In earlier research the vertical migration of zooplankton into lower and darker water layers was explained by the avoidance of visually oriented predators (e.g., fish). Today UV exposure is assumed to be a contributing, hazardous factor.[125]

The sensitivity of zooplankton to UV radiation was tested for several species of *Daphnia* that differed in their pigmentation.[126] Both melanin and carotenoid pigments protect these organisms from UV. Under UV, all *Daphnia* species moved deeper into the water, but the extent of the response was inversely correlated with the pigmentation - the lighter pigmented species migrating deeper into the water column.[127] In another experiment *Daphnia* was found to migrate away from the surface at midday and in late afternoon, while animals in UV shielded controls remained closer to the surface. However, the vertical swimming behavior itself, as well as their phototactic orientation, is impaired by exposure to full spectrum solar radiation.[128, 129]

Large variability was found in the concentration of the photoprotective compounds, MAAs, among zooplankton from lakes located along an elevation gradient.[130] The concentration of these photoprotective compounds was inversely related to the attenuation coefficient of the water and in the lakes. MAAs, together with other photoprotective compounds, play a major role in minimizing the damaging effects of solar UV radiation in zooplankton from transparent lakes. UV-B is a major stress factor for zooplankton, particularly in high mountain lakes, which have high transparency, especially above the tree line.[40]

The copepod *Calanus* is a key component in marine zooplankton communities in the Gulf of St. Lawrence (Figure 4-2). Eggs are released in spring and summer in shallow water and incubate for 1 – 3 days. At current levels, UV radiation has a negative impact on eggs residing in the first few meters of the water column.[131] Again, variability in cloud cover, water transparency and vertical distribution may have a greater effect on UV-B exposure than ozone depletion. Kuhn and coworkers[132] have modeled the UV induced

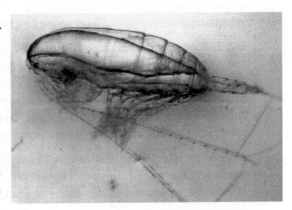

mortality in the early life stages of *Calanus finmarchicus*. The lowest modeled daily survival was 59% under ambient ozone and 49% under simulated 50% ozone loss.

Figure 4-2. Photograph of the fifth copepodite of *Calanus marshallae* Frost. (Photo by Jaime Gomez-Gutiérrez).

The copepod *Diaptomus* showed no increased mortality during food shortage when incubated at 0.5 m in a clear-water lake, but food-replete animals did. These results show that UV tolerance is not affected by short-term lack of energy or nutrients. Under artificial UV the animals showed high mortality, which could not be improved by feeding.[133]

Usually organisms tolerate damaging UV better if they are exposed to low irradiances for a longer time (in the presence of UV-A or visible light) than to high irradiances for a short time (indicating the lack of reciprocity), because their photorepair system keeps up with the damage.[134] However, in some strains there is reciprocity, due to a lack of photorepair. In *Asplancha* and *Daphnia* the offspring died if no photorepair-inducing radiation was provided.

Secondary Consumers

Although humans use about 8% of the productivity of the oceans, that fraction increases to more than 25% for upwelling areas and to 35% for temperate continental shelf systems. For about one-sixth of the world's population (primarily developing nations), the oceans provide more than one-third of their animal protein. Many of the fisheries that depend upon the oceanic primary productivity are unsustainable. Although the primary causes for a decline in fish populations are predation and poor food supply for larvae, overfishing of adults, increased water temperature and pollution and disease; exposure to increased UV-B radiation may also contribute to that decline. The eggs and larvae of many fish are sensitive to UV-B exposure. However, imprecisely defined habitat characteristics and the unknown effect of small increases in UV-B exposure on the naturally high mortality rates of fish larvae are major barriers to a more accurate assessment of ozone depletion on marine fish populations.

In the Gulf of Maine, UV-A penetrates to 23 m and UV-B to 7-12 m where the embryos and larvae of the Atlantic cod develop. Exposure to UV equivalent to 10 m depth resulted in a significant mortality of developing embryos and a significant decrease in length of larvae.[135] These irradiances occur in many temperate latitudes where these ecologically and commercially important fish spawn.

After exposure to solar UV larvae had lower concentrations of UV absorbing compounds and greater DNA damage. However, they had higher activities of the antioxidant superoxide dismutase and transcriptional activator p53. p53 is expressed in response to DNA damage and can result in cellular growth arrest during the cell cycle or to programmed cell death (apoptosis). Cellular death caused by apoptosis is the most likely cause of mortality in embryos and larvae in these experiments, while the smaller size at hatching in those larvae that survived is caused by permanent cellular arrest in response to DNA damage.

In another experiment, the effect of UV on the success of early life history stages of bluegills was tested for fish from two lakes with different underwater UV environment. Survival was as low as 20% at 0.1 m, but higher at 1 m depth. Embryos responded similarly to UV exposure regardless of the lake of origin. UV-B is an important factor in the success of early life history stages especially in high transparency lakes. Bluegills constructed their nests deeper in a lake with high UV transparency than in a less transparent lake.[136]

Fingerling channel catfish were found to be quite sensitive to solar UV-B.[137] After a 24-h exposure, thinning of the dorsal epidermis was observed accompanied by edema and sunburn cells. After 48-h exposure, cell death and sloughing of the outer epidermal layer were widespread.

The impact of UV on Atlantic cod eggs and larvae was studied in the estuary and Gulf of St. Lawrence[22] in comparison with the ambient levels of UV radiation and penetration in this subarctic marine ecosystem. Exposure to UV-B produced a significant negative effect; however, these direct effects are likely to be minimal within the context of all the other environmental factors that produce the very high levels of mortality typically observed in their planktonic early life stages.

Also in the Gulf of St. Lawrence, certain larval stages of the American lobster spend the daylight hours in the top two meters of the water column throughout the breeding season. Lobster larvae may therefore be exposed to heavy doses of UV radiation; yet larvae exposed to radiation had a mortality rate comparable to that of protected larvae.[138] This outcome suggests that lobster larvae are tolerant to UV radiation. A combination of adaptations to planktonic life near the surface, such as production of light-blocking pigments and other effective mechanisms, may account for the relative resistance of lobster larvae to UV radiation.

There is quantitative evidence for global amphibian population declines.[139] One extensive study was based on large-scale temporal and spatial variations in amphibian population trends from 936 populations in North America and Western Europe.[140] On a global scale, the data indicate rapid declines from the late 1950s to the late 1960s with subsequent slower declines. These declines have complex causes, including pathogen outbreaks, interannual variability in precipitation, climate-induced changes and possibly UV-B exposure.[141] Climate-induced reductions in water depth at sites where eggs are laid have caused high mortality of embryos due to increased exposure to solar UV-B radiation and subsequent vulnerability to infection. Precipitation is strongly linked to El Niño events underscoring the role of large-scale climatic patterns. Elevated surface temperatures affect the climate over much of the world and if warming continues this could be responsible for future pathogen-mediated amphibian declines in many regions. While a number of studies have not found evidence for negative effects of UV radiation on amphibian early embryonic development,[142] sublethal effects that can manifest themselves at later developmental stages can occur.[143] In addition, another study on frogs did not find clear evidence for reduced hatchability or increased frequency of developmental anomalies of embryos exposed to ambient

UV-B.[144] However, hatchling size was significantly larger when UV-B was blocked, indicating that solar UV-B has a negative effect on early hatchling growth. In yet another study, enhanced UV-B was found to induce high mortality and damage to the skin and ocular system of two other species of tadpoles.[145] After 1 month of hatching only 3-18% survived under enhanced UV-B as compared to 52-55% at ambient radiation and 44-65 % in the controls. A series of careful studies tried to assess the risk of solar ultraviolet radiation to the northern leopard frog (*Rana pipiens*) in 26 North American wetlands.[146, 147] Full sunlight caused approximately 50 % mortality of the frogs during early larval development and about 97 % hindlimb malformations. [146] Filtering the UV-B wavelengths out almost completely eliminated the effects. The difficulty arises when one tries to evaluate the radiation doses perceived by the organisms in their natural habitat. This depends on shading, the attenuation in the water column and the behavior of the animals.[147] On the basis of radiation monitoring over the year and behavioral observations, the authors conclude that estimated UV-B doses never exceeded detrimental levels in 21 of the 26 wetlands in Minnesota and Wisconsin.[147] However, continued reduction of ozone and other climate change effects may increase UV doses above the damage threshold.

The catastrophic declines in corals and sea urchins on a global scale are only partially offset by some local recoveries.[148, 149] Multiple factors seem to be responsible for these declines, including rising temperatures, pollution and other anthropogenic causes. While protection by UV absorbing pigments has been proven for many species,[150] a primary effect of increased solar radiation on survival and growth is still uncertain.

Ecosystems

All ecosystems are affected by gradual changes in important environmental factors including climate, nutrient loading, habitat fragmentation or biotic exploitation.[151] In addition, ecosystems are now being subjected to relatively rapid anthropogenic climate and UV-related changes which may lead to large shifts in the system.[148] Also, it is at the ecosystem level where assessment of anthropogenic climate change and UV-related effects are confounded and where there is the potential for both synergistic and antagonistic effects. Recent studies have shown that these changes may lead to loss of ecosystem resilience that often drives the system into a different structure. This is particularly important when strategies for sustainable management of ecosystems are developed. The seasonal timing of anthropogenic changes is critical. For example, in the Arctic and the Antarctic ecosystems as well as many temperate freshwater biotopes the onset of spring phytoplankton blooms and spawning in invertebrates as well as vertebrates coincides with ozone depletion as well as shifts in several climate-related parameters. Ozone monitoring and ground-based measurements show a clear downward trend of stratospheric ozone, with attendant increases in UV-B, over both polar regions.

Freshwater Ecosystems

Olesen and Maberly[152] have measured oxygen production in natural phytoplankton populations from a freshwater lake in situ at mid-summer. They show that fluxes of PAR, UV-A and UV-B accounted for 81 % of the variation in gross photosynthesis and that UV-A was more inhibitory than UV-B radiation. In another study the impact of UV-B on food quality in four western boreal toad breeding ponds was carried out.[153] These workers found that ambient solar UV-B exposure decreased protein concentration, shifted the community composition of algae and reduced the food quality within the ponds.

Williamson and co-workers have shown that in order to evaluate anthropogenic impacts on lakes a variety of parameters need to be assessed. These parameters should include acid precipitation, heavy metal and toxic organic contaminants, and the concentration of cDOC (colored dissolved organic carbon), in addition to increased UV radiation and changes due to global warming.[154] Further, the anthropogenic acidification often causes changes in zooplankton community structure, which in turn also affects zooplanktivorous predators.[155]

The Antarctic Aquatic Ecosystem

An assessment of UV-B effects for polar aquatic ecosystems is complex and requires consideration of the ecosystem as a whole (Figure 4-3). In particular, climate variability has been shown to have important synergistic influences on UV-B. Because of being close to freezing temperatures, polar ecosystems are particularly sensitive to change because the freeze/thaw boundary applies critical limits to subsequent environmental responses including: air and water temperature, the timing, extent and duration of ice and snow cover, changes in the surface albedo, changes in water column cDOM concentrations and the level of solar radiation and its penetration depth. Such changes, driven by climate variability, may be more important for UV-B exposure levels and spectral balance between UV-B and PAR than ozone depletion. In addition, the known increases in UV-B from reduction of stratospheric ozone may be augmented or reduced by changes in cloud cover related to climate variability. A summary of nearly a decade of ship and satellite observations along the western Antarctic Peninsula showed a very large (nearly an order of magnitude) interannual variability both spatially and temporally.[156] From the perspective to trying to understand the possible influence of a multitude of environmental factors, such as ozone-related enhanced UV-B, cloud cover and sea ice season, this large interannual variability makes it difficult do attribute cause and effect.

Recent work confirms changes in UV effects consistent with the physiological effects of temperature, both directly on photosynthesis as well as indirectly through the enzymes involved in repair of UV damage.[98] These authors concluded that changes in temperature can have strong effects on UV sensitivity, and point out the importance of repair processes. Thus, ecological response to climate variability with attendant indirect UV-related effects may mask direct ozone-related UV effects.

Figure 4-3. Antarctic ecosystem with research vessel Tangaroa, New Zealand, in the background.

While the ecological significance of enhanced ozone-related UV radiation continues to be debated, the ecological response to a statistically significant warming trend in the western Antarctic Peninsula region over the past half century, with corresponding reduction in sea ice extent, has been demonstrated for several trophic levels.[157, 158] It is well documented that changes in underwater UV exposure have the capacity to directly affect the species composition of aquatic biota at various trophic levels and to cause effects that may cascade throughout the trophic structure.[159] It is also clear that this complex combination of direct and indirect effects will result in future changes in aquatic ecosystem structure. However, the individual contribution of climate variability and ozone-related increases in UV radiation are extremely difficult to untangle and/or predict.

Marine plankton can be used as sensitive indicators of UV-B fluctuations at the Earth's surface. Significant UV-B penetration occurs to 20 – 30 m.[160] A first report indicated a close correlation between DNA damage and UV-B irradiance in Antarctica.[161] DNA dosimeters were 2 – 4 times more sensitive than small phytoplankton indicating that photoprotective and DNA repair mechanisms reduce DNA damage in bacterioplankton and phytoplankton. However, phytoplankton had higher DNA damage levels after daily exposure than bacterioplankton. This is in contrast to the findings by Jeffrey et al. in the Gulf of Mexico.[162] This could indicate a more efficient photorepair in bacteria, depending on temperature.

The Arctic Aquatic Ecosystem

Ozone monitoring and ground-based measurements show a clear downward trend of total column ozone of -6.1 % per decade for April and -3 % per decade for June (1979-1999); however, there is large variability.[163] Calculations using a multiple scattering radiation transfer model for the period from 1979 to 1999 predict increases in ground-based UV of 8 % per decade (April); however, high surface albedo and cloud cover may strongly affect the UV level.

Aas and co-workers have characterized the attenuation of solar radiation both in Atlantic and coastal waters of the Barents Sea and Nordic Seas.[164] They have documented both the spatial and seasonal variability of water transparency and the attenuation of UV radiation for these waters. Available data suggest that Arctic marine phytoplankton populations may be more sensitive to solar UV radiation than their Antarctic counterparts;[165] however, the role of long term acclimation processes is not clear. In both areas there was a shift in species composition to diatom-dominated assemblages, which are capable of synthesizing UV screening compounds. Available results indicate that currently measured UV levels do not seriously affect macroalgal communities in high Arctic coastal ecosystems. While growth and photosynthesis are affected by solar UV-B, all species studied so far have sufficient acclimation potential to cope with moderately increased UV levels.[166]

Sea ice and snow are highly scattering and absorbing and therefore their presence or absence has a very large influence on the penetration of UV radiation. Perovich has measured the spectral transmittance of snow and sea ice.[167] He shows, for example, that 10 cm of snow reduces UV-B transmittance by about a factor of 40, which protects the biota from UV but which allows a substantial amount of visible radiation to penetrate. The potential risk is that there is a large step-up in UV impact on non-adapted organisms when the ice melts. UV albedos can range from above 0.9 for fresh snow to 0.7 for ice and 0.2 for ice with melted surface areas (ponded ice).

Due to the extreme climatic conditions in combination with anthropogenic contamination, increased solar UV-B may have a considerable impact on freshwater ecosystems.[168] Most Arctic freshwater ecosystems are characterized by low nutrient concentration, low temperature - and consequently low productivity and low DOC - making them particularly vulnerable to UV stress. These characteristics are also found in high alpine lakes.[169] Changes in underwater UV exposure directly affect species composition of the biota at each trophic level. The abundance of cyanobacteria in microbial mats indicates their efficient defense mechanisms including absorbing pigments and vertical migration.[170] In the future the largest changes in UV exposure in the Arctic may be associated with changes in water quality and vegetation linked with climate change, and there is evidence of substantial warming over the last 30 years in some regions of the Arctic.[171] In addition, this warming has lead to a statistically significant reduction in the temporal period of ice cover in many circumarctic lakes which results in increasing periods of UV exposure in the water column.[172] Changes in UV exposure may influence not only species composition but also cause a shift in the balance between benthic and pelagic primary production as has been shown by paleo-optical studies of subarctic lakes during the Holocene.[173]

The zooplankton food chains are rather simple with only few species dominated by melanic (pigmented) morphs of *Daphnia* species.[174] While a number of potential effects can be deduced from laboratory and field studies, well founded conclusions on UV-induced community effects are premature at this stage. Synergistic effects of UV and other stress factors as well as lack of food due to low primary productivity or change in food quality under increased UV radiation may make zooplankton more vulnerable.[175]

Interactions Between UV-B Increases and Other Environmental Factors

In addition to higher levels of solar UV-B radiation, aquatic ecosystems are confronted with other environmental stress factors including increased nutrient input, pollution, acidification and global climate change. In turn, climate change will result in water temperature and sea level change; shifts in the timing and extent of sea ice cover; changes in salinity and altered stratification of the water column, wave climate and ocean circulation; and these effects will be linked by feedback mechanisms which are not yet completely understood.[176] These complex changes are likely to have significant impacts, that will vary both spatially and temporally, including biological production (including human marine resources) as well as changes in the global hydrological cycle, vertical mixing and efficiency of CO_2 uptake by the ocean. Ozone-related increases in UV-B are an important additional ecological stress that will have both positive and negative impacts in association with the other factors.

Several recent reviews have tackled the interaction between climate change and ozone depletion.[174, 177-179] Ozone depletion has occurred only during the last few decades,[180] exceeding 50 % of the pre-ozone hole concentrations at some locations. Because of the strict control measures imposed, the concentrations of ozone depleting substances will decrease during the next decades.[181] However, increasing CO_2 concentrations will result in warming of the troposphere and simultaneous cooling of the stratosphere, which favors further ozone destruction.[182, 183] One of the possible feedback mechanisms is changes in cloud cover and increased rainfall, but this is not well understood.

Direct monitoring of the ambient and yearly average temperatures are restricted to about 120 years in Europe and much less in other parts of the world,[184-186] although information on past temperatures can be extracted from ice core and sediment records.[187] Non-anthropogenic changes of ambient temperature fluctuated over millennia, while the recent global climate change has occurred on the order of a few decades. Expected and already measured temperature changes are not uniform over the surface of the earth. While on the Antarctic Peninsula a decrease in sea ice was observed over the last two decades,[188] increases in ice cover were monitored over most of the Antarctic continent.[189] Temperature changes significantly affect carbon assimilation, and even small changes could alter species competition, timing of reproduction and hatching success.[190-192]

Changing temperatures can lead to sea ice variability, altered nutrient cycling, food availability and trophic interactions.[32] Melting of sea ice, with relatively fresh water, provides water column stability, thus enhancing springtime phytoplankton blooms. Recent work has shown that glacial melt water (enhanced due to the past century's warming trend in the Antarctic peninsula) is associated with enhanced productivity, extending over 100 km offshore.[193] Field experiments have shown that higher temperatures increase colonization by cyanobacteria and increase arthropod populations. Changes in species composition and expansions of macroalgae populations have been reported in response to local temperature increases.[194] Changes in ice cover will modify gas and heat exchange between the ocean and the atmosphere,[195, 196] and incident light and UV penetration into the water column will be affected. Consequently carbon fluxes and photosynthesis of phytoplankton and ice communities will be affected.[29] Thus, changing temperatures affect primary consumers as well as secondary consumers, trophic dynamics and biogeochemical cycling.[197-200]

There are major feedback loops between climate change and other environmental variables and primary productivity. The primary producers are responsible for large uptake of atmospheric CO_2, part of which is sunk into the marine sediments as oceanic snow. Because of physiological differences in the substrate affinity of the CO_2 fixing enzymes in different organisms changes in the partial pressure will alter autotroph diversity.[201] With phytoplankton productivity being affected by climate change, this will simultaneously modify the degree of climate change.[199, 202-204] Increasing temperatures enhance rainfall and melting of glaciers and ice shelves augmenting the runoff of melt water and stabilizing the stratification of the water column, which in turn increases the sedimentation of particulate organic matter. Pronounced stratification decreases nutrient concentrations of coastal waters and increases UV-B exposure of phytoplankton.[205, 206]

Conclusions and Consequences

All ecosystems are likely to be affected by gradual changes in important environmental factors, including climate, nutrient loading, habitat fragmentation or biotic exploitation. As with other environmental stress factors, UV-B elicits species-specific responses with a high degree of intraspecies variation. Potential consequences of enhanced levels of exposure to UV-B radiation, demonstrated in recent experiments, include loss of biomass, including food sources for humans; changes in species composition; decrease in availability of nitrogen and other nutrients; and reduced uptake capacity for atmospheric carbon dioxide, resulting in the potential augmentation of global warming. Temperature changes in Antarctica can, for example, significantly affect carbon assimilation, and even small changes could alter species competition, timing of reproduction, and hatching success. Changing temperatures also have indirect effects, such as changes in sea ice variability, and altered nutrient cycling and food availability within the food web. In addition, there is emerging evidence that global warming and acid precipitation may allow increased penetration of UV-B and UV-A radiation into aquatic environments, predominantly through decreases in attenuation of radiation by dissolved organic carbon. Although there is significant evidence that increased UV-B exposure is harmful to aquatic organisms, damage at the whole ecosystem level is still uncertain. In the Arctic, however, while growth and photosynthesis are affected by solar UV-B, all species studied so far have sufficient acclimation potential to cope with moderately increased UV levels. One of the most important concepts for assessing the impacts of enhanced levels of UV-B exposure on aquatic ecosystems is that complex rather than simple responses are likely to be the rule. Responses will not be limited to simple decreases in primary production. In fact, shifts in community structure may initially be more common and result in small, yet detectable differences in ecosystem biomass.

References

1   L. J. Rothschild, in *Origin, Evolution and Versatility of Microorganisms* ed.: J. Seckbach, Kluwer, Dordrecht, The Netherlands, 1999, pp. 551-562.

2   F. Garcia-Pichel, Solar ultraviolet and the evolutionary history of cyanobacteria, *Origins Life Evol. Biosphere*, 1998, **28**, 321-347.

3   C. S. Cockell, in *Ecosystems, Evolution and Ultraviolet Radiation* eds.: C. S. Cockell and A. R. Blaustein, Springer-Verlag, New York, 2001, pp. 1-35.

4   L. J. Rothschild and R. L. Mancinelli, Life in extreme environments, *Nature*, 2001, **409**, 1092-1101.

5   E. G. Nisbet and N. H. Sleep, The habitat and nature of early life, *Nature*, 2001, **409**, 1083-1091.

6   K. Hoyer, U. Karsten, T. Sawall and C. Wiencke, Photoprotective substances in Antarctic macroalgae and their variation with respect to depth distribution, different tissues and developmental stages, *Mar. Ecol. Progr. Ser.*, 2001, **211**, 117-129.

7   S. J. Newman, W. C. Dunlap, S. Nicol and D. Ritz, Antarctic krill (*Euphausia superba*) acquire a UV-absorbing mycosporine-like amino acid from dietary algae, *J. Exp. Mar. Biol. Ecol.*, 2000, **255**, 93-100.

8   J. G. Dillon and R. W. Castenholz, Scytonemin, a cyanobacterial sheath pigment protects against UVC radiation: implications for early photosynthetic life, *J. Phycol.*, 1999, **35**, 673.

9   Y.-Y. He and D.-P. Häder, Involvement of reactive oxygen species in the UV-B damage to the cyanobacterium *Anabaena* sp., *J. Photochem. Photobiol. B.*, 2002, **66**, 73-80.

10   A. R. Blaustein, L. K. Belden, A. C. Hatch, L. B. Kats, P. D. Hoffman, J. B. Hays, A. Marco, D. P. Chivers and J. M. Kiesecker, in *Ecosystems, Evolution and Ultraviolet Radiation* eds.: C. S. Cockell and A. R. Blaustein, Springer-Verlag, New York, 2001, pp. 63-79.

11   A. G. J. Buma, E. W. Helbling, M. K. de Boer and V. E. Villafañe, Patterns of DNA damage and photoinhibition in temperate South-Atlantic picophytoplankton exposed to solar ultraviolet radiation, *J. Photochem. Photobiol. B.*, 2001, **62**, 9-18.

12   F. L. Figueroa, in *Role of Solar UV-B Radiation on Ecosystems, Ecosystem Research Report No. 30* eds.: C. V. Nolan and D.-P. Häder, European Communities, Belgium, 1998, pp. 121-133.

13   D.-P. Häder, in *Ecosystems, Evolution and Ultraviolet Radiation* eds.: C. S. Cockell and A. R. Blaustein, Springer-Verlag, New York, 2001, pp. 150-169.

14   A. U. Bracher and C. Wiencke, Simulation of the effects of naturally enhanced UV radiation on photosynthesis of Antarctic phytoplankton, *Mar. Ecol. Progr. Ser.*, 2000, **196**, 127-141.

15   B. B. Prezelin, M. A. Moline and H. A. Matlick, in *Antarctic Sea Ice Biological Processes, Interactions, and Variability, Antarctic Research Series*, **Vol. 73** eds.: M. P. Lizotte and K. R. Arrigo, American Geophysical Union, Washington D.C., 1998, pp. 45-83.

16   P. S. Huovinen, A. O. J. Oikari, M. R. Soimasuo and G. N. Cherr, Impact of UV radiation on the ealy development of the giant kelp (*Macrocystis pyrifera*) gametophytes, *Photochem. Photobiol.*, 2000, **72**, 308-313.

17   U. Karsten, D. Hanelt, K. Bischof, H. Tüg, P. E. M. Brouwer and C. Wiencke, in *The Arctic and Global Change, Proceedings from the Fourth Ny-Alesund Seminar* eds.: R. Casacchia, H. Koutsileos, M. Morbidoni, P. D. Petrelli, M. R. Pettersen, R. Salvatori, R. Sparapani and E. S. Larsen, Ravello, Italy, 1998, pp. 177-180.

18   V. Dethlefsen, H. von Westernhagen, H. Tüg, P. D. Hansen and H. Dizer, Influence of solar ultraviolet-B on pelagic fish embryos: osmolality, mortality and viable hatch, *Helgol. Mar. Res.*, 2001, **55**, 45-55.

19   J. H. M. Kouwenberg, H. I. Browman, J. J. Cullen, R. F. Davis, J.-F. St-Pierre and J. A. Runge, Biological weighting of ultraviolet (280-400 nm) induced mortality in marine zooplankton and fish. I. Atlantic cod (*Gadus morhua*) eggs, *Mar. Biol.*, 1999, **134**, 269-284.

20   J. H. M. Kouwenberg, H. I. Browman, J. A. Runge, J. J. Cullen, R. F. Davis and J. F. St-Pierre, Biological weighting of ultraviolet (280-400 nm) induced mortality in marine zooplankton and fish. II. *Calanus finmarchicus* (Copepoda) eggs, *Mar. Biol.*, 1999, **134**, 285-293.

21   D.-P. Häder, H. D. Kumar, R. C. Smith and R. C. Worrest, Effects on aquatic ecosystems, *J. Photochem. Photobiol. B.*, 1998, **46**, 53-68.

22   H. I. Browman, C. A. Rodriguez, F. Bèland, J. J. Cullen, R. F. Davis, J. H. M. Kouwenberg, P. S. Kuhn, B. McArthur, J. A. Runge, J.-F. St-Pierre and R. D. Vetter, Impact of ultraviolet radiation on marine crustacean zooplankton and ichthyoplankton: a synthesis of results from the estuary and Gulf of St. Lawrence, Canada, *Mar. Ecol. Prog. Ser.*, 2000, **199**, 293-311.

23   D. F. Gleason, in *Ecosystems, Evolution and Ultraviolet Radiation* eds.: C. S. Cockell and A. R. Blaustein, Springer-Verlag, New York, 2001, pp. 118-149.

24   T. Takahashi, R. A. Feely, R. F. Weiss, R. H. Wanninkhof, D. W. Chipman, S. C. Sutherland and T. T. Takahashi, Global air-sea flux of CO_2: an estimate based on measurements of sea-air pCO_2 difference, *Proc. Natl. Acad. Sci. USA*, 1997, **94**, 8292-8299.

25   R. Sommaruga and A. G. J. Buma, UV-induced cell damage is species-specific among aquatic phagotrophic protists, *J. Eukar. Microbiol.*, 2000, **47**, 450-455.

26   M. E. Feder, A. F. Bennett and R. B. Huey, Evolutionary physiology, *Ann. Rev. Ecol. Syst.*, 2000, **31**, 315-341.

27   D. Tilman, The ecological consequences of changes in biodiversity: a search for general principles, *Ecology*, 1999, **80**, 1455-1474.

28   D. S. Woodruff, Declines of biomes and biotas and the future of evolution, *Proc. Natl. Acad. Sci. USA*, 2001, **98**, 5471-5476.

29   P. G. Falkowski, R. T. Barber and V. Smetacek, Biogeochemical controls and feedbacks on ocean primary production, *Science*, 1998, **281**, 200-206.

30   J. Hilty and A. Merenlender, Faunal indicator taxa selection for monitoring ecosystem health, *Biol. Cons.*, 2000, **92**, 185-197.

31   S. Naeem, F. S. Chapin III, R. Costanza, P. R. Ehrlich, F. B. Golley, D. U. Hooper, J. H. Lawton, R. V. O'neill, H. A. Mooney, O. E. Sala, A. J. Symstad and D. Tilman, Biodiversity and ecosystem functioning: maintaining natural life support processes, *Issues Ecol.*, 1999, **4**, 1-14.

32   K. Reid and J. P. Croxall, Environmental response of upper trophic-level predators reveals a system change in an Antarctic marine ecosystem, *Proc. R. Soc. Lond. B*, 2001, **268**, 377-384.

33   J. E. Frederick, Z. Qu and C. R. Booth, Ultraviolet radiation at sites on the Antarctic coast, *Photochem. Photobiol.*, 1998, **68**, 183-190.

34   A. E. Waibel, T. Peter, K. S. Carslaw, H. Oelhaf, G. Wetzel, P. J. Crutzen, U. Pöschl, A. Tsias, E. Reimer and H. Fischer, Arctic ozone loss due to denitrification, *Science*, 1999, **283**, 2064-2069.

35   M. Lebert, M. Schuster and D.-P. Häder, The European Light Dosimeter Network: four years of measurements, *J. Photochem. Photobiol. B.*, 2002, **66**, 81-87.

36   EC, *European research in the stratosphere 1996-2000*, **Vol. EUR 19867**, European Commission, 2001.

37   C. S. Zerefos, C. Meleti, D. S. Balis, A. F. Bais and D. Gillotay, On changes of spectral UV-B in the 90's in Europe, *Adv. Space Res.*, 2000, **26**, 1971-1978.

38   D.-P. Häder, M. Lebert, R. Marangoni and G. Colombetti, ELDONET - European Light Dosimeter Network hardware and software, *J. Photochem. Photobiol. B.*, 1999, **52**, 51-58.

39   A. A. Sabziparvar, K. P. Shine and P. M. F. de Forster, A model-derived global climatology of UV irradiation at the earth's surface, *Photochem. Photobiol.*, 1999, **69**, 193-202.

40   I. Laurion, M. Ventura, J. Catalan, R. Psenner and R. Sommaruga, Attenuation of ultraviolet radiation in mountain lakes: factors controlling the among- and within-lake variability, *Limnol. Oceanogr.*, 2000, **45**, 1274-1288.

41   P. Kuhn, H. Browman, B. McArthur and J.-F. St-Pierre, Penetration of ultraviolet radiation in the waters of the estuary and Gulf of St. Lawrence, *Limnol. Oceanogr.*, 1999, **44**, 710-716.

42   D. Conde, L. Aubriot and R. Sommaruga, Changes in UV penetration associated with marine intrusions and freshwater discharge in a shallow coastal lagoon of the Southern Atlantic Ocean, *Mar. Ecol. Prog. Ser.*, 2000, **207**, 19-31.

43   M. J. Dring, A. Wagner, L. A. Franklin, R. Kuhlenkamp and K. Lüning, Seasonal and diurnal variations in ultraviolet-B and ultraviolet-A irradiances at and below the sea surface at Helgoland (North Sea) over a 6-year period, *Helgol. Mar. Res.*, 2001, **55**, 3-11.

44   V. S. Kuwahara, H. Ogawa, T. Toda, T. Kikuchi and S. Taguchi, Variability of bio-optical factors influencing the seasonal attenuation of ultraviolet radiation in temperate coastal waters of Japan, *Photochem. Photobiol.*, 2000, **72**, 193-199.

45   M. T. Arts, R. D. Robarts, F. Kasai, M. J. Waiser, V. P. Tumber, A. J. Plante, H. Rai and H. J. de Lange, The attenuation of ultraviolet radiation in high dissolved organic carbon waters of wetlands and lakes on the northern Great Plains, *Limnol. Oceanogr.*, 2000, **45**, 292-299.

46   H. E. Zagarese, M. Diaz, F. Pedrozo, M. Ferraro, W. Cravero and B. Tartarotti, Photodegradation of natural organic matter exposed to fluctuating levels of solar radiation, *J. Photochem. Photobiol. B.*, 2001, **61**, 35-45.

47   G. J. Herndl, J. M. Arrieta, I. Obernosterer and C. Pausz, in *Role of Solar UV-B Radiation on Ecosystems, Ecosystem Research Report No. 30* eds.: C. V. Nolan and D.-P. Häder, European Communities, Belgium, 1998, pp. 69-77.

48   D. O. Hessen and P. J. Faerovig, in *Plant Ecology. Special Issue: Responses of Plants to UV-B Radiation,* **Vol. 154** eds.: J. Rozema, Y. Manetas and L. O. Björn, Kluwer Academic Publishers, Dordrecht, Boston, London, 2001, pp. 263-273.

49   R. F. Whitehead, S. deMora, S. Demers, M. Gosselin, P. Monfort and B. Mostajir, Interactions of ultraviolet-B radiation, mixing, and biological activity on photobleaching of natural chromophoric dissolved organic matter: A mesocosm study, *Limnology and Oceanography*, 2000, **45**, 278-291.

50   H. Piazena, E. Perez-Rodrigues, D.-P. Häder and F. Lopez-Figueroa, Penetration of solar radiation into the water column of the central subtropical Atlantic Ocean - optical properties and possible biological consequences, *Deep-Sea Res. II*, 2002, **49**, 3513-3528.

51   R. Sommer, A. Cabaj, T. Sandu and M. Lhotsky, Measurement of UV radiation using suspensions of microorganisms, *J. Photochem. Photobiol. B.*, 1999, **53**, 1-6.

52   K. Koussoulaki, D. Danielidis, D.-P. Häder and R. Santas, Assessment of *Euglena gracilis* as a biological dosimeter for solar UVA and UVB under field conditions. Proceedings of the First Internet Conference on Photochemistry and Photobiology. Reviewed publication, in *Proceeding of the First InternetConference on Photochemistry and Photobiology*, 1998.

53   Y. Huot, W. H. Jeffrey, R. F. Davis and J. J. Cullen, Damage to DNA in bacterioplankton: a model of damage by ultraviolet radiation and its repair as influenced by vertical mixing, *Photochem. Photobiol.*, 2000, **72**, 62-74.

54   T. Douki, M. Court, S. Sauvaigo, F. Odin and J. Cadet, Formation of the main UV-induced thymine dimeric lesions within isolated and cellular DNA as measured by high performance liquid chromatography-tandem mass spectrometry, *J. Biol. Chem.*, 2000, **275**, 11678-11685.

55   T. Douki and J. Cadet, Individual determination of the yield of the main UV-induced dimeric pyrimidine photoproducts in DNA suggests a high mutagenicity of CC photolesions, *Biochem.*, 2001, **40**, 2495-2501.

56   F. Thoma, Light and dark in chromatin repair: repair of UV-induced DNA lesions by photolyase and nucleotide excision repair, *Embo J.*, 1999, **18**, 6585-6598.

57   C. Winter, M. M. Moeseneder and G. J. Herndl, Impact of UV radiation on bacterioplankton community composition, *Appl. Environm. Microbiol.*, 2001, **67**, 665-672.

58   M. Radman, F. Taddei and I. Matic, DNA repair systems and bacterial evolution, *Cold Spring Habor Symposia on Quantitative Biology*, 2000, **65**, 1-9.

59   A. Vaishampayan, R. P. Sinha, D.-P. Häder, T. Dey, A. K. Gupta, U. Bhan and A. L. Rao, Cyanobacterial biofertilizers in rice agriculture, *Bot. Rev.*, 2002, **67**, 453-516.

60   C. Kruschel and R. W. Castenholz, The effect of solar UV and visible irradiance on the vertical movements of cyanobacteria in microbial mats of hypersaline waters, *FEMS Microbiol. Ecol.*, 1998, **27**, 53-72.

61   M. A. Moran and R. G. Zepp, in *Microbial Ecology of the Oceans* ed.: D. L. Kirchman, Wiley-Liss Inc., New York, 2000, pp. 201-228.

62   R. P. Sinha, M. Klisch, A. Gröniger and D.-P. Häder, Responses of algae and cyanobacteria to solar UV-B, *Plant Ecol.*, 2001, **154**, 189-204.

63   R. P. Sinha and D.-P. Häder, in *Advances in Phycology* eds.: B. N. Verma, A. N. Kargupta and S. K. Goyal, APC Publ., New Delhi, 1998, pp. 71-80.

64   R. P. Sinha, M. Dautz and D.-P. Häder, A simple and efficient method for the quantitative analysis of thymine dimers in cyanobacteria, phytoplankton and macroalgae, *Acta Protozool.*, 2001, **40**, 187-195.

65   B. K. Kolli, S. Tiwari and P. Mohanty, Ultraviolet-B induced damage to photosystem II in intact filaments of *Spirulina platensis*, *Z. Naturf.*, 1998, **53c**, 369-377.

66   D. Campbell, M.-J. Eriksson, G. Öquist, P. Gustafsson and A. K. Clarke, The cyanobacterium *Synechococcus* resists UV-B by exchanging photosystem II reaction-center D1 proteins, *Proc. Natl. Acad. Sci. USA*, 1998, **95**, 364-369.

67   T. Han, R. P. Sinha and D.-P. Häder, UV-A/blue light-induced reactivation of photosynthesis in UV-B irradiated cyanobacterium, *Anabaena* sp., *J. Plant Physiol.*, 2001, **158**, 1403-1413.

68   S. W. Hansucker, B. M. Tissue, M. Potts and R. F. Helm, Screening protocol for the ultraviolet-photoprotective pigment scytonemin, *Analyt. Biochem.*, 2001, **288**, 227-230.

69   D. D. Wynn-Williams, H. G. M. Edwards and F. Garcia-Pichel, Functional biomolecules of Antarctic stromatolitic and endolithic cyanobacterial communities, *Eur. J. Phycol.*, 1999, **34**, 381-391.

70   S. Steiger, L. Schäfer and G. Sandmann, High-light-dependent upregulation of carotenoids and their antioxidative properties in the cyanobacterium *Synechocystis* PCC 6803, *J. Photochem. Photobiol. B.*, 1999, **52**, 14-18.

71   A. Canini, D. Leonardi and M. G. Caiola, Superoxide dismutase activity in the cyanobacterium *Microcystis aeruginosa* after bloom formation, *New Phytol.*, 2001, **152**, 107-116.

72   T. Lindahl and R. D. Wood, Quality control by DNA repair, *Science*, 1999, **286**, 1897-1905.

73   R. Araoz and D.-P. Häder, Enzymatic antioxidant activity in two cyanobacteria species exposed to solar radiation, *Recent Res. Devel. Photochem. Photobiol.*, 1999, **3**, 123-132.

74   R. Sommaruga and F. Garcia-Pichel, UV-absorbing mycosporine-like compounds in planktonic and benthic organisms from a high-mountain lake, *Arch. Hydrobiol.*, 1999, **144**, 255-269.

75   R. P. Sinha, J. P. Sinha, A. Gröniger and D.-P. Häder, Polychromatic action spectrum for the induction of a mycosporine-like amino acid in a rice-field cyanobacterium, *Anabaena* sp., *J. Photochem. Photobiol. B.*, 2002, **66**, 47-53.

76   J. Rozema, L. O. Björn, J. F. Bornman, A. Gaberšèik, D.-P. Häder, T. Trošt, M. Germ, M. Klisch, A. Gröniger, R. P. Sinha, M. Lebert, Y.-Y. He, R. Buffoni-Hall, N. V. J. de Bakker, J. van de Staaij and B. B. Meijkamp, The role of UV-B radiation in aquatic and terrestrial ecosystems-an experimental and functional analysis of the evolution of UV-absorbing compounds, *J. Photochem. Photobiol. B.*, 2002, **66**, 2-12.

77   A. Yamazawa, H. Takeyama, D. Takeda and T. Matsunaga, UV-A-induced expression of GroEL in the UV-A-resistant marine cyanobacterium *Oscillatoria* sp. NKBG 091600, *Microbiol.*, 1999, **145**, 949-954.

78   A. Gröniger, R. P. Sinha, M. Klisch and D.-P. Häder, Photoprotective compounds in cyanobacteria, phytoplankton and macroalgae - a database, *J. Photochem. Photobiol. B.*, 2000, **58**, 115-122.

79   A. L. George, A. W. Murray and P. O. Montiel, Tolerance of Antarctic cyanobacterial mats to enhanced UV radiation, *FEMS Microbiol. Ecol.*, 2001, **37**, 91-101.

80   L. C. Rai, B. Tyagi, P. K. Rai and N. Mallick, Interactive effects of UV-B and heavy metals (Cu and Pb) on nitrogen and phosphorus metabolism of a N_2-fixing cyanobacterium *Anabaena doliolum*, *Environm. Experim. Bot.*, 1998, **39**, 221-231.

81   P. Falkowski, The ocean's invisible forest, *Scientific American*, 2002, **August 2002**, 38-45.

82   S.-A. Wängberg, J.-S. Selmer and K. Gustavson, Effects of UV-B radiation on carbon and nutrient dynamics in marine plankton communities, *J. Photochem. Photobiol. B.*, 1998, **45**, 19-24.

83   M. S. Estevez, G. Malanga and S. Puntarulo, UV-B effects on Antarctic *Chlorella* sp. cells, *J. Photochem. Photobiol. B.*, 2001, **62**, 19-25.

84   W. W. Gregg and M. E. Conkwright, Decadal changes in global ocean chlorophyll, *Geophys. Res. Lett.*, 2002, **29**.

85   F. Ghetti, H. Hermann, D.-P. Häder and H. K. Seidlitz, Spectral dependence of the inhibition of photosynthesis under simulated global radiation in the unicellular green alga *Dunaliella salina*, *J. Photochem. Photobiol. B.*, 1999, **48**, 166-173.

86   M. Klisch and D.-P. Häder, Effects of solar radiation on phytoplankton, *Recent Res. Devel. Photochem. Photobiol.*, 1999, **3**, 113-121.

87   W. M. Bandaranayake, Mycosporines: are they nature's sunscreens?, *Nat. Prod. Rep.*, 1998, 59-172.

88   N. Noguchi, A. Watanabe and H. Shi, Diverse functions of antioxidants, *Free Rad. Res.*, 2000, **33**, 809-817.

89   S. W. Jeffrey, H. S. MacTavish, W. C. Dunlap, M. Vesk and K. Groenewoud, Occurrence of UVA- and UVB-absorbing compounds in 152 species (206 strains) of marine microalgae, *Mar. Ecol. Progr. Ser.*, 1999, **189**, 35-51.

90   M. Klisch, R. P. Sinha, P. R. Richter and D.-P. Häder, Mycosporine-like amino acids (MAAs) protect against UV-B-induced damage in *Gyrodinium dorsum* Kofoid, *J. Plant Physiol.*, 2001, **158**, 1449-1454.

91   A. C. Sigleo, P. J. Neale and A. M. Spector, Phytoplankton pigments at the Weddell-Scotia confluence during the 1993 austral spring, *J. Plankt. Res.*, 2000, **22**, 1989-2006.

92   A. M. Chekalyuk, F. E. Hoge, C. W. Wright, R. N. Swift and J. K. Yungel, Airborne test of laser pump-and-probe technique for assessment of phytoplankton photochemical characteristics, *Photosynth. Res.*, 2000, **66**, 45-56.

93   D. Karentz and H. J. Spero, Response of a natural *Phaeocystis* population to ambient fluctuations of UVB radiation caused by Antarctic ozone depletion, *J. Plankt. Res.*, 1995, **17**, 1771-1789.

94   A. T. Davidson and H. J. Marchant, in *Antarctic Research Series. Ultraviolet Radiation in Antarctica: Measurements and Biological Effects*, **Vol. 62** eds.: C. S. Weiler and P. A. Penhale, 1994, pp. 187-205.

95   T. A. Moisan and B. G. Mitchell, UV absorption by mycosporine-like amino acids in *Phaeocystis antarctica* Karsten induced by photosynthetically available radiation, *Mar. Biol.*, 2001, **138**, 217-227.

96   F. Xiong, Evidence that UV-B tolerance of the photosynthetic apparatus in microalgae is related to the D1-turnover mediated repair cycle in vivo, *J. Plant Physiol.*, 2001, **158**, 285-294.

97   A. Kaplan, Y. Helman, D. Tchernov and L. Reinhold, Acclimation of photosynthetic microorganisms to changing ambient CO_2 concentration, *Proc. Natl. Acad. Sci. USA*, 2001, **98**, 4817-4818.

98   P. J. Neale, Modeling the effects of ultraviolet radiation on estuarine phytoplankton production: impact of variations in exposure and sensitivity to inhibition, *J. Photochem. Photobiol. B.*, 2001, **62**, 1-8.

99   O. Arino, K. Boushaba and A. Boussouar, Modelization of the role of currents and turbulence on the growth and dispersion of marine phytoplankton, *C. R. Acad. Sci. Paris, Sciences de la vie/ Life Sciences*, 2000, **323**, 113-118.

100   V. E. Villafañe, E. W. Helbling and H. E. Zagarese, Solar ultraviolet radiation and its impact on aquatic systems of Patagonia, South America, *Ambio*, 2001, **30**, 112-117.

101   E. W. Helbling, V. E. Villafane, A. G. J. Buma, M. Andrade and F. Zaratti, DNA damage and photosynthetic inhibition by solar ultraviolet radiation in tropical phytoplankton (Lake Titicaca, Bolivia), *Eur. J. Phycol.*, 2001, **36**, 157-166.

102   I. Sobolev, Effect of column ozone on the variability of biologically effective UV radiation at high southern latitudes, *Photochem. Photobiol.*, 2000, **72**, 753-765.

103   E. van Donk, B. A. Faafeng, H. J. de Lange and D. O. Hessen, in *Plant Ecology. Special Issue: Responses of Plants to UV-B Radiation*, **Vol. 154** eds.: J. Rozema, Y. Manetas and L. O. Björn, Kluwer Academic Publishers, Dordrecht, Boston, London, 2001, pp. 249-259.

104   C. W. Grobe and T. M. Murphy, Solar ultraviolet-B radiation effects on growth and pigment composition of the intertidal alga *Ulva expansa* (Setch.) S. & G. (Chlorophyta), *J. Exp. Mar. Biol. Ecol.*, 1998, **225**, 39-51.

105   M. J. Dring, A. Wagner and K. Lüning, Contribution of the UV component of natural sunlight to photoinhibition of photosynthesis in six species of subtidal brown and red seaweeds, *Plant Cell Environ.*, 2001, **24**, 1153-1164.

106   D.-P. Häder, in *Landmarks in Photobiology, Proceedings of the 12th Congress on Photobiology (ICP '96), OEMF spa, Italy* eds.: H. Hönigsmann, R. M. Knobler, F. Trautinger and G. Jori, Milano, 1998, pp. 31-33.

107   A. Gröniger, C. Hallier and D.-P. Häder, Influence of UV radiation and visible light on *Porphyra umbilicalis*: photoinhibition and MAA concentration, *J. Appl. Phycol.*, 1999, **11**, 437-445.

108   J. A. Segui, V. Maire, I. S. Gabashvili and M. Fragata, Oxygen evolution loss and structural transitions in photosystem II induced by low intensity UV-B radiation of 280 nm wavelength, *J. Photochem. Photobiol. B.*, 2000, **56**, 39-47.

109   W. H. van de Poll, A. Eggert, A. G. J. Buma and A. M. Breeman, Effects of UV-B-induced DNA damage and photoinhibition on growth of temperate marine red macrophytes: habitat-related differences in UV-B tolerance, *J. Phycol.*, 2001, **37**, 30-37.

110   D.-P. Häder, M. Lebert and E. W. Helbling, Effects of solar radiation on the Patagonian macroalga *Enteromorpha linza* (L.) J. Agardh - Chlorophyceae, *J. Photochem. Photobiol. B.*, 2001, **62**, 43-54.

111   U. Karsten, K. Bischof and C. Wiencke, Photosynthetic performance of Arctic macroalgae after transplantation from deep to shallow waters, *Oecologia*, 2001, **127**, 11-20.

112   M. Altamirano, A. Flores-Moya, F. Conde and F. L. Figueroa, Growth seasonality, photosynthetic pigments, and carbon and nitrogen content in relation to environmental factors: a field study of *Ulva olivascens* (Ulvales, Chlorophyta), *Phycologia*, 2000, **39**, 50-58.

113   M. L. Quartino, H. Klöser, I. R. Schloss and C. Wiencke, Biomass and associations of benthic marine macroalgae from the inner Potter Cove (King George Island, Antarctica) related to depth and substrate, *Polar Biol.*, 2001, **24**, 349-355.

114   D. Hanelt, H. Tüg, K. Bischof, C. Groß, H. Lippert, T. Sawall and C. Wiencke, Light regime in an Arctic fjord: a study related to stratospheric ozone depletion as a basis for determination of UV effects on algal growth, *Marine Biol.*, 2001, **138**, 649-658.

115   U. Karsten and C. Wiencke, Factors controlling the formation of UV-absorbing mycosporine-like amino acids in the marine red alga *Palmaria palmata* from Spitsbergen (Norway), *J. Plant Physiol.*, 1999, **155**, 407-415.

116   F. R. Conde, M. S. Churio and C. M. Previtali, The photoprotector mechanism of mycosporine-like amino acids. Excited-state properties and photostability of porphyra-334 in aqueous solution, *J. Photochem. Photobiol. B.*, 2000, **56**, 139-144.

117   A. Gröniger and D.-P. Häder, Stability of mycosporine-like amino acids, *Recent Res. Devel. Photochem. Photobiol.*, 2000, **4**, 247-252.

118   A. Gröniger and D.-P. Häder, Induction of the synthesis of an UV-absorbing substance in the green alga *Prasiola stipitata*, *J. Photochem. Photobiol. B.*, 2002, **66**, 54-59.

119   L. A. Franklin, G. Kräbs and R. Kuhlenkamp, Blue light and UV-A radiation control the synthesis of mycosporine-like amino acids in *Chondrus crispus* (Florideophyceae), *J. Phycol.*, 2001, **37**, 257-270.

120   E. Perez-Rodriguez, I. Gomez, U. Karsten and F. L. Figueroa, Effects of UV radiation on photosynthesis and excretion of UV-absorbing compounds of *Dasycladus vermicularis* (Dasycladales, Chlorophyta) from southern Spain, *Phycologia*, 1998, **37**, 379-387.

121   S. Coelho, J. W. Rijstenbil, I. Sousa-Pinto and M. T. Brown, Cellular responses to elevated light levels in *Fucus spiralis* embryos during the first days after fertilization, *Plant Cell Environ.*, 2001, **24**, 801-810.

122   C. Wiencke, I. Gómez, H. Pakker, A. Flores-Moya, M. Altamirano, D. Hanelt, K. Bischof and F. L. Figueroa, Impact of UV radiation on viability, photosynthetic characteristics and DNA of brown algal zoospores: implications for depth zonation, *Mar. Ecol. Progr. Ser.*, 2000, **197**, 217-229.

123   M. J. Dring, V. Makarov, E. Schoshina, M. Lorenz and K. Lüning, Influence of ultraviolet radiation on chlorophyll fluorescence and growth in different life history stages of three species of *Laminaria* (Phaeophyta), *Mar. Biol.*, 1996, **126**, 183-191.

124   N. de Bakker, J. Rozema and R. Aerts, UV effects on a charophycean algae, *Chara aspera*, *Plant Ecol.*, 2001, **154**, 205-212.

125   M. P. Vega and R. A. Pizarro, Oxidative stress and defence mechanisms of the freshwater cladoceran *Daphnia longispina* exposed to UV radiation, *J. Photochem. Photobiol. B.*, 2000, **54**, 121-125.

126   S. C. Rhode, M. Pawlowski and R. Tollrian, The impact of ultraviolet radiation on the vertical distribution of zooplankton of the genus *Daphnia*, *Nature*, 2001, **412**, 69-72.

127   L. De Meester, P. Dawidowicz, E. van Gool and C. J. Loose, eds.: R. Tollrian and C. D. Harvell, Princeton University Press, Princeton, NJ, 1999, pp. 160-176.

128   U. C. Storz and R. J. Paul, Phototaxis in water fleas (*Daphnia magna*) is differently influenced by visible and UV light, *J. Comp. Physiol. A*, 1998, **183**, 709-717.

129   D. M. Leech and C. E. Williamson, In situ exposure to ultraviolet radiation alters the depth distribution of *Daphnia*, *Limnol. Oceanogr.*, 2001, **46**, 416-420.

130   B. Tartarotti, I. Laurion and R. Sommaruga, Large variability in the concentration of mycosporine-like amino acids among zooplankton from lakes located across an altitude gradient, *Limnol. Oceanogr.*, 2001, **46**, 1546.

131   C. A. Rodriguez, H. I. Browman, J. A. Runge and J.-F. St-Pierre, Impact of solar ultraviolet radiation on hatching of a marine copepod, *Calanus finmarchicus*, *Mar. Ecol. Prog. Ser.*, 2000, **193**, 85-93.

132   P. S. Kuhn, H. I. Browman, R. F. Davis, J. J. Cullen and B. L. McArthur, Modeling the effects of ultraviolet radiation on embryos of *Calanus finmarchicus* and Atlantic cod (*Gadus morhua*) in a mixing environment, *Limnol. Oceanogr.*, 2000, **45**, 1797-1806.

133   P. L. Stutzman, An examination of the potential effects of food limitation on the ultraviolet radiation (UVR) tolerance of *Diaptomus minutus*, *Freshwater Biol.*, 2000, **44**, 271-277.

134   G. Grad, C. E. Williamson and D. M. Karapelou, Zooplankton survival and reproduction responses to damaging UV radiation: a test of reciprocity and photoenzymatic repair, *Limnol. Oceanogr.*, 2001, **46**, 584-591.

135   M. P. Lesser, J. H. Farrell and C. W. Walker, Oxidative stress, DNA damage and p53 expression in the larvae of Atlantic cod (*Gadus morhua*) exposed to ultraviolet (290-400 nm) radiation, *J. Exp. Biol.*, 2001, **204**, 157-164.

136   C. Gutiérrez-Rodrìguez and C. E. Williamson, Influence of solar ultraviolet radiation on early life-history stages of the bluegill sunfish, *Lepomis macrochirus*, *Environ. Biol. Fish.*, 1999, **55**, 307-319.

137   M. S. Ewing, V. S. Blazer, D. L. Fabacher, E. E. Little and K. M. Kocan, Channel catfish response to ultraviolet-B radiation, *J. Aquat. Anim. Hlth.*, 1999, **11**, 192-197.

138   C. A. Rodriguez, H. I. Browman and J.-F. St-Pierre, High survival of neustonic zoea I larvae of American lobster *Homarus americanus* following short-term exposure to ultraviolet radiation (280 to 400 nm), *Mar. Ecol. Progr. Ser.*, 2000, **193**, 305-309.

139   R. A. Alford, P. M. Dixon and J. H. K. Pechmann, Global amphibian population declines, *Nature*, 2001, **412**, 499-500.

140   J. E. Houlahan, C. S. Findlay, B. R. Schmidt, A. H. Meyer and S. L. Kuzmin, Quantitative evidence for global amphibian population declines, *Nature*, 2001, **404**, 752-755.

141   J. M. Kiesecker, A. R. Blaustein and L. K. Belden, Complex causes of amphibian population declines, *Nature*, 2001, **410**, 681-683.

142   R. Hofer and C. Mokri, Photoprotection in tadpoles of the common frog, *Rana temporaria*, *J. Photochem. Photobiol. B.*, 2000, **59**, 48-53.

143   M. Pahkala, A. Laurila and J. Merilä, Carry-over effects of ultraviolet-B radiation on larval fitness in *Rana temporaria*, *Proc. R. Soc. Lond. B*, 2001, **268**, 1699-1706.

144   M. Pahkala, A. Laurila and J. Merilä, Ambient ultraviolet-B radiation reduces hatchling size in the common frog *Rana temporaria*, *Ecography*, 2000, **23**, 531-538.

145   I. N. Flamarique, K. Ovaska and T. M. Davis, UV-B induced damage to the skin and ocular system of amphibians, *Biol. Bull.*, 2000, **199**, 187-188.

146   G. T. Ankley, S. A. Diamond, J. E. Tietge, G. W. Holcombe, K. M. Jensen, D. L. Defoe and R. Peterson, Assessmet of the risk of solar ultraviolet radiation to amphibians. I. Hindlimb malformations in the Northern Leopard frog (Rana pipiens), *Environ. Sci. Technol.*, 2002, **36**, 2853-2858.

147   G. S. Peterson, L. B. Johnson, R. P. Axler and S. A. Diamond, Assessment of the risk of solar ultraviolet radiation to amphibians. II. In situ characterization of exposure in amphibian habitats, *Environ. Sci. Technol.*, 2002, **36**, 2859-2865.

148   B. E. Brown, R. P. Dunne, M. S. Goodson and A. E. Douglas, Bleaching patterns in reef corals, *Nature*, 2000, **404**, 142-143.

149   N. Knowlton, Sea urchin recovery from mass mortality: new hope for Caribbean coral reefs?, *Proc. Natl. Acad. Sci. USA*, 2001, **98**, 4822-4824.

150   A. Salih, A. Larkum, G. Cox, M. Kühl and O. Hoegh-Guldberg, Fluorescent pigments in corals are photoprotective, *Nature*, 2000, **408**, 850-853.

151   M. Scheffer, S. Carpenter, J. A. Foley, C. Folke and B. Walker, Catastrophic shifts in ecosystems, *Nature*, 2001, **413**, 591-596.

152   B. Olesen and S. C. Maberly, The effect of high levels of visible and ultra-violet radiation on the photosynthesis of phytoplankton from a freshwater lake, *Arch. Hydrobiol.*, 2001, **151**, 301-315.

153   K. Rogers, A. Schmidt, J. Wilkinson and T. Merz, Effects of incident UV-B radiation on periphyton in four alpine freshwater ecosystems in central Colorado: impacts on boreal toad tadpoles (*Bufo boreas*), *J. Freshwater Ecol.*, 2001, **16**, 283-301.

154   C. E. Williamson, D. P. Morris, M. L. Pace and O. G. Olson, Dissolved organic carbon and nutrients as regulators of lake ecosystems: resurrection of a more integrated paradigm, *Limnol. Oceanogr.*, 1999, **44**, 795-803.

155   C. E. Williamson, B. R. Hargreaves, P. S. Orr and P. A. Lovera, Does UV play a role in changes in predation and zooplankton community structure in acidified lakes?, *Limnol. Oceanogr.*, 1999, **44**, 774-783.

156   R. C. Smith, K. S. Baker, H. M. Dierssen, S. E. Stammerjohn and M. Vernet, Variability of primary production in an Antarctic marine ecosystem as estimated using muli-scale sampling strategy, *Am. Zool.*, 2001, **41**, 40-56.

157   R. C. Smith and S. E. Stammerjohn, Variations of surface air temperature and sea-ice extent in the western Antarctic Peninsula region, *Ann. Glaciol.*, 2001, **33**, 493-500.

158   W. C. Quayle, L. S. Peck, H. Peat, J. C. Ellis-Evans and P. R. Harrigan, Extreme responses to climate change in Antarctic lakes, *Science*, 2002, **295**, 645.

159   S. de Mora, S. Demers and M. Vernet, *The effect of UV radiation in the marine environment*, **Vol. 10**, Cambridge University Press, Cambridge, 2000.

160   R. C. Smith, B. B. Prezelin, K. S. Baker, R. R. Bidigare, N. P. Boucher, T. Coley, D. Karentz, S. MacIntyre, H. A. Matlick, D. Menzies, M. Ondrusek, Z. Wan and K. J. Waters, Ozone depletion: ultraviolet radiation and phytoplankton biology in Antarctic waters, *Science*, 1992, **255**, 952-959.

161   J. Meador, W. H. Jeffrey, J. P. Kase, J. D. Pakulski, S. Chiarello and D. L. Mitchell, Seasonal fluctuation of DNA photodamage at Palmer Station, Antarctica, *UNEP*, 2002.

162   W. H. Jeffrey, R. J. Pledger, P. Aas, S. Hager, R. B. Coffin, R. Von Haven and D. L. Mitchell, Diel and depth profiles of DNA photodamage in bacterioplankton exposed to ambient solar ultraviolet radiation, *Mar. Ecol. Prog. Ser.*, 1996, **137**, 283-291.

163   A. Dahlback, in *UV Radiation and Arctic Ecosystems. Ecological Studies,* **Vol. 153** ed.: D. Hessen, Springer-Verlag, Berlin, Heidelberg, 2002, pp. 3-22.

164   E. Aas, J. Høkedal, N. K. Højerslev, R. Sanvik and E. Sakshaug, in *UV Radiation and Arctic Ecosystems. Ecological Studies,* **Vol. 153** ed.: D. Hessen, Springer-Verlag, Berlin, Heidelberg, 2002, pp. 23-56.

165   W. E. Helbling and V. E. Villafañe, in *UV Radiation and Arctic Ecosystems. Ecological Studies,* **Vol. 153** ed.: D. Hessen, Springer-Verlag, Berlin, Heidelberg, 2002, pp. 204-226.

166   K. Bischof, D. Hanelt and C. Wiencke, in *UV Radiation and Arctic Ecosystems. Ecological Studies,* **Vol. 153** ed.: D. Hessen, Springer Verlag, Berlin, Heidelberg, 2002, pp. 227-243.

167   D. K. Perovich, in *UV Radiation and Arctic Ecosystems. Ecological Studies,* **Vol. 153** ed.: D. Hessen, Springer-Verlag, Berlin, Heidelberg, 2002, pp. 73-89.

168   W. F. Vincent and C. Belzile, in *UV Radiation and Arctic Ecosystems. Ecological Studies,* **Vol. 153** ed.: D. Hessen, Springer-Verlag, Berlin, Heidelberg, 2002, pp. 137-155.

169   R. Sommaruga, The role of solar UV radiation in the ecology of alpine lakes, *J. Photochem. Photobiol. B.*, 2001, **62**, 35-42.

170   W. F. Vincent, in *The Ecology of Cyanobacteria* eds.: B. A. Whitton and M. Potts, Kluwer Academic Publishers, 2000, pp. 321-340.

171   G. Weller, Regional impacts of climate change in the Arctic and Antarctic, *Ann. Glac.*, 1998, **27**, 543-552.

172   J. J. Magnuson, D. M. Robertson, B. J. Benson, R. H. Wynne, D. M. Livingstone, T. Arai, R. A. Assel, R. G. Barry, V. Card, E. Kuusisto, N. G. Granin, T. D. Prowse, K. M. Stewart and V. S. Vuglinski, Historical trends in lake and river ice cover in the Northern hemisphere, *Science*, 2000, **289**, 1743-1746.

173   R. D. Vinnebrooke and P. R. Leavitt, Phytobenthos and phytoplankton as potential indicators of climate change in mountain lakes and ponds: an HPLC-based pigment approach, *J. North Am. Benth. Assoc.*, 1999, **10**, 1065-1081.

174   D. Hessen, *UV Radiation and Arctic Ecosystems. Ecological Studies,* **Vol. 153**, Springer-Verlag, Berlin, Heidelberg, 2002.

175   D. O. Hessen and N. A. Rukke, Increased UV-susceptibility in *Daphnia* at low calcium concentrations, *Limnol. Oceanogr.*, 2000, **45**, 1834-1838.

176   R. Pienitz and W. F. Vincent, Effect of climate change relative to ozone depletion on UV exposure in subarctic lakes, *Nature*, 2000, **404**, 484-487.

177   R. T. Watson, M. C. Zinyowera and R. H. Moss, IPCC Special Report on the Regional Impacts of Climate Change: An Assessment of Vulnerability, Intergovernmental Panel on Climate Change (IPCC) Report No.

178   D. Karentz and I. Bosch, Influence of ozone-related increases in ultraviolet radiation on Antarctic marine organisms, *Am. Zool.*, 2001, **41**, 3-16.

179   H. D. Kumar and D.-P. Häder, *Global Aquatic and Atmospheric Environment*, Springer-Verlag, Berlin, Heidelberg, New York, 1999.

180   J. Staehelin, N. R. P. Harris, C. Appenzeller and J. Eberhard, Ozone trends: a review, *Rev. Geophys.*, 2001, **39**, 231-290.

181   S. A. Montzka, J. H. Butler and L. T. Lock, Present and future trends in the atmospheric burden of ozone-depleting halogens, *Nature*, 1999, **398**, 690-694.

182   D. L. Hartmann, J. M. Wallace, V. Limpasuvan, D. W. J. Thompson and J. R. Holton, Can ozone depletion and global warming interact to produce rapid climate change, *Proc. Natl. Acad. Sci. USA*, 2000, **97**, 1412-1417.

183   W. J. Randel and F. Wu, Cooling of the Arctic and Antarctic polar stratospheres due to ozone depletion, *J. Climate*, 1999, **12**, 1467-1479.

184   W. F. Vincent, I. Laurion and R. Pienitz, Arctic and Antarctic lakes as optical indicators of global change, *Ann. Glac.*, 1998, **27**, 691-696.

185   J. R. Petit, J. Jouzel, D. Raynaud, N. I. Barkov, J.-M. Barnola, I. Basile, M. Benders, J. Chappellaz, M. Davis, G. Delaygue, M. Delmotte, V. M. Kotlyakov, M. Legrand, V. Y. Lipenkov, C. Lorius, L. Pepin, C. Ritz, E. Saltzman and M. Stievenard, Climate and atmospheric history of the past 420,000 years from the Vostok ice core, Antarctica, *Nature*, 1999, **399**, 429-436.

186   K. Alverson and F. Oldfield, Pages - past global changes and their significance for the future: an introduction, *Quat. Sci. Rev.*, 2000, **19**, 3-7.

187   S. D. Emslie, W. Fraser, R. C. Smith and W. Walker, Abandoned penguin colonies and environmental change in the Palmer Station area, Anvers Island, Antarctic Peninsula, *Antarctic Sci.*, 1998, **10**, 257-268.

188   M. van den Broeke, On the interpretation of Antarctic temperature trends, *J. Climate*, 2000, **13**, 3385-3389.

189   R. Bindschadler and P. Vornberger, Changes in the West Antarctic ice sheet since 1963 from declassified satellite photography, *Science*, 1998, **279**, 689-692.

190   M. Simon, F. O. Glockner and R. Amann, Different community structure and temperature optima of heterotrophic picoplankton in various regions of the Southern Ocean, *Aquat. Micro. Ecol.*, 1999, **18**, 275-284.

191   S. L. Chown and K. J. Gaston, Exploring links between physiology and ecology at macroscales: the role of respiratory metabolism in insects, *Biol. Rev.*, 1999, **74**, 87-120.

192   J. Cuzin-Roudy, Seasonal reproduction, multiple spawning, and fecundity in northern krill, *Meganyctiphanes norvegica*, and Antarctic krill, *Euphausia superba*, *Can. J. Fish. Aq. Sci.*, 2000, **57 suppl. 3**, 6-15.

193   H. M. Dierssen, R. C. Smith and M. Vernet, Glacial meltwater dynamics in coastal waters west of the Antarctic peninsula, *Proc. Nat. Acad. Sci. USA*, 2002, **99**, 1790-1795.

194   C. W. Grobe, C. T. Ruhland and T. A. Day, A new population of *Colobanthus quitensis* near Arthur Harbor, Antarctica: correlating recruitment with warmer summer temperatures, *Arctic Alpine Res.*, 1997, **29**, 217-221.

195   D. H. Bromwich, B. Chen and K. M. Hines, Global atmospheric impacts induced by year-round open water adjacent to Antarctica, *J. Geophys. Res. D*, 1998, **103**, 11173-11189.

196   B. S. Britton and R. F. Keeling, The influence of Antarctic sea ice on glacial - interglacial CO_2 variations, *Nature*, 2000, **404**, 171-174.

197   R. G. Zepp, T. V. Callaghan and D. J. Erickson, Effects of enhanced solar ultraviolet radiation on biogeochemical cycles, *J. Photochem. Photobiol. B.*, 1998, **46**, 69-82.

198   P. Falkowski, R. J. Scholes, E. Boyle, J. Canadell, D. Canfield, J. Elser, N. Gruber, K. Hibbard, P. Högberg, S. Linder, F. T. Mackenzie, B. Moore III, T. Pedersen, Y. Rosenthal, S. Seitzinger, V. Smetacek and W. Steffen, The global carbon cycle: a test of our knowledge of earth as a system, *Science*, 2000, **290**, 291-296.

199   P. G. Falkowski and Y. Rosenthal, Biological diversity and resource plunder in the geological record: casual correlations or causal relationships?, *Proc. Natl. Acad. Sci. USA*, 2001, **98**, 4290-4292.

200   A. S. Brierley and J. L. Watkins, Effects of sea ice cover on the swarming behaviour of Antarctic krill, *Euphausia superba*, *Can. J. Fish. Aq. Sci.*, 2000, **57 suppl. 3**, 24-30.

201   P. D. Tortell, Evolutionary and ecological perspectives on carbon acquisition in phytoplankton, *Limnol. Oceanogr.*, 2000, **45**, 744-750.

202   J. L. Sarmiento, T. M. C. Hughes, R. J. Stouffer and S. Manabe, Simulated response of the ocean carbon cycle to anthropogenic climate warming, *Nature*, 1998, **393**, 245-249.

203   F. Louanchi and M. Hoppema, Interannual variations of the Antarctic Ocean CO_2 uptake from 1986 to 1994, *Mar. Chem.*, 2000, **72**, 103-114.

204   J. Beardall, S. Beer and J. A. Raven, Biodiversity of marine plants in an era of climate change: some predictions based on physiological performance, *Bot. Mar.*, 1998, **41**, 113-123.

205   P. J. Neale, R. F. Davis and J. J. Cullen, Interactive effects of ozone depletion and vertical mixing on photosynthesis of Antarctic phytoplankton, *Nature*, 1998, **392**, 585-589.

206   K. R. Arrigo, D. H. Robinson, D. L. Worthen, R. B. Dunbar, G. R. DiTullio, M. VanWoert and M. P. Lizotte, Phytoplankton community structure and the drawdown of nutrients and CO_2 in the Southern Ocean, *Science*, 1999, **283**, 365-367.

CHAPTER 5. INTERACTIVE EFFECTS OF OZONE DEPLETION AND CLIMATE CHANGE ON BIOGEOCHEMICAL CYCLES

R. G. Zepp[a], T. V. Callaghan[b,c], and D. J. Erickson III[d]

[a]United States Environmental Protection Agency, 960 College Station Road, Athens, Georgia 30605-2700, USA

[b]Abisko Scientific Research Station, SE-98107 Abisko, Sweden

[c]Sheffield Centre for Arctic Ecology, Department of Animal and Plant Sciences, University of Sheffield, Tapton Experimental Gardens, 26 Taptonville Road, Sheffield, S10 5BR, UK

[d]Computational Climate Dynamics Group, Computer Science and Mathematics Division, Oak Ridge National Laboratory, P.O. Box 2008, MS 6367 Oak Ridge, TN 37831-6367, USA

Summary

The effects of ozone depletion on global biogeochemical cycles, via increased UV-B radiation at the Earth's surface, have continued to be documented over the past 4 years. In this report we also document various effects of UV-B that interact with global climate change because the detailed interactions between ozone depletion and climate change are central to the prediction and evaluation of future Earth environmental conditions.

There is increasing evidence that elevated UV-B has significant effects on the terrestrial biosphere with important implications for the cycling of carbon, nitrogen and other elements. Increased UV has been shown to induce carbon monoxide production from dead plant matter in terrestrial ecosystems, nitrogen oxide production from Arctic and Antarctic snowpacks, and halogenated substances from several terrestrial ecosystems. New studies on UV effects on the decomposition of dead leaf material confirm that these effects are complex and species-specific. Decomposition can be retarded, accelerated or remain unchanged. It has been difficult to relate effects of UV on decomposition rates to leaf litter chemistry, as this is very variable. However, new evidence shows UV effects on some fungi, bacterial communities and soil fauna that could play roles in decomposition and nutrient cycling. An important new result is that not only is nitrogen cycling in soils perturbed significantly by increased UV-B, but that these effects persist for over a decade. As nitrogen cycling is temperature dependent, this finding clearly links the impacts of ozone depletion to the ability of plants to use nitrogen in a warming global environment. There are many other potential interactions between UV and climate change impacts on terrestrial biogeochemical cycles that remain to be quantified.

There is also new evidence that UV-B strongly influences aquatic carbon, nitrogen, sulfur, and metals cycling that affect a wide range of life processes. UV-B accelerates the decomposition of colored dissolved organic matter (CDOM) entering the sea via terrestrial runoff, thus having important effects on oceanic carbon cycle dynamics. Since UV-B influences the distribution of CDOM, there is an impact of UV-B on estimates of oceanic productivity based on remote sensing of ocean color. Thus, oceanic productivity estimates based on remote sensing require estimates of CDOM distributions.

Recent research shows that UV-B transforms dissolved organic matter to dissolved inorganic carbon and nitrogen, including carbon dioxide and ammonium and to organic substances that are either more or less readily available to micro-organisms. The extent of these transformations is correlated with loss of UV absorbance by the organic matter. Changes in aquatic primary productivity and decomposition due to climate-related changes in circulation and nutrient supply, which occur concurrently with increased UV-B exposure, have synergistic influences on the penetration of light into aquatic ecosystems. New research has confirmed that UV affects the biological availability of iron, copper and other trace metals in aquatic environments thus potentially affecting the growth of phytoplankton and other microorganisms that are involved in carbon and nitrogen cycling. There are several instances where UV-B modifies the air-sea exchange of trace gases that in turn alter atmospheric chemistry, including the carbon cycle.

Introduction

Former UNEP reports have assessed the impacts of UV-B on biogeochemical cycling in terrestrial and aquatic ecosystems.[1, 2] The term "biogeochemical cycles" is used here to refer to the complex interaction of biological, chemical, and physical processes that control the exchange and recycling of matter and energy at and near the Earths surface. Research on biogeochemical cycles focuses on the transport and transformation of substances in the natural environment. Here, we report on new findings that highlight the importance of UV-B impacts on biogeochemistry or modify our earlier understanding. UV effects on biogeochemical cycling also have the potential to interact with effects on carbon and nutrient cycling mediated through current climate changes and predicted changes in climate (IPCC)[3]. We present evidence here for such interactive effects as well as the basis for expecting potentially important effects that have not yet been demonstrated.

Terrestrial ecosystems

Changes in solar UV radiation can affect terrestrial biogeochemistry in at least two important interconnected ways. Firstly, the effects can involve the cycling of carbon including its capture (photosynthesis), storage (biomass and soil organic matter content) and release (plant and soil organism respiration). Secondly, UV exposure can affect the cycling of mineral nutrients such as nitrogen upon which plant production and ecosystem productivity are dependent (Figure 5-1).

A review of UV effects on biogeochemical cycles[4] published since the last UNEP report[1], demonstrated the complexity of UV impacts on decomposition processes which are species and system-specific, and suggested that, overall, the effects were small and transient. However, there have been new studies, some of which show that particular effects of UV-B on carbon and nitrogen cycling, that are likely to be important in the long term. The implications of this recent research are presented here.

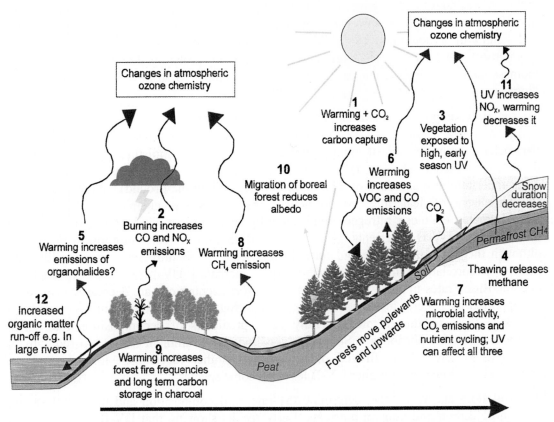

Figure 5-1. Conceptual model illustrating the potential effects of enhanced UV radiation and climate change on biogeochemical cycles in terrestrial ecosystems. The evidence and bases for numbered hypotheses and processes relating to specific effects are discussed in the text. Key: CO = carbon monoxide, NOx = oxides of nitrogen, CH_4 = methane, CO_2 = carbon dioxide, VOC = volatile organic compounds

UV Effects on Terrestrial Biogeochemistry

Carbon cycling

The capture of atmospheric carbon dioxide by green plants in photosynthesis and its storage in plant tissues (phytomass) is the fundamental process that supports life in the biosphere. The accumulation of dead organic matter in soils also stores carbon, making it less available as a greenhouse gas in the atmosphere. In contrast, the microbial respiration of organisms that decompose dead organic matter in the soil, together with the respiration of other organisms in the biosphere, return carbon to the atmosphere where it adds to existing greenhouse gases. Sometimes the gases released, such as methane and carbon monoxide, are chemically active and could alter atmospheric chemistry.

A quantitative review by Searles *et al.*[5] of experiments seeking to identify the effect of UV on plants showed that shoot biomass and leaf area were decreased modestly by UV-B enhancement. However, shoot biomass was reduced only under very high levels of UV-B. Increased UV-B radiation was suggested to have little direct impact on carbon capture and storage in phytomass. Specific systems might, however, deviate from this general trend. Shoot density (number per m^2) and height of a bog moss (*Sphagnum fuscum*) in a Subarctic mire were reduced, although productivity was not affected over a two year period, probably due to high variability in the biomass data.[6] However, changes in the number of shoots could have long-term implications for biomass.

Microbial decomposition controls carbon and nutrient storage in soils, release to the atmosphere and availability to plants. Decomposition is controlled by numerous physical and biological parameters. Among the most important are temperature, soil moisture and the chemistry of the dead organic matter substrate. UV-B affects the chemistry of living leaves and these changes are often inherited by litter (dead organic material that falls to the ground).[1] Paul *et al.*[4] showed that the chemistry of leaf litter as influenced by UV-B are chemical and species specific. Carbohydrates, cellulose, nitrogen, tannins and lignin vary greatly in both magnitude and direction in response to UV-B treatments. UV-B usually decreased the concentration of nitrogen in litter, although the effect is variable and often insignificant.[4] As nitrogen content of litter is usually positively correlated with decomposition rate, increased UV would be expected to reduce decomposition rates in those litters where nitrogen concentrations are decreased. This expectation is supported by general increases in the carbon:nitrogen and carbon:lignin ratios under elevated UV-B as these parameters are generally good predictors of decomposition rate. In addition, increases in soluble phenolics in Scots pine seedlings under ambient UV, compared with exclusion treatments (where UV is filtered out),[7] suggest another mechanism for expected decreased decomposition rates under higher UV-B levels in some species.

The soil flora and fauna also determine the rate of decomposition and the transformations and cycling of carbon and mineral nutrients. Early results showing that UV-B radiation can directly affect fungal and faunal communities associated with plant litter have been confirmed by recent studies. These show species-specific responses of soil fungi,[8] litter and leaf surface fungi[9] and fungi that are symbionts with oak. Overall, leaf surface fungi and the oak symbiont were more tolerant of elevated UV-B than soil and litter fungi. UV-B can also affect soil microfauna: amoebae were more numerous at near-ambient than in attenuated UV-B levels in UV filtration experiments on a southern Argentinian heathland.[5, 10] Soil microorganisms can also be affected indirectly.[11] After 5 years exposure of a subarctic heath to enhanced UV-B radiation, alone and in combination with elevated CO_2, there were striking changes in microbial carbon and bacterial community structure. Microbial carbon was decreased by 50% in the UV-B treatment. The use of various carbon sources exposed to soil microorganisms suggested either a lower or less active population of bacteria in the enhanced UV treatments. Also, sole carbon source utilization tests, in which a range of individual carbon sources are made available as bacterial substrates, showed that UV-B caused a change in the soil microbial community structure, resulting almost certainly from a change in the dominant bacterial species.

Recently, a coordinated series of field experiments decomposed standard birch leaf litter under ambient and elevated UV-B at sites ranging from 38°N in Greece to 78°N on Arctic Svalbard[12]. Transient changes in the fungal community decomposing the litter were found at a Subarctic site[12] and were similar to those recorded by Newsham *et al.*[13] on oak litter. Significant reductions in the mass loss of litter decomposing under enhanced UV-B occurred at two of the four sites.

UV-B can accelerate litter decomposition by photochemical processes. Although Moody *et al.*[9] showed no photodegradation of leaf litter by weight loss, other results have demonstrated that senescent and dead leaves from temperate deciduous plants and tropical grasses produce CO on exposure to solar UV radiation.[14] A recent study in Brazil provided additional evidence that CO is photoproduced from litter. Highest fluxes were late in the dry season, especially following burning of the Cerrado.[15] A recent estimate indicated that about 60 teragrams (1 teragram equals 10^{12} g) of CO may be produced annually from this process on a global basis.[16] This is similar to earlier estimates and is sufficiently large that it should not be neglected when considering the global CO budget, particularly as CO reacts in the troposphere to influence ozone, other oxidants and aerosols.

Nitrogen oxides can also be produced from photodegradation processes in polar snowpacks in Greenland[17], Michigan[18] and the Antarctic.[19] The process could result in destruction of tropospheric ozone in the snow pack but the extent and speed of ozone destruction probably also involve a catalytic destruction by bromide.[17] Experiments[20] and field observations[19] have shown that UV-B radiation induces the photochemical transformations of a variety of organic and inorganic substances containing nitrogen.

The release or storage of carbon and mineral nutrients depends on the final outcome of the indirect and direct effects of UV-B on decomposition.[21] New studies, since those reported by Zepp et al.[1] and Paul et al.,[4] confirm that UV-B effects are species and system-specific, with both increases[21-24], decreases[8, 12] (two of four sites) and no change in decomposition rates recorded[12] (two of four sites)[24] or inferred from lack of UV-B effects on leaf litter chemistry.[25] UV-B modifications of dead plant material of pine are not only vary from species to species, but also from seed source to seed source.[24] Overall, studies that show effects of enhanced UV-B on decomposition suggest that these effects are small and confined to initial stages of decomposition according to Moody et al.[12] Even so, small effects over large areas are likely to be important. Recent findings that UV-B affects microbial immobilization of nitrogen and the structures of microbial communities after 5 years[11], and that UV-B effects on oak litter decomposition rate are maintained after four years[23], emphasize that our understanding is limited by the low number of long-term UV-B field experiments.

Nutrient Cycling

In most natural and semi-natural terrestrial ecosystems, the availability of nitrogen in soil strongly constrains plant growth and productivity. In unmanaged and, to a lesser extent, managed ecosystems, the input of nitrogen to ecosystems by the fixation of atmospheric nitrogen is important. This process commonly occurs by the activity of cyanobacteria that are free living or grow in symbiotic relationships with plants such as algae and lichens, and symbiotic rhizobia that are symbionts of higher plants. It has been known for some time that UV-B radiation reduces the fixation of nitrogen by cyanobacteria in rice paddy fields and other aquatic environments,[26] and the activity of N-fixing rhizobia bacteria.[27] Recently, work in the Arctic where nitrogen availability to plants is particularly limiting, has shown that UV-B radiation can constrain potential N_2 fixation there. Nitrogen fixation potential by cyanobacteria associated with one moss exposed to enhanced UV-B in the Northern Arctic was reduced by 50% compared with natural conditions, whereas that associated with a Subarctic moss was not affected.[28] In addition, there was a 50% reduction in nitrogen fixation potential of a lichen exposed to enhanced UV-B in the Subarctic.[28]

UV-B induces changes in the assimilation and allocation of mineral nutrients and other chemicals within the tissues of some plant species (Chapter 3).[29] Changes in tissue chemistry that are inherited by litter affect decomposition[24] and nutrient cycling. However, not all species show changes in tissue chemistry when exposed to UV-B. Little impact of UV-B was expected on decomposition and nutrient cycling in mid-latitude dune grasslands[30] and oak woodlands[25] based on UV supplementation experiments that showed insignificant changes in plant tissue chemistry. Despite lack of change in tissue chemistry, however, decomposition was accelerated in the oak system.[22, 23] In contrast to studies showing no change, nitrogen concentrations in dead plant matter from several European heathlands, when decomposing under enhanced UV-B, were decreased.[4] Although the fate of this nitrogen (i.e. subsequent uptake by plants, microbial immobilization or leaching) was not investigated, a recent long-term study showed that enhanced UV-B resulted in a significant immobilization of nitrogen in microbial biomass in a subarctic heath soil.[11] Microbial N increased over 100% in UV-B exposed field plots compared to control plots and microbial biomass C:N ratio decreased by 320%. These effects could possibly be the result of UV-B impacts on exudation of microbial resources from roots of plants irradiated with enhanced UV-B as suggested by Klironomos and Allen[31]. Many plants increase their ability to take up nutrients by having a symbiotic relationship with a fungus (a mycorrhiza) that provides an efficient nutrient foraging and capture system for the plant. However, exposure to enhanced UV-B can reduce this potential by up to 20%.[27] The processes of microbial immobilization of nitrogen and reduced mycorrhizal infection are expected to further limit nutrient availability and plant productivity.

Interactions between Climate Change and UV-B Impacts on Terrestrial Biogeochemical Cycling

Models of future climate change predict significant changes in variables that are important to terrestrial ecosystems such as temperature, precipitation, radiation reaching the Earth's surface and increases in atmospheric CO_2 concentration. There are several areas where interactions between climate change and UV-B that are non-additive and complex in nature can lead to non-linear changes in the behavior of biogeochemical cycles. UV exposure may induce changes in biological systems that moderate or enhance species responses to changes in climate and their roles in element cycling. Also, changes in climate, such as earlier snow melt in spring, might increase the exposure of species and biogeochemical processes to potential damage from UV-B.

Carbon fluxes and pools in phytomass

Changes in climate and/or climate variability have already had significant effects on carbon dynamics in terrestrial ecosystems[32, 33], in that "greenness" of vegetation, length of the growing season and biomass have increased in middle and northern latitudes of the northern hemisphere. Such changes could potentially interact with UV-B effects. If moisture remains unaffected, climatic warming and increased atmospheric concentrations of CO_2 will increase carbon pools in phytomass, particularly in northern forests and tundra, due to increased growth of existing vegetation (Figure 5-1, pathway 1) and displacement of this existing vegetation by more productive vegetation (Figure 5-1).[34-37] Increased biomass production has already occurred in northern areas due to recent warming.[32] However, UV-B has the potential to reduce biomass in some ecosystems and should to some extent modify the increase in carbon in phytomass due to warming.

Climate change induces disturbance of vegetation, which is important because it increases forest fires (Figure 5-1, pathway 2), forest pest outbreaks, over-grazing, drought, and thawing permafrost. For example, defoliation of forests due to increased insect pest outbreaks resulting from greater pest survival in milder winters[38, 39] could interact with UV-mediated changes in food quality that increase [40-42] or decrease grazing[5] leading to changes in carbon and nitrogen pools over large areas. Earlier snow melt has been exposing plants in the Northern Hemisphere to higher UV levels in Spring[33] (Figure 5-1, pathway 3), and thawing permafrost and methane-containing clathrates have the potential to release large quantities of CH_4 (Figure 5-1, pathway 8).[43]

Plants of some ecosystems, particularly those of salt marshes, but also peatlands and forest floor vegetation, are important in enhancing fluxes of halogenated hydrocarbons from the biosphere to the atmosphere (Figure 5-1, pathway 5).[44] This is important in contributing to the global pool of these chemically reactive substances.[45, 46] Some plant species are particularly efficient at transporting halomethanes into the atmosphere. As this is an active physiological process, emissions should increase in response to warming. The emissions of halogenated compounds from coastal salt marshes also are likely to be affected by sea level rise associated with global warming. Any impact of elevated UV-B on plant species that emit halocarbons would modify expected responses due to global warming. Warming also induces significant changes in the production and emission of VOCs that are derived from terrestrial vegetation, resulting in an alteration in the tropospheric production of ozone and a resulting perturbation of the oxidative capacity of the troposphere[47] (Chapter 6)[48] (Figure 5-1, pathway 6).

Changes in the production of CO by UV-induced oxidation of plant matter could be affected by climate change in several ways. Climate-sensitive parameters such as humidity and temperature have important effects on the efficiency of CO photoproduction (Figure 5-1, pathway 6).[14-16] The efficiency increases as temperature and humidity increase. Also, CO production efficiencies increase sharply as plants start to senesce and die and so increased drought frequency associated with climate change in some regions could increase UV-induced CO emissions.[14]

Carbon pools and fluxes in soils

If moisture remains unaffected, climatic warming will lead to decreased carbon pools in soils, particularly in northern forests and tundra where global warming is amplified, and in peatlands and wetlands where carbon storage is most pronounced.[49-51] The mechanism involved increased rates of microbial decomposition and an increased flux of carbon as CO_2 from dryer areas (Figure 5-1, pathway 7) and CO_2 and CH_4 from wetter areas (Figure 5-1, pathway 8). Methane is an important greenhouse gas and a major source of hydrogen for the production of water vapor via reaction with hydroxyl radicals in the stratosphere. Thus, increased CH_4 may enhance ozone depletion on polar stratospheric clouds (PSCs). In contrast, higher UV-B should increase carbon storage in soils in which nutrients are particularly limiting to plant growth by changing litter quality and influencing decomposer organisms (Figure 5-1, pathway 7), although in some ecosystems, higher UV-B may reduce carbon storage in soil or remain neutral. Paul *et al.*[4] suggest that any changes in carbon storage will be small and they imply that small changes will be insignificant. However, even small changes in carbon storage in peatlands, northern boreal forests and tundra, where most of the earth's organic carbon is stored,[52] could be at least regionally important. In wetland ecosystems, e.g. rice paddies, the magnitude of emissions of CH_4 to the atmosphere depends on the particular plant species present.[53] Global methane emissions are likely to increase by 45% for a global $2^\circ C$ average warming (Figure 5-1, pathway 8).[54] Any negative impact of UV on the activity of those plants that efficiently transport CH_4 to the atmosphere could be important in reducing the impact of warming on CH_4 emissions as shown by Niemi *et al*[55]. In drier ecosystems, such as arid lands, with high UV-B, storage of soil carbon during warming will be reduced by increased UV-B and warming together, because of photodegradation of litter and reduced litter production through increased water stress. On the other hand, warming will result in increased carbon storage due to reduced microbial activity limited by water. The balances between these complex interactions are unknown.

Increased atmospheric CO_2[56, 57] and UV-B radiation (see above) both result in a change in litter chemistry that would suggest additive or even synergistic decreases in decomposition and increased carbon storage in soils (but see Norby and Cotrufo[58] for a cautionary viewpoint). Experimentally increased UV-B and CO_2 together are likely to increase microbial immobilisation of nitrogen that is, in turn, expected to reduce nitrogen availability for plant production.[11]

Fire reduces short term carbon storage but enhances the storage of a fraction for millennia by producing charcoal (Figure 5-1, pathway 9), a persistent form of carbon[59], but it also results in loss of nitrogen to the atmosphere[60], reducing productivity over the long term in nitrogen-limited ecosystems. Fires also increase the UV-mediated release of CO from vegetation and litter[15]. Fire frequency is increasing in some areas such as the boreal forests of North America and is expected to increase further as a result of global warming: this could affect atmospheric ozone chemistry.[47]

(Chapter 6) [48] Moreover, since many forest fires occur in the mid- to high-Northern latitudes, these burned regions are particularly subject to ozone depletion and increases in UV.

Effects of warming through impacts on surface energy and water balances

Increased atmospheric CO_2 concentrations result in less water use by plants which leads to less evaporative cooling and thus warming of the earth's surface in daytime.[61] Increased UV-B might also restrict water loss by plants through stomata (small pores in leaves)[62] and together with increased CO_2, there is potential to increase surface temperature additively. In addition, models of feedbacks from vegetation to the climate system calculate that decreases in albedo (reflectivity) associated with the displacement of tundra by evergreen forest will dominate over the negative feedback of increased carbon sequestration (Figure 5-1, pathway 10).[35, 36] If UV-B affects the optical properties of leaves, there could be an effect on albedo (reflectivity).

Nitrogen cycling

Climatic warming, assuming a constant moisture content, will stimulate nitrogen cycling rates in soils as a result of increased microbial decomposition of litter[51] and possibly increased activity of free-living and symbiotic nitrogen fixers. UV-B can reduce or increase nitrogen cycling rates through its effects on litter decomposition (overall the effect is to reduce nitrogen cycling) and it can also reduce nitrogen fixation by cyanobacteria directly. Again, the balance between the processes is unknown but warming effects are likely to dominate over UV effects (Figure 5-1, pathway 7). The results of changes in nitrogen cycling are two-fold. Firstly, there will be changes in the amount of N_2O, which participates in chemical reactions that affect stratospheric O_3, emitted from soil to atmosphere. Secondly, plant productivity will increase in response to increased temperature caused by greenhouse warming and to enhanced nitrogen availability in most mesic to dry terrestrial ecosystems. Also, NO_x production by snowpacks will be reduced because of reduced snow duration (Figure 5-1, pathway 11).[3]

Aquatic Ecosystems

Changes in UV can have significant effects on aquatic carbon cycling, nutrient cycling, and water-air trace gas exchange. In this section we discuss results on UV-aquatic biogeochemistry interactions that were obtained since our last report[1], taking into account the fact that co-occurring climate change can influence the UV effects (Figure 5-2). UV effects on aquatic ecosystems are further treated in Häder et al.[26] and Kerr et al.[63] provide additional updates on recent measurements of UV radiation in aquatic systems.

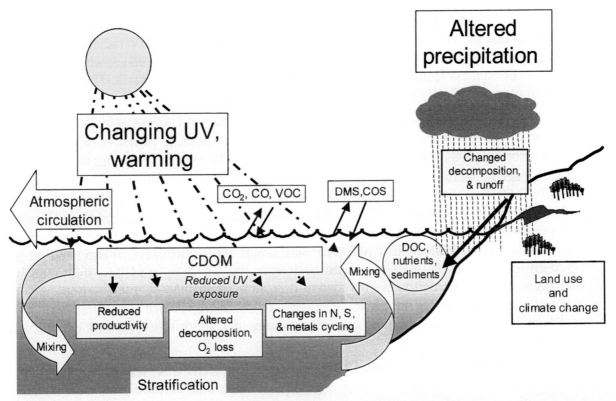

Figure 5-2. Aquatic biogeochemical cycles affected by UV radiation and their interaction with other co-occurring environmental changes such as global warming and land use change. Key: DMS dimethyl sulfide; CDOM colored dissolved organic matter, the primary UV absorbing substance in aquatic environments; DOC dissolved organic carbon (see text for explanation)

UV Effects on Aquatic Biogeochemistry

Carbon cycling

Phytoplankton communities are primarily responsible for the production of biomass in large lakes and the ocean. Direct DNA damage caused by UV-B has been observed in Antarctic marine phytoplankton and bacterioplankton during mid-summer, especially under stratified conditions related to melting shelf ice.[64] A recent study has shown that the UV sensitivity of mid-latitude estuarine phytoplankton photosynthesis is remarkably similar to that previously observed for Antarctic phytoplankton.[65] These results provide further evidence that UV reduces phytoplankton productivity globally in the ocean, although the UV sensitivity of open ocean phytoplankton is still poorly defined. On the other hand, UV photoinhibition of productivity may be partially offset by other indirect effects of UV on iron in the ocean. Photoreactions of complexed iron enhance its biological availability,[66] a process that may stimulate productivity in parts of the sea that are iron limited, such as the Southern Ocean.[67] Atmospheric iron deposition correlates closely with observed productivity in parts of the sea.[68]   Thus, the net impact of increased UV on phytoplankton productivity is unclear at this point. However, a recent study based on remote sensing indicates that global oceanic chlorophyll has decreased globally between the early 1980's and the late 1990's.[69]   The overall decrease was attributed to changes in upper ocean mixing, mixed layer depth, sea surface temperature and nutrient supply caused by climate change. [69] Based on other research that is discussed below, the decreases could have been partly attributable to increases in UV exposure in the upper ocean caused by ozone depletion and by climate-induced changes in mixing, stratification and UV penetration.

As discussed in this volume[26] and in the UNEP 1998 report[1, 70], other indirect effects involving trophic level interactions may also affect ecosystem productivity. For example, recent research indicates that the vertical migration of zooplankton is sensitive to UV radiation.[71, 72] This finding has important implications for the flux of carbon through the microbial food web, which involves transfer of biomass from the primary producers to metazoa and bacteria. Thus, the net impact on carbon capture is clearly not a linear function of UV exposure.

UV effects on decomposition of aquatic organic matter are caused by inhibition of microbial activity, by direct photodegradation of colored dissolved organic matter (CDOM) and particulate organic carbon (POC) to CO_2 and other gases, and by UV-induced photodegradation of CDOM to readily decomposable compounds that are referred to here as biologically-labile photoproducts (BLPs). Bacterial activity is inhibited by UV-B radiation and direct DNA damage has been demonstrated in field studies.[64, 73, 74]   The greatest damage to bacterioplankton is observed in the upper layer of poorly mixed, stratified waters. However, observations showed that the reduction in microbial activity is attenuated with increased winds and surface layer mixing and the activity is rapidly restored in the dark via repair and regrowth.[73, 74]   A modeling study concluded that changes in UV radiation caused by ozone depletion could have a more serious net impact on bacterial activity than UV increases attributable to decreased CDOM concentrations.[75] Viruses can influence microbial diversity and activity, including decomposition, and viral activity is sensitive to UV-B exposure.[76]

In freshwaters and the coastal ocean, a large part of the CDOM is "terrestrially-derived", i.e. it is derived from the decomposition of terrestrial plant matter that is transported from the land (Figure 5-1, pathway 2). Microorganisms do not readily decompose terrestrially-derived CDOM, but its transformation can be accelerated when it is exposed to solar ultraviolet radiation. Recent research has provided additional evidence that the two major decomposition processes induced by solar UV are direct photoproduction of both dissolved inorganic carbon (DIC)[77-79] and labile organic substances that are readily assimilated by microorganisms.[80-87]   UV exposure also enhances the decomposition of particulate organic carbon in freshwaters.[88]   Other recent results seem to indicate that the net effect of UV exposure on algal- or some plant-derived DOC is a reduction in biological lability.[83, 89-92] Exposure to solar UV radiation also causes changes in CDOM isotopic content,[93, 94] that are useful in understanding the fate and transport of carbon and oxygen in the environment.[77, 95]

The direct photodegradation processes involve, in part, reactive oxygen species (ROS) such as hydrogen peroxide, superoxide ions and hydroxyl radicals, as well as short-lived reductants such as hydrated electrons that are produced on absorption of UV radiation.[96-103] Complex interactions of the ROS with iron and copper complexes that are present in surface waters and in precipitation[103, 104] help control the nature and extent of carbon cycling in aquatic environments.[77, 100, 105]

Marine scientists have long debated the fate of terrestrially-derived organic matter on entry to the ocean. Experimental studies indicate that the DOC in the open ocean is primarily of marine origin, although some terrestrial character would have been expected.[87, 93, 106] Recent experimental and modeling research indicates that UV-stimulated decomposition can potentially consume all of the input of CDOM from land.[95, 107] Most of this decomposition potentially occurs in coastal areas of the Northern Hemisphere, with substantial contributions from high-latitude coastal regions.

Recent studies of a wide range of freshwater and marine environments have shown that CDOM, and, to a lesser extent in the open ocean, organic colloids, play an important role in the attenuation of solar UV and blue radiation.[108-111] CDOM effectively protects aquatic ecosystems from harmful UV-B radiation while permitting beneficial photorepairing (UV-A) and photosynthetically active radiation to be much more efficiently transmitted into the water. Changes in CDOM concentrations occur seasonally in freshwaters[112, 113] and the ocean[108, 111] and they also likely are linked to climate change, acid deposition[114] and land use changes. The UV absorbance and fluorescence of CDOM decreases with exposure to solar UV radiation and recent research has demonstrated that this "photobleaching" process is induced most efficiently by UV-B radiation.[115-117] A combination of photochemical and microbial processes is responsible for the photobleaching[77, 85, 99, 107, 115, 117] and the efficiency is affected by factors such as oxygen concentration[77, 95] and temperature.[93] Although one study in U.S. freshwaters has indicated that photobleaching rates are related to acid-neutralizing capacity[118], other investigations in Chilean, Argentinian and Antarctic freshwaters indicate that alkalinity has no detectable effect (H. Zagarese, personal communication, 2002). The UV-induced changes in CDOM concentrations can influence remote sensing of oceanic productivity, which is based on observations of ocean color. New results indicate that CDOM makes a major contribution to remotely-sensed ocean color.[108]

Nutrient cycling

UV radiation can affect nitrogen cycling in various ways: through effects on nitrogen-related enzymatic activity by microorganisms such as photoinhibition of nitrogen-fixing microorganisms[26] and, indirectly, through effects on the biological availability of essential trace elements, such as iron, that stimulate the growth of nitrogen fixers; and through enhanced decomposition of persistent dissolved organic nitrogen to biologically labile nitrogenous photoproducts. Nitrogen is a limiting nutrient in remote parts of the open ocean and thus impacts of UV radiation on important nitrogen fixing cyanobacteria such as *Trichodesmium*[119] or the newly discovered N-fixing marine nanoplankton[120] potentially could be ecologically significant. Iron plays a role in stimulating the growth of *Trichodesmium*.[121] It has been proposed that the iron deposited in the sea via long range transport of terrestrial dust[68] can stimulate rapid growth of this organism and that related increases in biologically-available nitrogen can trigger growth in toxic organisms such as *Gymnodinium breve*.[122] UV-induced photoreactions of iron are known to affect its biological availability in the sea.[66]

Biologically labile nitrogen compounds such as nitrate, ammonium and amino acids are rapidly recycled by the biota in aquatic systems, while N-containing substances whose structures are too complex or randomized to be readily assimilated accumulate in the water column. In aquatic environments with limited N fixation or low external inputs of labile N, the labile compounds drop to almost unmeasurable levels in the photic zone where productivity occurs, while the persistent dissolved organic nitrogen (DON) accumulates. Interactions of UV radiation and DON provide a pathway for the conversion of persistent DON to compounds that are more easily assimilated by aquatic microorganisms. Recent results suggest that photochemically-produced labile nitrogen compounds can be an important source of biologically available nitrogen in coastal regions.[123-125]

Phosphorus cycling can potentially also be affected by exposure to UV. The changes in microbial consortia that are discussed in the carbon cycling section likely influence phosphorus cycling as well. In addition, recent research has provided additional evidence that UV photolysis of phosphatase-humic substance complexes can enhance phosphorus cycling in aquatic environments.[126, 127]

UV-B and trace gas exchange

The aquatic environment is an important atmospheric source and sink of trace carbon, sulfur and other gases. Recent research on the air-sea exchange of trace gases has provided evidence that the sources and sinks of certain carbon and sulfur gases are strongly influenced by solar UV radiation.[128]

New research has appeared on the effects of UV radiation on the emissions of volatile organic compounds (VOC) and carbon monoxide from aquatic environments. These gases participate in chemical reactions that change air quality in the atmosphere. Isoprene emissions correlate with chlorophyll concentrations, indicating that phytoplankton or reactive DOM released by phytoplankton is the source[128, 129] and thus that phytoplankton inhibition by UV likely alters isoprene emissions. The sea is thought to be a net source of CO, but this source has been subject to a wide range of estimates. A recent study estimated a much lower CO photoproduction in the ocean than previously reported and that most of this CO production was consumed by microorganisms rather than escaping to the atmosphere.[130] CO is photoproduced most efficiently by UV-B radiation and the efficiencies for CO photoproduction from terrestrially-derived CDOM are much larger than those observed with open ocean CDOM. This difference in efficiencies, which largely accounts for the lower estimated CO photoproduction in the open ocean, suggests that the photoreactivity of open-ocean CDOM derived from algae may be quite different from that of terrestrially-derived CDOM.

Atmospheric sulfur plays an important role in the radiative balance of the atmosphere. Anthropogenic sources are dominant in highly industrialized regions and are reasonably well defined. Natural sources and sinks of sulfur gases are much less well defined than anthropogenic sources, but have received greater scrutiny in recent years due to their potential involvement in the regulation of climate in remote parts of the ocean. The major source of natural sulfur gases is the sea. Of particular interest are the sulfur gases, dimethylsulfide (DMS) and carbonyl sulfide (COS). Both of these compounds are formed predominantly in aerobic marine environments, *i.e.* the upper layers of the ocean, and their sources and sinks are affected by solar UV radiation.

DMS, the predominant volatile sulfur compound in the open ocean, is believed to be involved in the formation of marine aerosols. Thus, DMS emissions may lead to modification of the reflectivity of marine clouds and have a cooling influence on the atmosphere. One might expect that, since DMS is closely related to primary productivity of certain phytoplankton species and that phytoplankton photosynthesis is inhibited by UV, DMS concentrations may decrease as surface UV increases. This has indeed been found to be the case in Antarctica under the ozone hole.[128] On the other hand, a recent report provided evidence that DMS and dimethylsulfoniopropionate (DMSP), the oceanic precursor of DMS, has an antioxidant function in marine algae[131]. Thus, exposure of certain algae to UV, an important driver of cellular oxidant production, presumably would stimulate DMS production. The highest concentrations of DMS occur in the Southern Ocean during early to mid spring as the sea ice melts[132], a time in which that region also experiences high UV exposure due to ozone depletion. This indicates that the Southern Ocean may be a region of intense interactions between sulfur biogeochemistry and ozone depletion. Other recent research on the sensitivity of zooplankton to UV radiation[71, 72] suggests a potentially significant role of UV-zooplankton interactions in DMS production, whereby DMS emissions increase when the phytoplankton are stressed by zooplankton grazing. Recently it was also shown that changes in physical quantities such as mixed layer depth also influence DMS sea-to-air fluxes via UV-related biogeochemical interactions.[133] Photooxidation of DMS in the upper ocean is another significant sink that is induced by solar UV radiation.[134-136]

COS is the most concentrated sulfur gas in the troposphere and it is believed to play a role in the maintenance of the stratospheric sulfate layer, although this role may be more limited than was originally believed.[1, 128] COS is primarily produced in surface seawater by the UV-related degradation of dissolved organic matter and it is degraded mainly by hydrolysis. In a modeling effort to describe global air-sea fluxes of COS based on known information about its sources and sinks, it was estimated that the open ocean was a net source of COS.[137]

Interactions between Climate Change and UV-B Impacts on Biogeochemical Cycles in Freshwater, Estuarine and Coastal Systems

UV penetration and global warming

Aquatic biogeochemical cycles can be affected in several ways through effects of various global environmental changes on UV exposure. Climate and land use change affect the movement of UV-attenuating dissolved and particulate substances from land into water (Figure 5-1, pathway 12, Figure 5-2). Such substances, particularly CDOM, control the penetration of UV-B into many aquatic environments.[26, 112, 113, 138-140] Microorganisms that are often exposed to UV-B radiation can develop cellular UV-protective substances such as mycosporine-like amino acids that absorb in the UV region.[26] Such organisms or detritus derived from them can contribute significantly to UV attenuation in ecosystems that have low concentrations of DOC.[141] Observed seasonal changes have provided evidence for the important influence of climatic change on UV penetration into freshwaters[112, 113, 138, 142, 143] and the ocean.[110, 111] Droughts, for example, reduce terrestrial inputs of CDOM and sediments into aquatic environments.[138, 142] In contrast, increased precipitation may reduce UV penetration by enhancing runoff (see Figure 5-1, pathway 12 and Figure 5-2). Shifts in soil moisture content and related changes in oxygen content affect the microbial production of soil humic substances and thus can alter inputs of this important source of CDOM in freshwaters. Moreover, global warming, through changes in atmospheric circulation, precipitation patterns, temperature, and length of warm season, can affect stratification and vertical mixing dynamics in freshwaters and the sea.[144] Stratification can result in increased UV penetration and exposure in the upper water column, a phenomenon that is driven in part by UV-induced decomposition of UV-absorbing substances in the surface water.[109-111, 139, 143] Changes in vertical mixing dynamics also can affect phytoplankton photosynthesis.[145] Reductions in oceanic primary productivity over the past decade have been attributed to climate change effects on the upper ocean[69] and this effect may be caused in part by increased UV penetration. The interactions of bacteria, organic matter, temperature and UV changes are complex and it is impossible at this point to predict how climate warming might affect UV penetration into aquatic environments. However, recent observations have shown that the warm upper layers of freshwaters and the ocean that develop under stratified conditions are generally much more UV transparent than deeper, cooler waters.[109-111, 113, 139, 143]

The past effects of climate change on UV exposure have had an impact on freshwater sedimentary records in a remarkable way. Careful analysis of fossil diatom assemblages in Canadian subarctic lake sediments has provided clear evidence of the impacts of climate change on UV penetration in Canadian lakes during the Halocene.[146, 147]

Carbon and nitrogen cycling

The possible effects of climatic warming on carbon capture and decomposition have been recently discussed in several reviews of freshwater[138, 148, 149] and oceanic ecosystems.[144] Increasing temperatures tend to increase the rates of biological production and decomposition, but other factors such as reductions in nutrient concentrations in freshwaters related to altered hydrology could limit the increases. In the case of the oceans, the expected increase in the efficiency of phytoplankton photosynthesis and biological carbonate production due to warming may be counteracted by the effects of increased stratification that likely will lead to reduced CO_2 uptake.[69, 144] Stratification can affect CO_2 air-sea exchange by reducing uptake caused by the "solubility pump," i.e. the transport of carbon from the upper ocean to the deep ocean, and it also may result in decreased photosynthesis and changed microbial decomposition caused by reduced nutrient upwelling[69] and increased exposure of microorganisms to UV-B. Vertical transport is the primary determinant of what chemical constituents and organisms are brought into the UV-illuminated layer and how long they stay there and stratification greatly slows vertical transport. Transport can be important when certain biogeochemical processes are slow compared to movement into and back out of the photic zone, e.g. for processes in which the overall impact depends on the sequence and timing of UV exposure. An example of processes likely to be affected by climate-related changes is decomposition by bacteria that are susceptible to strong UV damage but have weak repair capability.

Other UV interactions with co-occurring environmental changes can include: (1) pH related changes on productivity caused by increases in atmospheric CO_2 or acid deposition[114, 138] (2) increased UV phototoxicity caused by pollution of aquatic environments by substances such as polycyclic aromatic hydrocarbons (PAH) derived from the usage of fossil fuels,[150, 151] (3) large-scale changes in organic carbon movement from land to the sea caused by climate change, such as the increased Arctic inputs of CDOM to the coastal ocean that will affect UV induced carbon cycling in this region[152] and climate-related and UV-induced changes on the decomposition of the CDOM in the Arctic Ocean.[95, 107, 152]

Sulfur cycling

Any UV-B related changes at the surface of the ocean that result in the alteration in DMS flux to the atmosphere and the subsequent formation of particles will also alter the atmospheric radiation budget for the affected region. UV effects on vertical migration of zooplankton can reduce the amount and timing of grazing induced release of DMS from marine phytoplankton. Recent results indicate that DMS emissions are possibly enhanced by an interaction between upper ocean stratification and UV inhibition of bacterioplankton that degrade DMS before it can escape the sea into the atmosphere.[133] DMS concentrations in the upper ocean also are affected by UV-related photooxidation.[134] The net effect is a feedback whereby climate warming and changing UV influence DMS release to the atmosphere. DMS conversion to particles in the atmosphere then results in a net change in radiative forcing. Carbonyl sulfide (COS) is formed by UV-induced photoreactions of dissolved organic sulfur in the upper ocean. Changes in climate-related vertical mixing dynamics and upper ocean temperature can greatly alter COS sea to air flux.[137] Model projections indicate that climate warming (mainly by decreasing COS solubility) and increased CO_2 levels (with resulting decreased pH and reduced hydrolysis of COS) should result in increased COS emissions from the open ocean.

Metal, oxygen and halogen cycling

Metals, especially iron and copper, play an important role in the upper ocean and freshwater biogeochemistry both by participating in UV-induced processes that produce and consume peroxides and other oxidants that participate in biogeochemical processes and also as essential trace elements for plankton. Inputs of metals and peroxides to aquatic systems change with changing precipitation patterns.[103, 104, 153] UV-induced photoreactions of organic complexes of metals increase their biological availability.[66, 154] Changes in the biotic sources of such complexes as well as pH changes related to climate change would likely affect metal-UV biogeochemistry.

Oxygen cycling is also induced by UV interactions with dissolved organic matter. UV absorption by CDOM results in oxygen consumption[77, 83, 95] and the production of reactive oxygen species (ROS) such as hydrogen peroxide, superoxide ions, singlet molecular oxygen, and hydroxyl radicals. ROS derived from the interactions of UV and DOM can participate in a variety of reactions with metals that help determine the oxidative capacity of the surface waters and the cycling of metals. Increased global temperatures are likely to change the rates and mechanisms of these reactions but the net effects are poorly defined.

The interactions of global warming and UV in halogen cycling are complex. The oceans are a net sink for organic halides[155] and, because hydrolytic loss of the halides is more sensitive to temperature change than biological production, global warming is likely to increase this sink. Increased UV may reduce production of the organic halides by inhibiting algal synthesis of these compounds or it may stimulate production by partly abiotic pathways, e.g. by UV-induced photoreactions that produce methyl iodide in the upper ocean [156] and or by enhancing formation of brominated methane derivatives such as bromoform via reactions of hydrogen peroxide with bromoperoxidases.[157, 158]

Acknowledgments

We wish to thank D. Gwynn Jones, T. Christensen, W. Helbling, H. Zagarese and P. Neale for helpful input and to A. Kristofersson for help with Fig 1. We are grateful to N. Blough, W. Miller, D. Koopmans, D. Bronk and O. Zafiriou for making as yet unpublished material available. The U.K. Department for Environment, Food and Rural Affairs kindly supported the participation of T.V.C. This paper has been reviewed in accordance with the U.S. Environmental Protection Agency's peer and administrative review policies and approved for publication. Mention of trade names or commercial products does not constitute endorsement or recommendation for use by the U.S. EPA.

References

1   R. G. Zepp, T. V. Callaghan and D. J. Erickson, III, Effects of enhanced solar ultraviolet radiation on biogeochemical cycles, *J. Photochem. Photobiol. B*, 1998, **46**, 69-82.

2   R. G. Zepp, T. V. Callaghan and D. J. Erickson, III, Effects of increased solar ultraviolet radiation on biogeochemical cycles, *Ambio*, 1995, **24**, 181-187.

3   IPCC, *IPCC guidelines for national greenhouse gas inventories*, OECD, Paris, France, 1997.

4   N. D. Paul, T. V. Callaghan, S. Moody, D. Gwynn-Jones, U.Johanson and C. Gehrke, in *Stratospheric ozone depletion: the effects of enhanced UV-B radiation on terrestrial ecosystems* ed.: J. Rozema, Backhuys Press, Leiden, 1999, pp. 117-134.

5   C. L. Ballaré, M. C. Rousseaux, P. S. Searles, J. G. Zaller, C. V. Giordano, T. M. Robson, M. M. Caldwell, O. E. Sala and A. L. Scopel, Impacts of solar ultraviolet-B radiation on terrestrial ecosystems of Tierra del Fuego (Southern Argentina). An overview of recent progress, *J. Photochem. Photobiol. B*, 2001, **62**, 67-77.

6   C. Gehrke, Effects of enhanced UV-B radiation on production-related properties of a *Sphagnum fuscum* dominated subarctic bog, *Funct. Ecol.*, 1998, **12**, 940-947.

7   M. Turunen, W. Heller, S. Stich, H. Sandermann, M.-L. Sutinen and Y. Norokorpi, The effects of UV exclusion on the soluble phenolics of young Scots pine seedlings in the subarctic., *Environ. Poll.*, 1999, **106**, 219-228.

8   K. J. Duguay and J. N. Klironomos, Direct and indirect effects of enhanced UV-B radiation on the decomposition and competitive abilities of saprobic fungi, *Appl. Soil. Ecol.*, 2000, **14**, 157-164.

9   S. A. Moody, K. K. Newsham, P. G. Ayres and N. D. Paul, Variation in the responses of litter and phylloplane fungi to UV-B radiation (290-315 nm). *Mycol. Res.*, 1999, **103**, 1469-1477.

10   P. S. Searles, S. D. Flint, S. B. Diaz, M. C. Rousseaux, C. L. Ballaré and M. M. Caldwell, Solar ultraviolet-B radiation influence on *Sphagnum* bog and *Carex* fen ecosystems: first field season findings in Tierra del Fuego, Argentina, *Global Change Biology*, 1999, **5**, 225-234.

11   D. Johnson, C. D. Campbell, D. Gwynn-Jones, J. A. Lee and T. V. Callaghan, Arctic soil microorganisms respond more to long-term ozone depletion than to atmospheric CO2, *Nature*, 2002, **416**, 82-83.

12   S. Moody, N. D. Paul, L. O. Björn, T. V. Callaghan, J. A. Lee, Y. Manetas, J. Rozema, D. Gwynn-Jones, U. Johanson, A. Kyparissis and A. Oudejans, The direct effects of UVB radiation on Betula pubescens litter decomposing at four European field sites., *Plant Ecol.*, 2001, **154**, 29-36.

13   K. K. Newsham, A. R. McLeod, J. D. Roberts, P. D. Greenslade and B. A. Emmet, Direct effects of elevated UV-B radiation on the decomposition of *Quercus robur* leaf litter, *Oikos*, 1997, **79**, 592-602.

14   D. W. Schade, R. M. Hoffman and P. J. Crutzen, CO emissions from degrading plant matter: measurements (I), *Tellus*, 1999, **51B**, 889-908.

15   K. Kisselle, R. Zepp, R. Burke, A. Pinto, M. Bustamante, S. Opsahl, R. Varella and L. Viana, Seasonal soil fluxes of carbon monoxide in burned and unburned Brazilian savannas, *J. Geophys. Res. D*, 2002, in press.

16   D. W. Schade and P. J. Crutzen, CO emissions from degrading plant matter: estimate of a global source strength (II), *Tellus*, 1999, **51B**, 909-918.

17   M. C. Peterson and R. E. Honrath, Observations of rapid photochemical destruction of ozone in snowpack interstitial air, *Geophys. Res. Lett.*, 2001, **28**, 511-514.

18   R. E. Honrath, M. C. Peterson, M. P. Dziobak, J. E. Dibb, M. A. Arsenault and S. A. Green, Release of NOx from sunlight-irradiated midlatitude snow, *Geophys. Res. Lett.*, 2000, **27**, 2237-2240.

19   A. E. Jones, R. Weller, P. S. Anderson, H. W. Jacobi, E. W. Wolff, O. Schrems and H. Miller, Measurements of NO_x emissions from the Antarctic snowpack, *Geophys. Res. Lett.*, 2001, **28**, 1499-1502.

20   Y. Dubowski and M. R. Hoffmann, Photochemical transformations in ice: implications for the fate of chemical species, *Geophys. Res. Lett.*, 2000, **27**, 3321-3324.

21   J. Rozema, B. Kooi, R. Broekman and L. Kuijper., in *Stratospheric ozone depletion: the effects of enhanced UV-B radiation on terrestrial ecosystems* ed.: J. Rozema, Backhuys Press, Amsterdam, 1999, pp. 135-156.

22   K. K. Newsham, P. D. Greenslade, V. H. Kennedy and A. R. McLeod, Elevated UV-B radiation incident on *Quercus robur* leaf canopies enhances decomposition of resulting leaf litter in soil, *Global Change Biology*, 1999, **5**, 403-409.

23   K. K. Newsham, J. M. Anderson, T. H. Sparks, P. Splatt, C. Woods and A. R. McLeod, UV-B effect on *Quercus robur* leaf litter decomposition persists over four years, *Global Change Biology*, 2001, **7**, 479-483.

24   W. J. Cybulski, W. T. Peterjohn and J. H. Sullivan, The influence of elevated ultraviolet-B radiation (UV-B) on tissue quality and decomposition of loblolly pine (*Pinus taeda* L.) needles, *Environ. Exp. Bot.*, 2000, **44**, 231-241.

25   K. K. Newsham, P. Platt, P. A. Coward, P. D. Greenslade, A. R. McLeod and J. M. Anderson, Negligible influence of elevated UV-B radiation on leaf litter quality of *Quercus robur*, *Soil Biol. Biochem.*, 2001, **33**, 659-665.

26   D.-P. Häder, H. D. Kumar, R. C. Smith and R. C. Worrest, Aquatic ecosystems: effects of increased solar ultraviolet radiation and interactions with other climatic change factors., *Photochem. Photobiol.*, 2002.

27   J. W. M. Van de Staaij, J. Rozema and R. Aerts, in *Stratospheric ozone depletion: the effects of enhanced UV-B radiation on terrestrial ecosystems* ed.: J. Rozema, Backhuys Press, Amsterdam, 1999, pp. 159-171.

28   B. Sølheim, U. Johanson, T. V. Callaghan, J. A. Lee, D. Gwynn Jones and L. O. Björn, The nitrogen fixation potential of arctic cryptogam species is influenced by enhanced UV-B radiation, *Oecologia*, 2002, **133**, 90-93.

29   M. M. Caldwell, C. L. Ballare, J. F. Bornman, S. D. Flint, L. O. Bjorn, A. H. Teramura, G. Kulandavailu and M. Tevini, Terrestrial ecosystems, increased solar ultraviolet radiation and interactions with other climatic change factors, *Photochem. Photobiol.*, 2002 In press.

30   H. A. Verhoef, J. M. H. Verspangen and H. R. Zoomer, Direct and indirect effects of ultraviolet-B radiation on soil biota, decomposition and nutrient fluxes in dune grassland soil systems, *Biol. Fert. Soils*, 2000, **31**, 366-371.

31   J. N. Klironomos and M. F. Allen, UV-B mediated changes on below-ground communities associated with the roots of *Acer saccharum.*, *Funct. Ecol.*, 1995, **9**, 923-930.

32   R. B. Myneni, J. Dong, C. J. Tucker, R. K. Kaufmann, P. E. Kauppi, J. Liski, L. Zhou, V. Alexeyev and M. K. Hughes, A large carbon sink in the woody biomass of northern forests, *Proc. Nat. Acad. Sci. USA*, 2001, **98**, 14784-14789.

33   R. B. Myneni, C. D. Keeling, C. J. Tucker, G. Asrar and R. R. Nemani, Increased plant growth in the northern high latitudes from 1981-1991, *Nature*, 1997, **386**, 698-702.

34   J. M. Melillo, A. D. McGuire, D. W. Kicklighter, B. Moore, III, C. J. Vorosmarty and A. L. Schloss, Global change and terrestrial net primary production, *Nature*, 1993, **363**, 234-240.

35   R. A. Betts, P. M. Cox, S. E. Lee and F. I. Woodward, Contrasting physiological and structural vegetation feedbacks in climate change simulations, *Nature*, 1997, **387**, 796-799.

36   P. Cox, R. Betts, C. Jones, S. Spall and I. Totterdell, Acceleration of global warming due to carbon-cycle feedbacks in a coupled climate model, *Nature*, 2000, **408**, 184-187.

37   R. Harding, P. Kuhry, T. R. Christensen, M. T. Sykes, R. Dankers and S. van der Linden, Climate feedbacks at the tundra-taiga interface., *Ambio Special Report*, 2002, 47-55.

38   O. Tenow, Hazards to a mountain birch forest--Abisko in perspective. Plant ecology in the subarctic Swedish Lapland, *Ecol. Bulls.*, 1996, **45**, 104-114.

39   S. Neuvonen, P. Niemelä and T. Virtanen, Climate change and insect outbreaks in boreal forests: the role of winter temperatures, *Ecol. Bulls.*, 1999, **47**, 63-67.

40   N. Buck and T. V. Callaghan, Impacts of increased UV-B radiation on the autumn moth caterpillar Epirrita autumnata. In: Animal responses to global change, *Ecol. Bulls.*, 1999, **47**, 68-76.

41   A. Lavola, R. Julkunen-Tiitto, P. Aphalo, T. de la Rosa and T. Lehto, The effect of UV-B radiation on UV-absorbing secondary metabolites in birch seedlings grown under simulated forest soil conditions, *New. Phytol.*, 1997, **137**, 617-621.

42   A. Lavola, R. Julkunen-Tiitto, H. Roininen and P. Aphalo, Host-plant preference of an insect herbivore mediated by UV-B and CO_2 in relation to plant secondary metabolites, *Biochem. Syst. Ecol.*, 1998, **26**.

43   K. A. Kvenvolden, Gas hydrate and humans, *Ann. NY Acad. Sci.*, 2000, **912**, 17-22.

44   C. H. Dimmer, P. G. Simmonds, G. Nickless and M. R. Bassford, Biogenic fluxes of halomethanes from Irish Peatland ecosystems, *Atmos. Environ.*, 2001, **35**, 321-330.

45   R. C. Rhew, B. J. Miller and R. Weiss, Natural methyl bromide and methyl chloride emissions from coastal salt marshes, *Nature*, 2000, **403**, 292-295.

46   Y. Yokouchi, Y. Noijiri, L. A. Barrie, D. Toom-Sauntry, T. Machida, Y. Inuzuka, H. Akimoto, H.-J. Li, Y. Fujinuma and S. Aoki, A strong source of methyl chloride to the atmosphere from tropical coastal land, *Nature*, 2000, **403**, 295-298.

47   R. L. McKenzie, L. O. Björn, A. Bais and M. Ilyas, in *******UNEP 2002 report on effects of ozone depletion* ed.: J. Van der Leun, 2003.

48   K. R. Solomon, X. Tang, S. R. Wilson, P. Zanis and A. F. Bais, Changes in tropospheric composition and air quality due to ozone depletion, *Photochem. Photobiol.*, 2002, in press.

49   W. C. Oechel, S. T. Hastings, G. Vourlitis, M. Jenkins, G. Riechers and N. Grulke, Recent change of Arctic tundra ecosystems from a net carbon dioxide sink to a source, *Nature*, 1993, **361**, 520-523.

50   W. C. Oechel, G. L. Vourlitis, S. J. Hastings and S. A. Bochkarev, Change in arctic CO2 flux over two decades: Effects of climate change at Barrow, Alaska, *Ecol. Apps*, 1995, **5**, 846-855.

51   J. M. Melillo, D. W. Kicklighter, A. D. McGuire, W. T. Peterjohn and K. M. Newkirk, in *Role of nonliving organic matter in the earth's carbon cycle* eds.: R. G. Zepp and C. H. Sonntag, John Wiley & Sons, New York, 1995, pp. 175-189.

52   A. D. McGuire and J. E. Hobbie, in *Modeling the Arctic System: A Workshop Report of the Arctic System Science Program*, The Arctic Research Consortium of the United States, Fairbanks, Alaska, 1997, pp. 53-54.

53   M. G. Öqvist and B. H. Svensson, Vascular plants as regulators of emissions from a subarctic mire ecosystem., *Geophys. Res. Lett.*, In press.

54   T. R. Christensen, A. Joabsson, L. Ström, N. Panikov, M. Mastepanov, M. Öquist, B. H. Svensson, H. Nykänen, P. Martikainen and H. Oskarsson, Factors Controlling Large Scale Variations in methane Emissions from Wetlands., submitted.

55   R. Niemi, P. J. Martikainen, J. Silvola, A. Wulff, S. Turtola and T. Holopainen, Elevated UV-B radiation alters fluxes of methane and carbon dioxide in peatland microcosms., *Global Change Biology*, 2002, **8**, 361.

56   M. M. Couteaux, M. Mousseau, M.L.Celerier and P. Bottner, Increased atmospheric CO2 and litter quality: decomposition of sweet chestnut leaf litter with animal food webs of different complexities., *Oikos*, 1991, **61**.

57   M. F. Cotrufo, P. Ineson and A. P. Rowland, Decomposition of tree litters grown under elevated CO2: effect of litter quality., *Plant and Soil*, 1994, **163**, 121-130.

58   R. L. Norby and M. F. Cotrufo, A question of litter quality, *Nature*, 1998, **396**, 17-18.

59   T. A. J. Kuhlbusch and P. J. Crutzen, A global estimate of black carbon in residues of vegetation fires representing a sink of atmospheric CO2 and a source of O2, *Global Biogeochem. Cycles*, 1996, **9**, 491-501.

60   T. A. J. Kuhlbusch, J. M. Lobert, P. J. Crutzen and P. Warneck, Molecular nitrogen emissions from denitrification during biomass burning, *Nature*, 1991, **351**, 135-137.

61   B. A. Kimball, P. I. Pinter, R. Garcia, R. LaMorte, G. W. Wall, D. J. Hunsaker, G. Wechsung, F. Wechsung and T. Kartschall, Productivity and water use of wheat under free-air CO2 enrichment., *Global Change Biology*, 1995, **1**, 429-442.

62   L. Negash and L. O. Björn, Stomatal closure by ultraviolet radiation, *Physiol. Plant.*, 1986, **66**, 360-364.

63   J. B. Kerr, G. Seckmeyer, A. F. Bais, G. Bernhard, M. Blumthaler, S. B. Diaz, N. Krotkov, D. Lubin, S. Madronich, R. L. McKenzie, A. A. Sabziparvar and J. Verdebout, in *Scientific Assessment of Ozone Depletion: 2002*, WMO (World Meteorological Organization), Global Ozone Research and Monitoring Project, Report No. 47, 2003, p. in press.

64   A. G. J. Buma, M. K. d. Boer and P. Boelen, Depth distributions of DNA damage in Antarctic marine phyto- and bacterioplankton exposed to summertime UV radiation., *J. Phycol.*, 2001, **37**, 200-208.

65   A. T. Banaszak and P. J. Neale, Ultraviolet radiation sensitivity of photosynthesis in phytoplankton from an estuarine environment, *Limnol. Oceanogr.*, 2001, **46**, 592-603.

66   K. Barbeau, E. L. Rue, K. W. Bruland and A. Butler, Photochemical cycling of iron in the surface ocean mediated by microbial iron(III)-binding ligands, *Nature*, 2001, **413**, 409-413.

67   S. W. Chisholm, Stirring times in the Southern Ocean, *Nature*, 2000, **407**, 685-687.

68   D. J. Erickson, III, J. L. Hernandez, P. Ginoux, W. Gregg, R. Kawa, M. Behrenfeld, W. Esaias, C. McClain and J. Christian, Atmospheric iron deposition to the surface ocean and remotely sensed color: A global satellite correlation analysis, *EOS Trans. AGU*, 2001, **81**, F57.

69   W. W. Gregg and M. E. Conkwright, Decadal changes in global ocean chlorophyll, *Geophys. Res. Lett.*, 2002, **29**.

70   D. P. Häder, H. D. Kumar, R. C. Smith and R. C. Worrest, Effects on aquatic ecosystems, *J. Photochem. Photobiol. B*, 1998, **46**, 53-68.

71   D. M. Leech and C. E. Williamson, In situ exposure to ultraviolet radiation alters the depth distribution of Daphnia, *Limnol. Oceanogr.*, 2001, **46**, 416-420.

72   S. C. Rhode, M.Pawlowski and R. Tollrian, The impact of ultraviolet radiation on the vertical distribution of zooplankton of the genus *Daphnia*, *Nature*, 2001, **412**, 69-72.

73   W. H. Jeffrey, P. Aas, M. M. Lyons, R. B. Coffin, R. J. Pledger and D. L. Mitchell, Ambient solar-radiation induced photodamage in marine bacterioplankton, *Photochem. Photobiol.*, 1996, **64**, 419-427.

74   W. H. Jeffrey, R. J. Pledger, P. Aas, S. Hager, R. B. Coffin, R. Vonhaven and D. L. Mitchell, Diel and depth profiles of DNA photodamage in bacterioplankton exposed to ambient solar ultraviolet radiation, *Marine Ecol. Prog. Ser.*, 1996, **137**, 283-291.

75   Y. Huot, W. H. Jeffrey, R. F. Davis and J. J. Cullen, Damage to DNA in bacterioplankton: A model of damage by ultraviolet radiation and its repair as influenced by vertical mixing, *Photochem. Photobiol.*, 2000, **72**, 62-74.

76   S. W. Wilhelm, M. G. Weinbauer, C. A. Suttle and W. H. Jeffrey, The role of sunlight in the removal and repair of viruses in the sea, *Limnol. Oceanogr.*, 1998, **43**, 586-592.

77   H. Gao and R. G. Zepp, Factors influencing photoreactions of dissolved organic matter in a coastal river of the southeastern United States, *Environ. Sci. Technol.*, 1998, **32**, 2940-2946.

78   S. C. Johannessen and W. L. Miller, Quantum yield for the photochemical production of dissolved inorganic carbon in the ocean, *Mar. Chem.*, in press.

79   A. V. Vähätalo, M. S.-Salonen, P. Taalas and K. Salonen, Spectrum of the quantum yield for photochemical mineralization of dissolved organic carbon in a humic lake, *Limnol. Oceanogr.*, 2001, **45**, 664-676.

80   S. Bertilsson and L. J. Tranvik, Photochemically produced carboxylic acids as substrates for freshwater bacterioplankton, *Limnol. Oceanogr.*, 1998, **43**, 885-895.

81   S. Bertilsson and L. J. Tranvik, Photochemical transformation of dissolved organic matter in lakes, *Limnol. Oceanogr.*, 2000, **45**, 753-762.

82   I. Obernosterer and G. J. Herndl, Differences in the optical and biological reactivity of the humic and nonhumic dissolved organic carbon component in two contrasting coastal marine environments, *Limnol. Oceanogr.*, 2000, **45**, 1120-1129.

83   I. Obernosterer, B. Reitner and G. J. Herndl, Contrasting effects of solar radiation on dissolved organic matter and its bioavailability to marine bacterioplankton, *Limnol. Oceanogr.*, 1999, **44**, 1645-1654.

84   M. A. Moran, W. M. Sheldon and J. E. Sheldon, Biodegradation of riverine dissolved organic carbon in five estuaries of the southeastern United States, *Estuaries*, 1999, **22**, 55-64.

85   M. A. Moran, W. M. Sheldon and R. G. Zepp, Carbon loss and optical property changes during long-term photochemical and biological degradation of estuarine dissolved organic matter, *Limnol. Oceanogr.*, 2000, **45**, 1254-1264.

86   M. A. Moran and R. G. Zepp, in *Microbial Ecology Of The Oceans* ed.: D. Kirchman, Wiley, New York, 2000, pp. 201-228.

87   K. Mopper and D. J. Kieber, in *The effects of UV radiation in the marine environment* eds.: S. de Mora, S. Demers and M. Vernet, Cambridge University Press, 2000, pp. 101-129.

88   A. M. Anesio, L. J. Tranvik and W. Graneli, Production of inorganic carbon from aquatic macrophytes by solar radiation, *Ecology*, 1999, **80**, 1852-1859.

89   R. Benner and B. Biddanda, Photochemical transformations of surface and deep marine dissolved organic matter: Effects on bacterial growth, *Limnol. Oceanogr.*, 1998, **43**, 1373-1378.

90   A. M. Anesio, C. M. T. Denward, L. J. Tranvik and W. Graneli, Decreased bacterial growth on vascular plant detritus due to photochemical modification, *Aquat. Microb. Ecol.*, 1999, **17**, 159-165.

91   L. J. Tranvik and S. Kokalj, Decreased biodegradability of algal DOC due to interactive effects of UV radiation and humic matter, *Aquat. Microb. Ecol.*, 1998, **14**, 301-307.

92   S. Ziegler and R. Benner, Effects of solar radiation on dissolved organic matter in a subtropical seagrass meadow, *Limnol. Oceanogr.*, 2000, **45**, 257-266.

93   S. Opsahl and R. G. Zepp, Photochemically-induced alteration of stable carbon isotope ratios ($*^{13}$C) in terrigenous dissolved organic carbon, *Geophys. Res. Lett.*, 2001, **28**, 2417-2420.

94   C. L. Osburn, D. P. Morris, K. A. Thorn and R. E. Moeller, Chemical and optical changes in freshwater dissolved organic matter exposed to solar radiation, *Biogeochem.*, 2001, **54**, 251-278.

95   S. S. Andrews, S. Caron and O. C. Zafiriou, Photochemical oxygen demand in marine waters: A major sink for colored dissolved organic matter?, *Limnology and Oceanography*, 2000, **45**, 267-277.

96   P. P. Vaughan and N. V. Blough, Photochemical formation of hydroxyl radical by constituents of natural waters, *Environ. Sci. Technol.*, 1998, **32**, 2947-2953.

97   B. H. Yocis, D. J. Kieber and K. Mopper, Photochemical production of hydrogen peroxide in Antarctic waters, *Deep Sea Res. Pt 1-Oceanog. Res. Pap.*, 2000, **47**, 1077-1099.

98   J. V. Goldstone and B. M. Voelker, Chemistry of superoxide radical in seawater: CDOM associated sink of superoxide in coastal waters, *Environ. Sci. Technol.*, 2000, **34**, 1043-1048.

99   J. V. Goldstone, M. J. Pullin, S. Bertilsson and B. M. Voelker, Reactions of hydroxyl radical with humic substances: Bleaching , mineralization, and production of bioavailable carbon substrates, *Environ. Sci. Technol.*, 2002, **36**, 364-372.

100   B. M. Voelker, D. L. Sedlak and O. C. Zafiriou, Chemistry of superoxide radicals (O_2^-) in seawater: Reactions with organic Cu complexes, *Envir. Sci. Technol.*, 2000, **34**, 1036-1042.

101   J. G. Qian and D. J. Kieber, Photochemical production of the hydroxyl radical in Antarctic water Deep-Sea Res. Part 1, *Oceanog. Res. Pap.*, 2001, **48**, 741-759.

102   T. E. Thomas-Smith and N. V. Blough, Photoproduction of hydrated electron from constituents of natural waters, *Envir. Sci. Technol.*, 2001, **35**, 2721-2726.

103   R. J. Kieber, W. J. Cooper, J. D. Willey and G. B. Avery, Hydrogen peroxide at the Bermuda Atlantic Time Series Station. Part 1: Temporal variability of atmospheric hydrogen peroxide an its influence on seawater concentrations., *J. Atmos. Chem.*, 2001, **39**, 1-13.

104   R. J. Kieber, K.Williams, J. D. Willey, S. Skrabal and G. B. Avery, Iron speciation in coastal rainwater:concentration and deposition to seawater, *Mar. Chem.*, 2001, **73**, 83-95.

105   L. Emmenegger, R. Schwarzenbach, L. Sigg and B. Sulzberger, Light-induced redox cycling of iron in circumneutral lakes, *Limnol. Oceanogr.*, 2000, **46**, 49-61.

106   W. Ludwig, The age of river carbon, *Nature*, 2001, **409**, 466.

107   W. L. Miller, M. A. Moran, W. M. Sheldon, R. G. Zepp and S. Opsahl, Determination of apparent quantum yield spectra for the formation of biologically labile photoproducts, *Limnol. Oceanogr.*, 2002, **47**, 343-352.

108   D. A. Siegel, S. Maritorena, N. B. Nelson, D. A. Hansell and M. Lorenzi-Kayser, Global distribution and dynamics of colored dissolved and detrital organic materials, *J. Geophys. Res.*, 2002, **107**, in press.

109   N. B. Nelson and D. A. Siegel, in *Biogeochemistry of Marine Dissolved Organic Matter* eds.: D. A. Hansell and C. A. Carlson, Academic Press, 2002.

110   N. B. Nelson, D.A.Siegel and A. F. Michaels, Seasonal dynamics of colored dissolved organic matter in the Sargasso Sea (Part I), *Deep Sea Res.*, 1998, **45**, 931-957.

111   A. Vodacek, N. V. Blough, M. D. DeGrandpre, E. T. Peltzer and R. K. Nelson, Seasonal variation of CDOM and DOC in the Middle Atlantic Bight: terrestrial inputs and photooxidation, *Limnol. Oceanogr.*, 1997, **42**, 674-686.

112   C. E. Williamson, R. S. Stemberger, D. P. Morris, T. M. Frost and S.G.Paulsen, Ultraviolet radiation in North American lakes: Attenuation estimates from DOC measurements and implications for plankton communities, *Limnol. Oceanogr.*, 1996, **41**, 1024-1034.

113   D. P. Morris, H. Zagarese, C. E. Williamson, E. G. Balseiro, B. R. Hargreaves, B. Modenutti, R. Moeller and C. Queimalinos, The attenuation of solar UV radiation in lakes and the role of dissolved organic carbon, *Limnol. Oceanogr.*, 1995, **40**, 1381-1391.

114   W. F. Donahue, D. W. Schindler, S. J. Page and M. P. Stainton, Acid induced changes in DOC quality in an experimental whole-lake manipulation, *Envir. Sci. Technol.*, 1998, **32**, 2954-2960.

115   R. F. Whitehead, S. d. Mora, S. Demers, M. Gosselin, P. Monfort and B. Mostajir, Interactions of ultraviolet-B radiation, mixing, and biological activity on photobleaching of natural chromophoric dissolved organic matter: A mesocosm study, *Limnol. Oceanogr.*, 2000, **45**, 278-291.

116   C. L. Osburn, H. E. Zagarese, D. P. Morris, B. R. Hargreaves and W. E. Cravero, Calculation of spectral weighting functions for the solar photobleaching of chromophoric dissolved organic matter in temperate lakes, *Limnol. Oceanogr.*, 2001, **46**, 1455-1467.

117   R. Del Vecchio and N. V. Blough, Photobleaching of chromophoric dissolved organic matter in natural waters: Kinetics and modeling, *Mar. Chem.*, 2003, In press.

118   I. Reche, M. L. Pace and J. J.Cole, Relationship of trophic and chemical conditions to photobleaching of dissolved organic matter in lake ecosystems, *Biogeochem.*, 1999, **44**, 259-280.

119   J. A. Fuhrman and D.G.Capone, Nifty nanoplanton, *Nature*, 2001, 593-594.

120   J. P. Zehr, J. B. Waterbury, P. J. Turner, J. P.Montoya, E. Omoregie, G. F. Steward, A. Hansen and D. M. Karl., Unicellular cyanobacteria fix N2 in the subtropical North Pacific Ocean, *Nature*, 2001, **412**, 635-638.

121   I. Berman-Frank, J. T.Cullen, Y. Shaked, R. M.Sherrell and P.G.Falkowski, Iron availability, cellular iron quotas, and nitrogen fixation in *Trichodesmium*, *Limnol. Oceanogr.*, 2001, **46**, 1249-1260.

122   J. M. Lenes, B. P. Darrow, C. Cattrall, C. A. Heil, M. Callahan, G. A. Vargo, R. H. Byrne, J. M. Prospero, D. E. Bates, K. A. Fanning and J. J. Walsh, Iron fertilization and the *Trichodesmium* response on the West Florida shelf, *Limnol. Oceanogr.*, 2001, **46**, 1261-1277.

123   K. L. Bushaw-Newton and M. A. Moran, Photochemical formation of biologically-available nitrogen from dissolved humic substances in coastal marine systems, *Aquat. Microb. Ecol.*, 1999, **18**, 185-292.

124   W. W. Wang, M. A.Tarr, T.S.Bianchi and E. Engelhaupt, Ammonium photoproduction from aquatic humic and colloidal matter, *Aquat. Geochem.*, 2000, **6**, 275-292.

125   D. J. Koopmans and D. A. Bronk, Photochemical production of inorganic nitrogen from dissolved organic nitrogen in waters of two estuaries and adjacent surficial groundwaters, *Aquat. Microb. Ecol.*, in press.

126   M. J. Boavida and R. G. Wetzel, Inhibition of phosphatase activity by dissolved humic substances and hydrolytic reactivation by natural ultraviolet light., *Freshwater Biol.*, 1998, **40**, 285-293.

127   E. M. Espeland and R. G. Wetzel, Complexation, stabilization, and UV photolysis of extracellular and surface-bound glucosidase and alkaline phosphatase: Implications for biofilm microbiota, *Microb. Ecol.*, 2001, **42**, 572-585.

128   D. J. Erickson, III, R. G. Zepp and E. Atlas, Ozone depletion and the air-sea exchange of greenhouse and chemically reactive trace gases, *Chemosphere-Global Change Science*, 2000, **2**, 137-149.

129   D. J. Erickson, III and J. L. Hernandez, in *American Geophysical Union Monograph: Gas Transfer at Water Surfaces* eds.: M. A. Donelan, W. M. Drennan, E. S. Saltzman and R. Wanninkhof, 2002, pp. 312-317.

130   O. C. Zafiriou, S. A. Andrews and W. Wang, Concordant estimates of oceanic carbon monoxide source and sink processes in the Pacific yield a balanced global "blue-water" CO budget, *Global Biogeochem. Cycles*, in press.

131   W. G. Sunda, D. J. Kieber, R. P. Kiene and S. A. Huntsman, An antioxidant function for DMSP and DMS in marine algae, *Nature*, 2002, **418**, 317-320.

132   M. A. J. Curran and G. B. Jones, Dimethyl sulfide in the Southern Ocean: Seasonality and flux, *J. Geophys. Res.*, 2000, **105**, 20,451-420,459.

133   R. Simó and C. Pedrós-Alió, Role of vertical mixing in controlling the oceanic production of dimethyl sulfide, *Nature*, 1999, **402**, 396-398.

134   D. A. Toole, D. J. Kieber, R. P. Kiene and D. A. Siegel, The quantum yield of dimethylsulfide (DMS) photooxidation in the Sargasso Sea, EOS Trans., *American Geophysical Union*, 2002, **83**.

135   D. Slezak, A. Brugger and G. J. Herndl, Impact of solar radiation on the biological removal of dimethylsuloniopropionate and dimethylsulfide in marine surface waters, *Aquat. Microb. Ecol.*, 2001, **25**, 87-97.

136   A. D. Hatton, Influence of photochemistry on the marine biogeochemical cycle of dimethylsulphide in the northern North Sea, *Deep Sea Res.*, 2002, **49**, 3039-3052.

137   D. Preiswerk and R. G. Najjar, A global, open-ocean model of carbonyl sulfide and its air-sea flux, *Global Biogeochem. Cycles*, 2000, **14**, 585-598.

138   D. W. Schindler, J. P. Curtis, B. R. Parker and M. P. Stainton, Consequences of climate warming and lake acidification for UV-B penetration in North American boreal lakes, *Nature*, 1996, **379**, 705-708.

139   D. A. Siegel and A. F. Michaels, Quantification of non-algal light attenuation in the Sargasso Sea: Implications for biogeochemistry and remote sensing, *Deep Sea Res.*, 1996, **43**, 321-346.

140   M. D. DeGrandpre, A. Vodacek, R. Nelson, E. J. Burce and N. V. Blough, Seasonal seawater optical properties of the U.S. Middle Atlantic Bight., *J. Geophys. Res.*, 1996, **101**, 22727-22736.

141   I. Laurion, M. Ventura, J. Catalan, R. Psenner and R.Sommaruga, Attenuation of ultraviolet radiation in mountain lakes: Factors controlling the among- and within-lake variability, *Limnol. Oceanogr.*, 2000, **45**, 1274-1288.

142   D. W. Schindler, Widespread effects of climatic warming on freshwater ecosystems in North America, *Hydrol. Process.*, 1997, **11**, 1043-1067.

143   D. P. Morris and B. R. Hargreaves, The role of photochemical degradation of dissolved organic matter in regulating UV transparency of three lakes on the Pocono Plateau, *Limnol. Oceanogr.*, 1997, **42**, 239-249.

144   P. Falkowski, R. J. Scholes, E. Boyle, J. Canadell, D. Canfield, J. Elser, N. Gruber, K. Hibbard, P. Högberg, S. Linder, F. T. Mackenzie, B. I. Moore, T. Pedersen, Y. Rosenthal, S. Seitzinger, V. Smetacek and W. Steffen, The global carbon cycle: A test of our knowledge of Earth as a system, *Science*, 2000, **290**, 291-296.

145   P. J. Neale, E. W. Helbling and H. Zagarese, in *UV effects in aquatic organisms and ecosystems* eds.: E. W. Helbling and H. Zagarese, Royal Society of Chemistry, Cambridge, UK, 2002, p. in press.

146   P. R. Leavitt, R. D. Vinebrooke, D. B. Donald, J. P. Smol and D. W. Schindler, Past ultraviolet radiation environments in lakes derived from fossil pigments, *Nature*, 1997, **388**, 457-459.

147   R. Pienitz and W. F. Vincent, Effect of climate change relative to ozone depletion on UV exposure in subarctic lakes, *Nature*, 2000, **404**, 484-487.

148   M. V. Moore, M. L. Pace, J. R. Mather, P. S. Murdoch, R. W. Howarth, C. L. Folt, C. Y. Chen, H. F. Hemond, P. A. Flebbe and C. T. Driscoll, Potential effects of climate change on freshwater ecosystems of the New England/Mid-Atlantic region, *Hydrol. Process.*, 1997, **11**, 925-947.

149   P. J. Mulholland, G. R. Best, C. C. Coutant, G. M. Hornberger, J. L. Meyer, P. J. Robinson, J. R. Stenberg, R. E. Turner, F. Veraherrera and R. G. Wetzel, Effects of climate change on freshwater ecosystems of the Southeastern United States and the Gulf Coast of Mexico, *Hydrol. Process.*, 1997, **11**, 949-970.

150   G. T. Ankley, S. A. Collyard, P. D. Monson and P. A. Kosian, Influence of ultraviolet light on the toxicity of sediments contaminated with polycyclic aromatic hydrocarbons., *Environ. Toxicol. Chem.*, 1994, **13**, 1791-1796.

151   G. T. Ankley, R. J. Erickson, G. L. Phipps, V. R. Mattson, P. A. Kosian, B. R. Sheedy and J. S. Cox, Effects of light intensity on the phototoxicity of fluoranthene to a benthic macroinvertebrate., *Environ. Sci. Technol.*, 1995, **29**, 2828-2833.

152   J. A. E. Gibson, W. F. Vincent, B. Nieke and R. Pienitz, Control of biological exposure to UV radiation in the Arctic Ocean: Comparison of the roles of ozone and riverine dissolved organic matter, *Arctic*, 2000, **53**, 372-382.

153   R. J. Kieber, B. Peake, J. D. Willey and B. Jacobs, Iron speciation and hydrogen peroxide concentration in New Zealand rainwater., *Atmos. Environ.*, 2001, **35**, 6041-6048.

154   W. G. Sunda, in *Role Of Non-Living Organic Matter in the Earth's Carbon Cycle* eds.: R. G. Zepp and C. Sonntag, Wiley, New York, 1994, pp. 191-207.

155   J. Butler, Atmospheric chemistry-Better budgets for methyl halides?, *Nature*, 2000, **403**, 260-261.

156   R. M. Moore and O. C. Zafiriou, Photochemical production of methyl iodide in seawater, *J. Geophys. Res.*, 1994, **99D**, 16415-16420.

157   R. M. Moore, R. Tokarczyk, V. K. Tait, M. Poulin and C. Green, in *Naturally-Produced Organohalogens* eds.: A. Grimvall and W. B. De Leer, Kluwer Academic Pub., 1995.

158   R. Wever, G. M. Tromp, B. E. Krenn, A. Marjani and Vantol, Brominating activity of the seaweed *Ascophyllum nodosum*, *Environ. Sci. Technol.*, 1991, **25**, 446-449.

CHAPTER 6. CHANGES IN TROPOSPHERIC COMPOSITION AND AIR QUALITY DUE TO STRATOSPHERIC OZONE DEPLETION

K. R. Solomon[a], X. Tang[b], S. R. Wilson[c], P. Zanis[d], and A. F. Bais[d]

[a]*Centre for Toxicology, University of Guelph, Guelph, ON, N1G 2W1, Canada.*

[b]*Peking University, Center of Environmental Sciences, Beijing 100871, China.*

[c]*Department of Chemistry, University of Wollongong, NSW, 2522, Australia.*

[d]*Aristotle University of Thessaloniki, Laboratory of Atmospheric Physics, Campus Box 149, 54006 Thessaloniki, Greece.*

Summary

Increased UV-B through stratospheric ozone depletion leads to an increased chemical activity in the lower atmosphere (the troposphere). The effect of stratospheric ozone depletion on tropospheric ozone is small (though significant) compared to the ozone generated anthropogenically in areas already experiencing air pollution. Modeling and experimental studies suggest that the impacts of stratospheric ozone depletion on tropospheric ozone are different at different altitudes and for different chemical regimes. As a result the increase in ozone due to stratospheric ozone depletion may be greater in polluted regions. Attributable effects on concentrations are expected only in regions where local emissions make minor contributions. The vertical distribution of NO_X ($NO + NO_2$), the emission of volatile organic compounds and the abundance of water vapor, are important influencing factors. The long-term nature of stratospheric ozone depletion means that even a small increase in tropospheric ozone concentration can have a significant impact on human health and the environment.

Trifluoroacetic acid (TFA) and chlorodifluoroacetic acid (CDFA) are produced by the atmospheric degradation of hydrochlorofluorocarbons (HCFCs) and hydrofluorocarbons (HFCs). TFA has been measured in rain, rivers, lakes, and oceans, the ultimate sink for these and related compounds. Significant anthropogenic sources of TFA other than degradation HCFCs and HFCs have been identified. Toxicity tests under field conditions indicate that the concentrations of TFA and CDFA currently produced by the atmospheric degradation of HFCs and HCFCs do not present a risk to human health and the environment.

The impact of the interaction between ozone depletion and future climate change is complex and a significant area of current research. For air quality and tropospheric composition, a range of physical parameters such as temperature, cloudiness and atmospheric transport will modify the impact of UV-B. Changes in the chemical composition of the atmosphere including aerosols will also have an impact. For example, tropospheric OH is the "cleaning" agent of the troposphere. While increased UV-B increases the OH concentration, increases in concentration of gases like methane, carbon monoxide and volatile organic compounds will act as sinks for OH in troposphere and hence change air quality and chemical composition in the troposphere. Also, changes in the aerosol content of the atmosphere resulting from global climate change may affect ozone photolysis rate coefficients and hence reduce or increase tropospheric ozone concentrations.

Introduction

Changes in air pollutants such as ozone (O_3), nitrogen oxides (NO_X), hydrogen peroxide (H_2O_2), formaldehyde (HCHO) and nitric acid (HNO_3) in the lower atmosphere (troposphere) have important implications for human and environmental health. Understanding the factors that influence the concentrations of these pollutants is important for the protection of humans and their environment. The relationship between ultraviolet-B radiation (UV-B, 280–315 nm) and the photolysis of atmospheric trace gases such as O_3, NO_2, H_2O_2, HCHO, and HNO_3 in the troposphere was reviewed in previous reports.[1, 2]

The previous report[1, 3] concluded that stratospheric ozone depletion causes changes in the chemical composition of the atmosphere through increased penetration of UV-B to the troposphere. Tropospheric ozone levels are sensitive to local concentrations of NO_X and hydrocarbons. Increased UV-B is expected to increase the concentration of hydroxyl and other peroxy radicals and result in faster removal of pollutants. The effects of UV-B increases on tropospheric constituents like ozone, while not negligible, will be difficult to detect because the concentrations of these species are also influenced by many other variable factors, such as anthropogenic emissions.

The replacement of the ozone-depleting chlorofluorocarbon (CFC) refrigerants with less persistent products such as the hydrochlorofluorocarbons (HCFCs) and hydrofluorocarbons (HFCs) has also raised the question of the environmental significance of their breakdown products. In the previous report the environmental and human health significance of these breakdown products were not completely understood.[1]

Here we present a brief review of relevant new information. In addition, a discussion of interactions between tropospheric composition, air quality, changes due to ozone depletion, and climate change has been added. The conclusions are based on the current state of the science.

Changes in Photodissociation Rate Coefficients due to Stratospheric Ozone Depletion

Reductions in stratospheric ozone cause increased penetration of UV-B radiation to the troposphere and increases the photodissociation rates of tropospheric ozone and other trace gases such as NO_X. The trends in photodissociation rates of tropospheric ozone and other chemical species were estimated by De Winter-Sorkina[4, 5] for the period 11/1978 to 4/1993, based on the TOMS/Nimbus-7 (version 7) total ozone data and Stratospheric Aerosol and Gas Experiment (SAGE) ozone trends together with experimental ozonesonde data. A three-dimensional chemical transport model was used to investigate the impact of changing photodissociation rates on tropospheric composition. The results showed that the trends in the daytime average photodissociation rate coefficient of ozone were + 18.0±4.7% (95% confidence interval) per decade in February at the surface for zonal averages between 40 and 50°N. More importantly, there were also significant tropospheric ozone photodissociation trends of between +3 and 15% per decade at the surface at northern mid-latitudes in spring, summer and the first half of autumn. Significant long-term trends in tropospheric ozone photodissociation rate coefficients below 50°S were predicted throughout the year, peaking at +42±15% per decade at the surface in October between 60 and 70°S. In general, the trends in ozone photodissociation rate coefficients due to stratospheric ozone depletion increased with altitude, reaching their maximum in winter-spring at about 8-12 km, the exact altitude depending on latitude. Overall, the trend in daytime average ozone photolysis rate coefficients is larger than the change in stratospheric ozone that caused them.

De Winter-Sorkina[5] found that the magnitude of the trends for the photodissociation rate coefficients for other atmospheric trace gases varied, although the regions and times of maximum impact were broadly the same as that for ozone photolysis. For example, at 40°N, the trends at the surface in January-April were calculated to be around +8 % per decade for the photolysis of CH_3CHO to produce CH_3, + 6% per decade for HNO_3 and + 2% per decade for H_2O_2, CH_3OOH and N_2O_5. Once again, much larger changes are observed at 60 to 70°S with a trend of near 25% per decade for the photolysis reaction for CH_3CHO listed above. The relative uncertainty in these estimates is similar to that of the ozone photolysis estimates.

Long-term global changes in tropospheric concentrations of ozone due to stratospheric ozone depletion have been calculated using the MOGUNTIA model[5] by assuming that trace gas emissions remained constant. This gave a trend of + 2.4±1.3% per decade for OH, - 1.8±1.3% per decade for CO and - 0.8±0.7% per decade for O_3 and CH_4. Thus, a small decrease in global tropospheric ozone was estimated due to stratospheric ozone reduction, with the tropospheric trends small or comparable to other factors, especially the changes due to anthropogenic emissions. The response of global OH concentrations to stratospheric ozone loss was found to be equivalent to the effect of a possible 10% NO_X emission increase and 85% of this response was found to be equal to an estimated 6.5% CO decrease or a possible 10% tropical H_2O increase.[6]

For all these chemical compounds, the observable impact of stratospheric ozone depletion on tropospheric trends can be overshadowed by local or regional emissions. Only in regions where local emissions make minor contributions will long-term effects due to stratospheric ozone reduction be clearly discernable from the changes due to other sources. However, the cumulative effect of long-term increases in ground level ozone concentrations may cause significant adverse environmental effects.

Changes in Chemical Composition of the Troposphere due to Stratospheric Ozone Depletion

The influence of increased UV-B photolysis on tropospheric chemical composition has been recognized more widely and has been examined in more detail recently through modeling and experimental studies. They include perturbations due to stratospheric ozone depletion as well as the influence of various tropospheric factors. The physical and chemical reactions involved in these processes have been reviewed previously.[1] The net ozone production or loss depends mainly on the NO_X concentration. Modeling studies suggest that an increase in UV-B (due to stratospheric ozone depletion) causes a decrease in tropospheric ozone in the clean environment of the southern hemisphere (very low NO_X), and an increase in tropospheric ozone in the polluted areas of the northern hemisphere.[7, 8] The near UV photolysis of other chemical species such as HCHO (λ<330 nm) or CH_3CHO (λ<330 nm), which are secondary sources of radicals, can also affect the surface ozone concentrations in an indirect way.[9]

However, in certain cases, the photochemical link between total and surface ozone can be perturbed by weather-related atmospheric transport. For example, low total-column ozone could be related to upper troposphere / lower stratosphere anticyclones associated on the one hand with large scale subsidence of ozone rich air masses, and on the other hand with fair weather conditions with large ozone formation.[10] Also, high total ozone column could be related to cut-off lows or upper troughs, synoptic systems associated with tropopause folds which may enhance the tropospheric ozone levels significantly within a few hours.[11]

Although the effects of change in UV intensity resulting from stratospheric ozone depletion on tropospheric chemistry are theoretically well understood from model calculations, there is a paucity of observational evidence. Stratospheric ozone is controlled by dynamical and chemical factors acting on different time scales and so the influence on surface UV-B and related tropospheric ozone chemistry should also act on different time scales. Long-term decreases in surface ozone in polar regions have been reviewed.[1] The first observational evidence of changes in tropical tropospheric ozone associated with stratospheric ozone changes on a time scale of an 11-year solar cycle has been identified using the TCO (tropospheric column ozone) data derived from the TOMS satellite data.[12]

On a day-to-day basis, i.e., when circulation in the upper troposphere / lower stratosphere causes variations in total ozone column,[13] there is even less observational evidence of the photochemical link between total and surface ozone due to the long lifetime of ozone and the fact that the photochemical link between total-column and surface ozone can be perturbed by dynamic coupling as discussed above. Thus, the photochemical influence of changing UV-B on in-situ ozone production and loss rate of 10% can easily be masked by transport effects, especially in late winter and at high latitudes.[14] In addition, the sensitivity of a regional scale photochemistry model to changes in UV radiation, caused by moderate variations in either the total ozone column (25 DU) or in the aerosol optical depth, was found to be small (<0.5nmol/mol for monthly average, June 1996).[15] Only under sufficiently large changes of UV-B (that is, a large change in total ozone column) and suitable meteorological conditions can such an influence be detected, as presented in a case study on Swiss mountains in late winter[14] and in a case study at Crete, Greece during the PAUR II (Photochemical Activity and solar Ultraviolet Radiation) campaign.[16]

A modeling study by Ma and Weele[17] emphasized that influences on tropospheric pollutants are not isolated from interactions with other factors. It was found that the response of net ozone production to stratospheric ozone depletion was different at different altitudes and for different chemical coherent regimes. In addition to the surface concentration of NO_X, the vertical distribution of NO_X as well as the emissions of non-methane hydrocarbons (NMHCs), the abundance of water vapor, and ozone itself, are important factors. The threshold NO_X concentration, at which the response to stratospheric ozone depletion of the net ozone production changes from negative to positive, depends on the chemical regime and varies during a day, but it is typically about 1 nmol/mol in a 24-h period. That is, it is around 100 times larger than the threshold NO_X concentration for ozone production. Water vapour and NMHCs can further modulate tropospheric ozone production.

The importance of the vertical distribution of NO_X on the net ozone production due to stratospheric ozone depletion in the polluted boundary region is illustrated in the observations of Brönnimann and co-authors[14, 18, 19] at two elevated sites in Europe (Chaumont; 1,140 m above sea level (ASL), and Rigi;1,030 m ASL) where enhanced near-surface ozone concentrations were recorded. Mean diurnal cycles of ozone concentration showed a strong increase from late morning to late afternoon and, at the same time a decrease at the high alpine site Jungfraujoch (3,580 m ASL). The different diurnal ozone cycles can both be explained photochemically by taking into account the large difference in NO_X concentrations (about two orders of magnitude). Brönnimann et al.[18] also attempted to quantify the effect of changing UV-B radiation on surface ozone peaks in a day-to-day scale using a time series of measurement at the mountain sites. Seven years of ozone, NO and NO_X data, meteorological measurements from Chaumont, total ozone and UV-B measurements from Arosa (1,847 m ASL), and surface albedo from satellite observations were investigated. The study was restricted to fair weather days with moderately high NO_X concentrations. The estimated net effect on ozone peaks is normally within a range of 4 nmol/mol, a range of about 6 nmol/mol is predicted for large UV-B changes. This is greater than 5% of the Swiss Air Quality 1 hour standard. Assuming that all other factors are constant, the trend due to the stratospheric ozone depletion observed in the last decades was found to be less than 0.12

nmol/mol/yr. A 3-D mesoscale photochemical model (Metphomod) gave similar results to these measurements.[20]

The Metphomod model calculations were performed for the entire Swiss Plateau,[20] , and for the large stratospheric ozone depletion used in their calculation the changes in near ground level ozone was 0-3 nmol/mol (See Figure 6-1). However, for the city of Zurich, they estimated changes of around + 5 nmol/mol for both the winter and summer "ozone event" they studied. In the urban airshed, such an increase could not simply be assigned, based on measurements, to stratospheric ozone depletion. However, it does represent a significant contribution to the overall ozone loading.

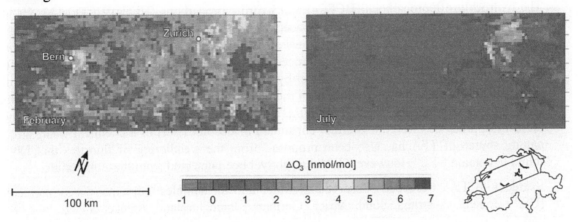

Figure 6-1 Ground level ozone production due to stratospheric ozone depletion. The calculations are for the region of Switzerland shown in the map. The left hand panel shows the calculated impact of ozone depletion from 400DU to 240DU for a simulation of an event in February 1998. The right hand panel shows a calculation for 30 July 1993, with an ozone decrease from 360DU to 280DU. (Figure based on the work of Brönnimann et al.[20])

Pirjola[21] used a Lagrangian model to assess the interaction of elevated UV-B, volatile organic compound (VOC) emissions from plants (isoprene and some terpenes) and SO_2. In the base case for emission rates of these organics, Pirjola reported a linear relationship between sulfate particle numbers and UV-B, with a 2.5-fold increase in particles for a 50% increase in UV-B. Under these conditions, the OH radical concentration increased by 9.8%. The concentration of biogenic organics is expected to increase with increasing CO_2, and Pirjola has investigated this also. The model shows a decrease in OH and particle formation and an increase in ozone with an increase in organics. The increase in particle formation through a UV-B (X_{UVB}(%)) enhancement can be offset by an increase in biogenic organics (Y_{Org}(%)) as described by

$$Y_{Org} = 1.23X_{UVB} + 3.34 \qquad (1)$$

Humidity, temperature, SO_2 emissions, and pre-existing particle concentrations were found to have little impact on the relationship.

The expected impact of stratospheric ozone depletion on formaldehyde (HCHO) is unclear, as both its production and destruction will be enhanced by ozone depletion. However, recent measurements of formaldehyde from Neumayer station in Antarctica[22] found roughly twice the HCHO concentration in the spring during the ozone hole period than observed at a corresponding time in autumn. This suggests that, at least under Antarctic conditions, the concentration is enhanced by stratospheric ozone depletion.

Over the past few years, significant advances have been made in understanding how aerosols affect actinic fluxes and therefore tropospheric chemistry. This advance benefited greatly from the UV monitoring networks that have been put in place to monitor stratospheric ozone depletion. Dickerson et al.[23] have shown that scattering by sulfate aerosols actually increases O_3 production in the planetary boundary layer (PBL) of the eastern USA. Absorbing aerosols will reduce photolysis rates and reduce PBL-O_3 production in polluted areas, but may actually reduce PBL-O_3 loss under low NO_X conditions, i.e. in more pristine regions.

Atmospheric Production, Fate, and Effects of Trifluoroacetic Acid and Related Substances

The hydrochlorofluorocarbons (HCFCs) and hydrofluorocarbons (HFCs) HCFC-123, HCFC-124 and HFC-134a degrade to give trifluoroacetic acid (TFA).[1] Use of HFCs may increase as the products are used to replace other products such SF_6, resulting in increased production of TFA. Environmental TFA can also be produced during the breakdown of other organofluorine compounds released to the atmosphere by human activities, e.g., halothane and isoflurane anesthetics. TFA is also produced through the breakdown of TFM (a lampricide), trifluoromethyl-containing agrochemicals such as trifluralin, and Teflon.[24, 25] TFA is widely used in the chemical industry in processes where it is either consumed or becomes part of a chemical waste stream. A natural source of TFA has also been proposed from the weathering of fluorites that have been found to contain CF_4.[26] However, TFA has not yet been detected from these materials.

Residues of TFA have been observed in water and air samples from many geographical areas (USA, Canada, Australia, South Africa, Germany, Israel, Ireland, France, Switzerland, Finland, and China) and show that TFA is a ubiquitous contaminant of the hydrosphere. Concentrations have been reported at up to 0.04 mg/L.[27] Another halogenated acetic acid with similar properties to TFA is chlorodifluoroacetic acid (CDFA), which is also the breakdown product of HCFCs, and is formed via degradative reactions occurring in the atmosphere.[28] Measured concentrations of CDFA are smaller than TFA. A maximum of 0.0002 ng/L was reported in water samples taken in Canada.[28] Both of these halogenated acetic acids (HAAs) are persistent in the environment.

Fate and Effects of TFA and CDFA in the Ecosystem

Fate

TFA and related products are water-soluble, have negligible vapor pressure, and accumulate in surface-waters (Figure 6-2).[1] Because of their great water solubility and low octanol-water partition coefficient (K_{OW}), TFA and related halogenated acetic acids (HAAs) are not likely to bioconcentrate, bioaccumulate, or biomagnify through the aquatic food chain, although accumulation in terrestrial plants has been observed following hydroponic exposures.[1] TFA is a stable ion in the aqueous phase and no significant loss process such as hydrolysis, photolysis, or formation of insoluble salts has been identified.[1] Degradation of TFA may occur under certain conditions in the laboratory.[1, 29] However, these processes appear to be less relevant in the

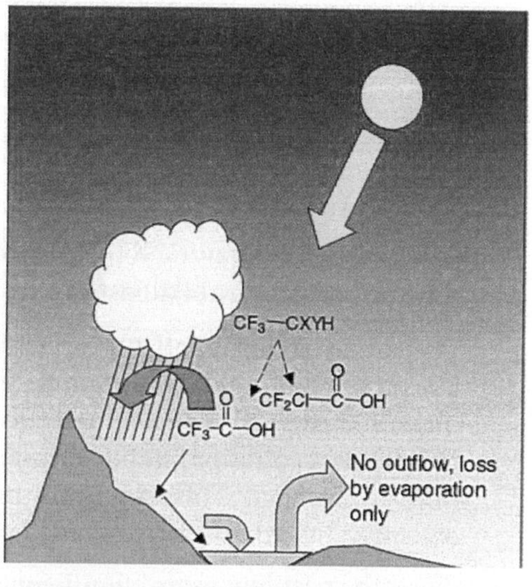

Figure 6-2 Illustration of the formation of persistent, water-soluble breakdown products of the HFCs and HCFCs (CF$_3$-CXYH) and their movement and concentration by evaporation, along with other water-soluble salts to surface waters

field. Studies in aquatic microcosms containing sediments and biota have not demonstrated any measurable dissipation of TFA over periods of up to two years.[30] Similarly, CDFA exhibited no degradation in outdoor aquatic microcosms over the period of almost a year.[31]

Toxicity to Aquatic Organisms

TFA is not considered highly toxic to aquatic plants and animals in acute laboratory studies.[1] Previous field studies on TFA showed that it did not alter the algal species composition in the stream microcosm.[1] Studies on the common aquatic plants *Myriophyllum spicatum* and *M. sibiricum* in outdoor microcosms exposed to TFA for 49 days showed no signs of toxicity at concentrations up to 10 mg/L TFA.[32]. Citrate concentrations in the plants were monitored and no increases were observed in exposed versus controls, implying that the citric acid cycle was not impacted at the concentrations used.[33] Similarly, CDFA demonstrated low toxicity to aquatic plants in laboratory studies EC25s of 14 – 18 mg/L in *Myriophyllum* spp.[28] and in microcosm studies, either on its own or in combination with TFA.[31]

Toxicity to Terrestrial Organisms

TFA is not considered highly toxic to terrestrial plants. No effects were observed in a variety of crop plants at concentrations ranging from 1 to 1,000 mg/L.[1] Effect concentrations for CDFA in terrestrial plants have not been reported in the literature. TFA is not metabolized in mammalian systems but is rapidly excreted. As the neutralized salt, TFA is not considered highly toxic to mammals via the inhalation or the oral route.[1] It is also not mutagenic and, although it has not been tested, is not considered a likely carcinogen.

Risk Assessment

The previous risk assessment of TFA was based on an estimated average concentration of 0.0001 mg/L in rainwater, by the year 2020.[1] With additional sources of TFA now identified, concentrations may be somewhat higher than this estimate. These concentrations are not expected to present risks to terrestrial plants through foliar soil absorption routes of exposure.

Based on a no observed effect concentration (NOEC) of about 0.10 mg/L (as TFA) for the most sensitive standard algal species, *Selenastrum capricornutum*, a predicted no effect concentration in aquatic systems (PNEC$_{aqua}$) of 0.1 mg/L was proposed.[1] Lack of effects of TFA on plants in aquatic microcosms under field conditions at concentrations up to 10 mg/L confirms low risk and the conservatism of the suggested PNEC$_{aqua}$.

On the basis of discussions in the previous review[1] and more recent information, risks from TFA in the ecosystem are judged to be low. Although less data exists for CDFA, risks from this substance are also judged to be low.

Uncertainties as to the sources of TFA in the environment have been reduced through the identification of other pathways of formation. However, CDFA has been identified as a persistent degradation product of the HCFCs. CDFA is not considered toxic to aquatic plants but sensitivity of other species has not been reported. Although additional data on environmental concentrations of TFA (and CDFA) have been reported, continuing monitoring is recommended to confirm trends in surface and rainwater.

Interactions with Global Climate Change

As discussed previously in this volume[34] and more fully elsewhere,[35, 36] interactions between climate change and stratospheric ozone depletion may occur through many chemical, radiative and dynamic mechanisms. For example, changes in temperature will change reaction rates, variations in cloudiness will have a direct impact upon photolysis rates, and long-range transport can change the chemical composition. Several authors have reviewed potential interactions between ozone depletion and climate change.[37-40] The review by Staehelin et al.[38] concluded that the interactions between stratospheric ozone depletion and climate change would be a productive research domain in the future. Only a few examples of the possible interactions will be given here.

Variations in ozone concentration, in particular in the upper troposphere and lower stratosphere, would be a crucial issue in the next decades because of links to climate change. Stratospheric ozone depletion leads to an increase in UV-B fluxes in the troposphere, which affect the photochemistry in the troposphere, especially the OH radicals. Increases in concentration of some greenhouse gases will act as sinks for OH in troposphere, thus changing air quality and composition in troposphere as suggested in the previous UNEP assessment[1] and by Ma and van Weele.[17] Studies by Prinn et al.[41] using methyl-chloroform, suggest a recent decrease in global OH that may be due to anthropogenic emissions. An increase in atmospheric CO_2 concentration would accelerate photosynthesis, (CO_2 fertilization) which might enhance the emissions of biogenic VOC's in forests and other natural ecological systems, and their oxidation reactions with hydroxyl radical which will act as a sink for OH.[21]

Other sources of tropospheric air pollutants may be affected by global warming. It is known that local and large-scale biomass fires such as are used for land-clearing are rich sources of NO_X, CO, CH_4, and other NMHCs, leading to enhanced tropospheric ozone production.[42] During the 1994 South-East Asian haze episode (September-October 1994), measurements in Asia showed increased tropospheric concentrations of NO_X (up to double) and ozone (~20%).[43] Besides extensive forest fires, local burning of biomass and fossil fuels also would have contributed to this. Thus, climate changes resulting from global warming may increase the risk of large-scale forest and brush-fires which affect concentrations of tropospheric air pollutants. Also, forest-fires induce haze aerosols that can increase multiple scattering, thus improving the efficiency of UV-B absorption of the boundary layer ozone. However, ozone production in the boundary layer may also be hindered by UV-B absorption by aerosols.[44]

Changes in the aerosol content of the atmosphere associated with global change may affect ozone photolysis rates[45] and hence the tropospheric ozone levels. It was calculated that soot particles and mineral dust particles can reduce the ozone photolysis rate by 6% to 11%[45], and reductions of up to 50% have been estimated elsewhere.[44, 46] During the Sahara dust events in the PAUR II campaign, Balis et al.[47] reported greatest effects on production of excited oxygen atoms ($J(O^1D)$) during days with high aerosol content. Box model calculations for a case study during the same experiment at Crete were carried out. The model indicated that the presence of absorbing aerosols offset part of the increase in local net ozone production rate caused by the decrease in total column ozone concentration when enough NO_X was present.[16] A sensitivity analysis of photolysis rates and ozone production in the troposphere in response to aerosol properties used a coupled transport-chemistry-radiative transfer model,[48] and reported reductions in ground level ozone concentrations of up to 70% in the presence of absorbing aerosols in the boundary layer (Figure 6-3).

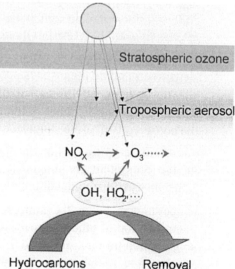

Figure 6-3 Illustration of the impact of tropospheric aerosols upon atmospheric chemistry. The aerosol can reduce the intensity of radiation, leading to a reduction in ozone production. Such a reduction offsets the impact of stratospheric ozone depletion

Although it is recognized that tropospheric ozone and other air pollutants are important with respect to human health and the environment, these pollutants are largely anthropogenic and concentrations vary in response local human activity. The impact of the coupling of stratospheric ozone depletion and climate change on concentrations of pollutant will be difficult to quantify experimentally, even though it could be significant, especially in the regions where air quality has a large impact on human health.

Since global warming is expected to increase demand for refrigerants, the breakdown products of these substances are likely to increase in concentration in the troposphere at a greater than expected rate. While this could increase concentrations of persistent breakdown products such as TFA and CDFA, inputs to most environments would still be small enough (by a factor of about 1,000) that biologically significant concentrations would not be expected to occur in flowing surface waters. However, in areas where there is little or no outflow and increased evaporation due to increased surface temperatures, these products are expected to increase in concentration. While this may present a risk to aquatic organisms, these areas would also experience increases in concentrations of other water-soluble materials such as has already occurred in salt lakes and playas. The effects of these naturally occurring salts and other materials would likely be greater and more biologically significant than those of TFA or CDFA and would occur in the absence of these substances anyway. The results of this interaction with global climate change are judged to be of low significance.

References

1   X. Tang, S. Madronich, T. Wallington and D. Calamari, Changes in tropospheric composition and air quality, *J. Photochem. Photobiol. B.*, 1998, **46**, 83–95.

2   D. L. Albritton, P. J. Aucamp, G. Megie and R. T. Watson, (Eds.), Scientific Assessment of Ozone Depletion: 1998, Global Ozone Research and Monitoring Project, World Meteorological Organization Report No. 44, Geneva.

3   J. C. van der Leun, M. Tevini, X. Tang and R. C. Worrest, Environmental Effects of Ozone Depletion: 1998 Update, United Nations Environment Programme, Nairobi, 1998, p. 192.

4   R. De Winter-Sorkina, Impact of ozone layer depletion I: Ozone depletion climatology, *Atmos. Environ.*, 2001, **35**, 1609-1614.

5   R. De Winter-Sorkina, Impact of ozone layer depletion II: Changes in photodissociation rates and tropospheric composition, *Atmos. Environ.*, 2001, **35**, 1615-1625.

6   M. Krol, P. J. Van Leeuwen and J. Lelieveld, Global OH trend inferred from methylchloroform measurements, *J. Geophys. Res.*, 1998, **103**, 10697-10711.

7   A. M. Thompson, R. W. Stewart, M. A. Owens and J. A. Herwehe, Sensitivity of tropospheric oxidants to global chemical and climate change, *Atmos. Environ.*, 1989, **23**, 519-532.

8   S. Madronich and C. Granier, Impact of recent total changes on tropospheric ozone photodissociation, hydroxyl radicals, and methane trends, *Geophys. Res. Lett*, 1992, **19**, 465-467.

9   A. Ruggaber, R. Dlugi and T. Nakajimax, Modelling radiation quantities and photolysis frequencies in the troposphere, *J. Atmos. Chem.*, 1994, **18**, 171-210.

10   P. Zanis, E. Schuepbach, H. W. Gaeggeler, S. Huebener and L. Tobler, Factors controlling berrylium-7 at Jungfraujoch in Switzerland, *Tellus*, 1999, **51**, 789-805.

11   G. Vaughan and G. D. Price, in *Ozone in the atmosphere* eds.: R. D. Bojkov and P. Fabian, Deepak Publ, 1989, pp. 415-418.

12   S. Chandra, J. R. Ziemke and R. W. Stewart, An 11-year solar cycle in tropospheric ozone from TOMS measurements, *Geophys. Res. Lett*, 1999, **26**, 185-188.

13   G. Vaughan and J. D. Price, On the relation between total ozone and meteorology, *J. Roy. Meteorol. Soc.*, 1991, **117**, 1281-1298.

14   S. Brönnimann and U. Neu, A possible photochemical link between stratospheric and near-surface ozone on Swiss mountain sites in late winter, *J. Atmos. Chem.*, 1998, **31**, 299-319.

15   J. E. Jonson, A. Kylling, T. Berntsen, I. S. A. Isaksen, C. S. Zerefos and K. Kourtidis, Chemical effects of UV fluctuations inferred from total ozone and tropospheric aerosol variations, *J. Geophys. Res.*, 2000, **105**, 14561-14574.

16   P. Zanis, K. Kourtidis, B. Rappenglueck, B. Balis, D. Melas, C. Zerefos, R. Schmitt, S. Rapsomanikis and P. Fabian, A case study on the link between surface ozone photochemistry and total ozone during the PAURII experiment at Crete - Comparison of observations with box model calculations, *J. Geophys. Res.*, 2002, **107**, 10.1029/2000JD000137.

17   J. Ma and M. van Weele, Effect of stratospheric ozone depletion on the net production of ozone in polluted rural areas, *Chemosphere Global Change Sci.*, 2000, **2**, 23-37.

18   S. Brönnimann, S. Voigt and H. Wanner, The influence of changing UVB radiation in near-surface ozone time series, *J. Geophys. Res.*, 2000, **105**, 8901-8913.

19   S. Brönnimann, Early spring ozone episodes: Occurrence and case study, *Phys. Chem. Earth*, 1999, **24**, 531-536.

20   S. Brönnimann, W. Eugster and H. Wanner, Photo-oxidant chemistry in the polluted boundary layer under changing UV-B radiation, *Atmos. Environ.*, 2001, **35**, 3789-3797.

21   L. Pirjola, Effects of the increased UV radiation and biogenic VOC emissions on ultrafine sulfate aerosol formation, *J. Aerosol Sci.*, 1999, **30**, 355-367.

22   K. Riedel, R. Weller and O. Schrems, The effect of UV-radiation on photo-oxidants and formaldehyde in the atmosphere, in *UV Radiation and its effects: An update* (Eds.: R. L. McKenzie, A. Reisinger and C. Watts), Royal Society of New Zealand, Christchurch, New Zealand, 2002, p.??

23   R. Dickerson, S. Kondragunta, G. Stenchikov, K. Civerolo, B. Doddridge and B. Holben, The impact of aerosol on solar UV radiation and photochemical smog, *Science*, 1997, **278**, 827-830.

24   D. A. Ellis, S. A. Mabury, J. W. Martin and D. C. G. Muir, Thermolysis of fluoropolymers as a potential source of halogenated organic acids in the environment, *Nature*, 2001, **412**, 321-324.

25   D. Ellis and S. A. Mabury, The aqueous photolysis of TFM and related trifluoromethylphenols. An alternate source of trifluoroacetic acid in the environment, *Environ. Sci. Technol.*, 2000, **34**, 632-637.

26   J. Harnisch, M. Frische, R. Borchers, A. Eisenhauer and A. Jordan, Naturally fluorinated organics in fluorite and rocks, *Geophys. Res. Lett*, 2000, **27**, 1883-1886.

27   D. Zehavi and J. N. Seiber, An analytical method for trifluoroacetic acid in water and air samples using headspace gas chromatographic determination of the methyl ester, *Anal. Chem.*, 1996, **68**, 3450-3459.

28   J. W. Martin, J. Franklin, M. L. Hanson, K. R. Solomon, S. A. Mabury, D. A. Ellis, B. F. Scott and D. C. G. Muir, Detection of chlorodifluoroacetic acid in precipitation: a possible product of fluorocarbon degradation, *Environ. Sci. Technol.*, 2000, **34**, 274-281.

29   B. R. Kim, M. T. Suidan, T. J. Wallington and X. Du, Biodegradability of trifluoroacetic acid, *Environ. Eng. Sci.*, 2000, **17**, 337-342.

30   D. A. Ellis, M. L. Hanson, P. K. Sibley, T. Shahid, N. A. Fineburg, K. R. Solomon, D. C. G. Muir and S. A. Mabury, The fate and persistence of trifluoroacetic and chloroacetic acids in pond waters, *Chemosphere*, 2001, **42**, 309-318.

31   M. L. Hanson, P. K. Sibley, K. R. Solomon, S. A. Mabury and D. C. G. Muir, Chlorodifluoroacetic acid (CDFA) fate and toxicity to the macrophytes *Lemna gibba*, *Myriophyllum spicatum* and *Myriophyllum sibiricum* in aquatic microcosms, *Environ. Toxicol. Chem.*, 2001, **20**, 2758-2767.

32   M. Hanson, P. K. Sibley, D. Ellis, N. Fineberg, S. Mabury, K. R. Solomon and D. Muir, Trichloroacetic acid (TCA) fate and toxicity to the macrophytes *Myriophyllum spicatum* and *Myriophyllum sibiricum* under field conditions, *Aquat. Toxicol.*, 2001, **56**, 241-255.

33   M. Hanson, P. K. Sibley, K. R. Solomon, S. Mabury and D. Muir, Trichloroacetic acid (TCA) and trifluoroacetic acid (TFA) mixture toxicity to the macrophytes *Myriophyllum spicatum* and *Myriophyllum sibiricum* in aquatic microcosms, *Sci. Tot. Environ.*, 2002, **285**, 247-259.

34   R. L. McKenzie, L. O. Bjorn, A. Bais and M. Ilyas, Changes in biologically active ultraviolet radiation reaching the Earth's surface, *Photochemical and Photobiological Science*, 2003, **In Press**.

35   WMO (World Meteorological Organization), Scientific Assessment of Ozone Depletion: 2002, Global Ozone Research and Monitoring Project, World Meteorological Organization Report No. 47, Geneva, Switzerland, 1999.

36   IPPC, *Climate Change 2001: The Scientific Basis. Contribution of Working Group I to the Third Assessment Report of the Intergovernmental Panel on Climate Change*, Cambridge University Press, Cambridge, UK, 2001.

37   P. Taalas, J. Kaurola and A. Kylling, The impact of greenhouse gases and halogenated species on future solar UV radiation doses, *Geophys. Res. Lett*, 2000, **27**, 1127-1130.

38   J. Staehelin, N. R. P. Harris and C. Appenzeller, Ozone trends: a review, *Rev. Geophys.*, 2001, **39**, 231-290.

39   D. T. Shindell, Climate and ozone response to increased stratospheric water vapor, *Geophys. Res. Lett*, 2001, **28**, 1551-1554.

40   D. T. Shindell, G. A. Schmidt, R. L. Miller and et al., Northern hemisphere winter climate response to greenhouse gas, ozone, solar and volcanic forcing, *J. Geophys. Res.*, 2001, **106**, 7193-7210.

41   R. G. Prinn, J. Huang, R. F. Weiss, D. M. Cunnold, P. J. Fraser, P. G. Simmonds, A. McCulloch, C. Harth, P. Salameh, S. O'Doherty, R. J. H. Wang, L. Porter and B. R. Miller, Evidence for substantial variations of atmospheric hydroxyl radicals in the past two decades, *Science*, 2001, **292**, 1881-1888.

42   W. J. Collins, D. S. Stephenson, C. E. Johnson and R. G. Derwent, Trophospheric ozone in a global-scale three-dimensional langrangian mode and its response to NO_x emission controls, *J. Atmos. Chem.*, 1997, **26**, 223-274.

43   M. Ilyas, A. Pandy and M. S. Jaafar, Changes to surface-level uvltaviolet-B radiation due to haze perturbation, *J. Atmos. Chem.*, 2001, **40**, 111-121.

44   J. P. Greenberg, A. B. Guenther, S. Madronich, W. Baugh, P. Ginoux, A. Druilhet, R. Delmas and C. Delon, Biogenic volatile organic compound emissions in central Africa during the Experiment for the Regional Sources and Sinks of Oxidants (EXPRESSO) biomass burning season, *J. Geophys. Res.*, 1999, **104**, 30659-30671.

45   H. Liao, Y. L. Yung and J. H. Seinfeld, Effects of aerosols on tropospheric photolysis rates in clear and cloudy atmospheres, *J. Geophys. Res.*, 1999, **104**, 23697-23707.

46   T. Castro, S. Madronich, S. Rivale, A. Muhlia and B. Mar, The influence of aerosols on photochemical smog in Mexico City, *Atmos. Environ.*, 2001, **35**, 1765-1772.

47   D. Balis, C. S. Zerefos, K. Kourtidis, A. F. Bais, A. Hofzumahaus, A. Kraus, R. Schmitt, K. Blumthaler and G. P. Gobbi, Measurements and modeling of the photolysis rates during the PAUR II campaign, *J. Geophys. Res.*, 2002, **107**, 10.1029/2000JD000136.

48   S. He and G. R. Carmichael, Sensitivity of photolysis rates and ozone production in the troposphere to aerosol properties, *J. Geophys. Res.*, 1999, **104**, 26307-26324.

CHAPTER 7. EFFECTS OF CLIMATE CHANGE AND UV-B ON MATERIALS

A. L. Andrady[a], H. S. Hamid[b] and A. Torikai[c]

[a]*Research Triangle Institute, Research Triangle Park, NC 27709 U.S.A.*

[b]*King Fahd University of Petroleum and Minerals, Dhahran, Saudi Arabia.*

[c]*Daido Institute of Technology, Minami-ku, Nagoaya 457-8630 Japan.*

Summary

The outdoor service life of common plastic materials is limited by their susceptibility to solar ultraviolet radiation. Of the solar wavelengths the UV-B component is particularly efficient in bringing about photodamage in synthetic and naturally occurring materials. This is particularly true of plastics, rubber and wood used in the building and agricultural industries. Any depletion in the stratospheric ozone layer and resulting increase in the UV-B component of terrestrial sunlight will therefore tend to decrease the service life of these materials. The extent to which the service life is reduced is, however, difficult to estimate as it depends on several factors. These include the chemical nature of the material, the additives it contains, the type and the amount of light-stabilizers (or protective coatings) used, and the amount of solar exposure it receives. Concomitant climate change is likely to increase the ambient temperature and humidity in some of the same regions likely to receive increased UV-B radiation. These factors, particularly higher temperatures, are also well known to accelerate the rate of photodegradation of materials, and may therefore further limit the service life of materials in these regions. To reliably assess the damage to materials as a consequence of ozone layer depletion, the wavelength sensitivity of the degradation process, dose-response relationships for the material and the effectiveness of available stabilizers need to be quantified. The data needed for the purpose are not readily available at this time for most of the commonly used plastics or wood materials. Wavelength sensitivity of a number of common plastic materials and natural biopolymers are available and generally show the damage (per photon) to decrease exponentially with the wavelength. Despite the relatively higher fraction of UV-A in sunlight, the UV-B content is responsible for a significant part of light-induced damage of materials.

The primary approach to mitigation relies on the effectiveness of the existing light stabilizers (such as hindered amine light stabilizers, HALS) used in plastics exposed to harsh solar UV conditions coupled with climate change factors. In developing advanced light-stabilizer technologies, more light-resistant grades of common plastics, or surface protection technologies for wood, the harsh weathering environment created by the simultaneous action of increased UV-B levels due to ozone depletion as well as the relevant climate change factors need to be taken into consideration. Recent literature includes several studies on synergism of HALS-based stabilizers, stabilizer effectiveness in the new m-polyolefins and elucidation of the mechanism of stabilization afforded by titania pigment in vinyl plastics.

Introduction

Materials that are deleteriously affected on exposure to UV-B radiation include man-made polymers (plastics and rubber materials)[1, 2] as well as naturally-occurring biopolymers such as wood[3], wool[4] skin proteins[5], and hair.[6] Both natural, and man-made materials are widely used in the building industry about a third of the plastics produced in Western Europe and in the US is used in building and agricultural applications. Some of the building products, for instance roofing materials, plastic or wood siding, window frames, glazing, water tanks, rain ware (gutters) and plastic conduit are routinely exposed to sunlight during regular use. Numerous plastic products exposed outdoors photodegrade slowly on exposure to solar radiation, steadily loosing their useful physical and mechanical attributes. This degradation is accelerated by higher ambient temperatures and in some polymers by the presence of moisture and pollutants in the atmosphere. The use of plastics outdoors is feasible only because of the use of efficient photostabilizers designed to slow down this degradation process. A large body of information exists on stabilizer technologies aimed at extending the service life of plastics exposed to outdoor environments.

Stratospheric ozone depletion and the ensuing increase in UV-B levels in terrestrial sunlight will tend to reduce the service life of plastic products used outdoors. With concurrent global warming, the service lifetimes of plastics are likely to be further affected as higher temperatures generally accelerate the chemical reactions responsible for the photodamage.[2, 7] The predicted average increase in ambient global air temperatures due to global warming (1.4 to 5.8° C above 1990 values by 2100[8]) is not expected to unduly accelerate the degradation of plastics or wood. Yet, the effect could be significant at locations with higher extreme temperatures. Also, the surface temperatures of materials exposed to direct sunlight is often much higher than that of the surrounding air due to heat build up.[9] As the relationship between the rate of degradation reactions and temperature is exponential, even a small increase in the temperature of an exposed plastic surface, already at a high temperature, can result in very significant increases in the rate of the photo damage.

In regions where climatic changes caused by global warming results in higher rainfall or humidity, the situation is even further exacerbated. In both wood[10] and moisture susceptible plastics[11, 12], photodegradation can be significantly accelerated by the presence of high humidity, particularly at the higher temperatures. The effect is well documented and higher temperatures and humidity are routinely used to accelerate the photodegradation of plastics and rubber in laboratory exposure tests. The geographic distribution of these modifying influences of temperature and humidity has not been fully investigated. Higher ambient temperature and rainfall due to climate change are expected in some of the same geographical regions likely to experience higher UV-B radiation. Regions that would experience particularly harsh exposure conditions, however, would include developing regions of the world that rely particularly heavily on wood and plastics for construction. Wood remains the primary material of residential construction in many parts of the developing world. Also, high volume users of plastics include many developing countries. For instance, China is presently the second largest producer of plastic resin in the world with 19 million tons produced in 2000.

Maintaining the service life of plastics products used outdoors at the same level despite harsh UV-environments due to ozone depletion and contributing climatic conditions may be possible with a combination of strategies. The use of higher concentrations of conventional UV stabilizers or the development of novel highly efficient UV-B stabilizers is the most likely response of the plastics industry. The use of surface protection, particularly in the case of wood, and substitution of materials with better UV-resistant grades of plastics, are also available strategies. These, however, add to the cost of the plastic products and in some markets can potentially affect the competitiveness of plastics as a material. A critical question, however, is whether the available photostabilizer technologies will function adequately with spectrally altered sunlight due to the stratospheric ozone loss. Materials substitution with more UV resistant plastics is feasible and candidate plastics are available for the purpose but at a significant cost. In the case of wood surfaces paints or coatings as well as UV-B stabilizers presents a feasible mitigation strategy.[13] While some success has been reported recently for the surface modification of wood to improve UV stability[8, 14], this is a more expensive and less satisfactory option.

A good assessment of the potential impact of stratospheric ozone depletion on the lifetimes of materials and the available strategies for mitigation requires key research information on at least the common polymers and wood. Of particular interest are: a) estimates of the increase in UV-B content expected in sunlight as well as the temperature/humidity variations due to global climate change; b) reliable wavelength sensitivity data and the dose-response relationships in the photodegradation of common polymers; and c) data on the efficacy of available UV stabilizers under spectrally altered sunlight conditions.[15] The data presently available on the topic is inadequate for a reliable assessment, but additional information is slowly being published in the literature.

Recent Findings

Wavelength Sensitivity of Photodegradation

It is important to quantify the relationship between the wavelength of UV radiation and the efficiency of degradation for common polymers. This would allow the estimation of damage to these materials under different UV environments (corresponding to various geographic locations or to different ozone-depletion scenarios) and help in the design of new light stabilizers. Published data on the wavelength sensitivity for the degradation processes in common polymers have been reviewed in recent years.[16] Data are presently available for a range of common materials (including polyethylene, polypropylene, poly(vinyl chloride) (PVC), polycarbonate, polystyrene), mechanical pulp (wood), wool, human hair, and skin proteins. The general relationship between the wavelength of UV-B radiation and the efficiency of photodamage for these materials is not linear. The degradation per available unit of UV radiation decreases exponentially as the wavelength of the UV radiation increases.[17] Given the high efficiency of photodamage, even small increases in UV-B content in sunlight can potentially result in marked increases in the rates of photodegradation in common polymer materials.

An important observation is that during processing, the plastics resin is mixed with a number of other chemicals (collectively referred to as additives) to impart key properties to the plastic material. For instance, the photostabilizer additives impart UV stability to the resin; other additives such as lubricants, fillers or heat stabilizers are used to obtain different properties. However, some of these additives can also alter the UV susceptibility of the material. Therefore, the more valuable wavelength sensitivity information is that pertaining to plastics materials that have the same composition (in terms of additives and stabilizers in the formulation) as the products of interest.

In the last few years, several publications have augmented the available information on wavelength sensitivity of polymeric materials. Two such studies focused on acrylic plastics[18] used in construction applications while another addressed the UV-induced damage to collagen[19] a key protein in human skin. Another, reported on the light-induced yellowing of mechanical pulps exposed to solar UV wavelengths.[17] The exposures were carried out at selected ultraviolet wavelengths between 270 and 400 nm and chemical changes indicative of degradation were monitored. The findings were consistent with data trends well established in the literature and summarized above. In a study on polyether-polyester elastomers, Nagai et al.[12] found UV-B wavelengths to be responsible for the chain-scission type damage that deteriorates the strength and elasticity of the material. Another important study was on light-induced damage to polystyrene plastics compounded with a flame retardant additive[1] that reduces the risk of fire when the plastic is used as building construction materials. Interestingly, this additive also acted as a catalyst accelerating the photodamage. Also, the waveband that resulted in the most efficient degradation shifted from UV-B into the UV-A when the flame retardant was used as an additive. An additive that shifts the most effective waveband to UV-A is generally undesirable. Although the longer UV-A wavelengths are not affected by stratospheric ozone depletion, the relatively higher fraction of UV-A, compared to UV-B, in terrestrial solar radiation is likely to increase the amount of photodamage. A drawback in these experiments on wavelength sensitivity is that the studies were generally carried out at ambient temperature and humidity.

New Light Stabilizers and Materials

The hindered amine light stabilizers (HALS) are presently the most effective class of stabilizers available and are used particularly in polyethylene and polypropylene products intended for outdoor use. Other classes of light stabilizers such as ultraviolet absorbers are also used with plastics, particularly the aromatic polymers. The harsh exposure conditions where the spectral content of sunlight has a larger UV-B component, and the ambient temperature and/or humidity is higher, generally indicates a higher concentration of the stabilizer to be used in the plastic. Also important are effective thermal stabilizers used to protect plastics from degradation during processing. Without these, high temperature processing can introduce chromophore species into polymers making them more susceptible to photodegradation.

HALS are relatively expensive additives and are used at a low concentration (0.1 to 0.2 percent in polyethylenes in mulch film applications). The protection from light-induced damage afforded by HALS is reported to increase linearly on its concentration in the plastic (up to about 0.6 weight percent).[20] While reported data on the issue are limited, it is likely that these stabilizers work well under a variety of different temperatures and humidity. Very little work has been done on their effectiveness and their own stability[21] in harsh UV environments (i.e. in sunlight with a higher than normal fraction of UV-B or that containing shorter than expected wavelengths of UV-B radiation).

 Recent studies do not directly address the issue of performance of stabilizers under altered sunlight conditions, but discuss how the optimum protective capacity of conventional HALS stabilizers might be exploited. Synergistic mixtures of HALS have gained increasing importance for UV stabilization of polyolefin. Synergism or antagonism between two HALS was detected by evaluating a single combination of the two HALS in propylene.[20] The mechanism involved, however, was not fully elucidated. The synergy depended on the particular combination of HALS and on the type of polyolefin.   Similarly, combinations of UV absorbers (an oxanilide with benzephenone or benzotriazole or a hydroxyphenyltriazine) were reported to be systematically synergistic in both polyethylene and polypropylene.[22] Combinations of oligomeric stabilizers with photostabilizer moieties (such as HALS) and heat stabilizer have also been tested for possible synergism.[23] While synergistic protection from photodamage was not obtained for these, some mixes showed synergistic heat stabilization in polypropylene. Other promising novel light stabilizer systems not presently in commercial use, such as HALS reacted with pyrenes[24], triazines, selenium, and selenium/triazine[25, 26] were recently studied for their potential as light stabilizers in polypropylene. While these are for the most part exploratory studies, research on fully exploiting the capability of HALS and attempting to develop even better stabilizers is an important undertaking.

With most of the 23 million tons of vinyl plastics (PVC) produced globally each year being used outdoors, and developing nations reporting an increasing demand for the material for building, their light stabilization is of particular interest. This plastic uses titania pigment (rutile titanium dioxide) as an opacifier at10-13 weight percent in compositions meant for outdoor use in the US. The pigment absorbs UV-B radiation in sunlight and reflects visible wavelengths making it a good photostabilzer.   The mechanism of protection of PVC with titania pigment was recently investigated with special emphasis on the role of water in promoting oxidative degradation.[27] The study compared the stabilizing effectiveness of nanocrystalline rutile powder, an anatase white pigment, and a photoactive as well as photostable grades of rutile pigment in PVC.

Using better UV-resistant varieties of plastics is an important strategy to mitigate the effects of increased UV radiation in sunlight. Metallocene-catalysed plastics (m-plastic) are slowly beginning to replace conventional polyolefins in several key applications within the last few years. The stabilizer effectiveness of existing UV stabilizers systems with the new m-polyolefins was recently reported.[28] The compatibility of the UV stabilizers at the concentration most commonly used in plastic film

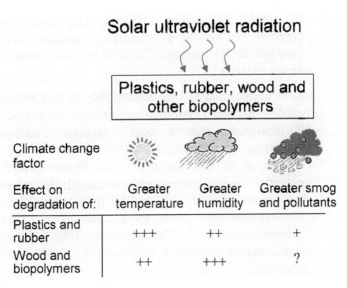

Figure 7-1. The anticipated effects of climatic change factors on the degradation of materials by solar ultraviolet radiation. The + symbols indicate the amount of published research data showing climatic factors to increase UV-induced degradation. +++ = High, ++ = Moderate, and + = Low

products, were found to be the same for both conventional polyolefin and the m-polyolefin. Furthermore, the synergism between two polymeric HALS reported earlier for conventional polyolefins is also found to be applicable to m-polyolefins. The main difference reported so far between the conventional and m-plastics is a small but systematic increase in lifetimes with m-plastics relative to conventional plastic, for the HALS-stabilized polyethylenes. This was reflected in the better weatherability of m-polyethylene relative to that of conventional polyethylene, in outdoor exposure studies.[29] These observations are important in that they suggest the trend towards the metallocene plastics with better characteristics, does not involve a compromise on the UV-stability of the material.

Influence of Temperature on UV-induced Effects

The outdoor degradation of common thermoplastic materials as well as the materials for construction such as wood, or even biopolymers like collagen (making up nearly a third of the body protein in mammals) is often the result of a combination of factors acting together. While the most important of these is the solar UV radiation, factors such as the temperature of the material and the presence of moisture shows a considerable synergistic effect on the photodegradation of materials. This is illustrated in Figure 7-1.

This suggests that the increase in ambient temperatures pursuant to global warming could play an important role in enhancing the rates of photodegradation in materials exposed to sunlight with higher levels of UV-B radiation. Global warming is also expected to alter rainfall and humidity in some locations, leading to longer periods of time where the material is in contact with moisture. A possible minor influence might be due to increased volatile organic compound, VOC, emissions and NOx/SOx releases that would increase the tropospheric ozone levels. The NOx/SOx species as well as smog ozone are well documented to promote UV-induced oxidative damage of common plastics.[30] The oxidative damage caused by even very low levels of ozone in the atmosphere, particularly in rubber products[31] is well documented; antiozonant additives are used in the industry to control this problem. In assessing damage scenarios associated with stratospheric ozone depletion as well as in evaluating measures available for mitigation of increased damage to materials due to increased UV-B levels, it is crucial to consider the modifying influence of climate change as well.

In a recent study[32], the weathering of polyethylene agricultural mulch films under high-UV outdoor exposure conditions at ambient temperature and at 25°C inside a controlled temperature UV-transparent chamber, were compared. Under ambient conditions, in Dhahran (Saudi Arabia), the surface temperature of the plastic rose as high as 60 °C depending on color and thickness, because of the absorption of solar IR wavelengths. The average elongation at break of the polyethylene was periodically measured; this property is particularly sensitive to degradation in this type of material. The rate of light-induced breakdown of the polyethylene under comparable UV exposure was slower by a factor of four when the temperature as controlled at the lower temperature of 25°C. The enhancing effect of temperature on degradation is generally the case with common plastics as evidenced by the low activation energies reported for the degradation processes.

A similar experiment was completed over a nearly-3 year period of exposure for 200-micrometer polycarbonate film, a plastic used in glazing applications because of its clarity and strength. As illustrated in Figure 7-2, the rate of photodamage (measured in terms of loss in the elongation at break) was markedly lower when high temperature was excluded from the test environment. The increase in ambient temperature as a result of global warming will be much smaller than the temperature differences between the two sets of samples referred to in the figure. Yet, at least in locations experiencing extremes of temperature change, a measurable change in service lifetimes of outdoor plastics might be expected.

Table 1. Loss in average elongation at break (percentage) in commercial polycarbonate sheets on exposure outdoors under different conditions.

	Exposure Conditions	0 months	15 months	29 months
1	Ambient UV radiation Ambient temperature	73.2	36.1	6.5
2	Reduced UV radiation (white film) Ambient temperature	73.2	57.5	56.3
3	No UV radiation (black film) Higher temperature	73.2	65.4	64.3
4	Ambient UV radiation 25°C temperature (in chamber)	73.2	54.0	49.7

Table 1 compares the values for the average elongation at break of commercial polycarbonate sheets (200 micrometers in thickness) exposed outdoors under different conditions. The location of exposure, Dhahran (Saudi Arabia), receives about 180 Kilo Langley's of sunlight annually. The average temperature in summer is about 40°C (with extremes of up to 60°C recorded) and the average humidity is 60-90 percent. The control samples were exposed to sunlight outdoors while the test samples were exposed to sunlight at the same location but in a UV-transparent chamber maintained at the lower temperature of 25°C and 50-60 percent humidity. The dramatic difference in the elongation at break of samples 1 and 4 is attributed to the enhancing effect of temperature under the same UV exposure. Also included in the Table are two other sets of samples both exposed under ambient conditions outdoors, but wrapped in either a black or a white 6-mil thick plastic films. The black film blocks out all UV (and visible light) but maintain the sample at an even a higher temperature than the control sample. This is a result of the absorption of solar infrared radiation in sunlight by the black film. The white film cut down most of the UV radiation, but maintained the sample at about the same temperature as the control sample. Of the two, the sample wrapped in black film degraded slower despite the higher sample temperature (see Table 1), illustrating UV to be the dominant influence in bringing about degradation.

Influence of Moisture on UV-Induced Effects

The presence of moisture can unexpectedly accelerate the degradation of polymers stabilized with titanium dioxide. Vinyl (PVC) extruded profile used in siding for instance, routinely use this pigment to maintain light stability during outdoor use. A recent study[27] found that neither anatase nor rutile form of this pigment catalyze photodegradation of the plastic under dry conditions when exposed to simulated solar radiation. But these pigments catalyzed the loss in surface gloss of the PVC (a practically relevant property) when exposed to UV radiation in the presence of moisture, illustrating the importance of moisture in promoting light-induced degradation. Another important consideration is that under high humidity soluble photostabilizers might leach out of the plastic matrix, reducing the effectiveness of the light stabilizer and leading to shorter service life. The presence of high humidity, particularly at the higher temperatures tends to increase the photodamage in polymers such as thermoplastic polyester elastomers.[12]

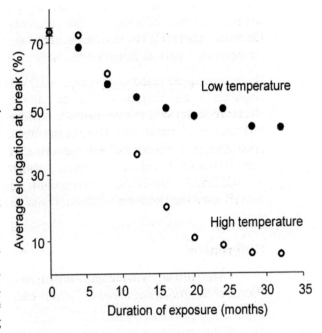

Figure 7-2 The loss in the elongation at break for Lexan® polycarbonate sheets on exposure to solar radiation under desert exposure conditions at high ambient temperature (open symbols) and at 25°C (closed symbols).

The accelerating effects of humidity on the UV-induced damage to wood is well known.[10, 33] This is true of changes in surface chemistry, color, and lignin content of the 80-100 micrometer layer through which UV radiation is able to penetrate into the wood. However, with plastics or wood [34] exposed simultaneously to both UV radiation and moisture, damage due to the radiation was clearly the dominant short-term effect. However, once the surface of wood has become more hydrophilic and oxygenated as a result of photodamage it becomes increasingly more accessible by microorganisms capable of biodegrading the wood. Common types of plastics are essentially non-biodegradable and therefore not affected by any biotic mechanism.

Conclusions

Damage to synthetic and biopolymer materials on exposure to solar radiation depends on the susceptibility of the polymer to solar UV wavelength as well as on the complexity of the weathering environment to which it is exposed. With common plastics products the inherent photodegradability of the polymer is an important factor, but the magnitude of damage is determined by the extent of processing used in the manufacturing of the product, as well as by the types of additives used in the plastics composition. The same polymer could potentially be compounded differently to have a range of different UV stabilities. However, the spectrally altered, UV-B enhanced, solar radiation that might be obtained consequent to disruption of the ozone layer, will consistently reduce the service life of these plastics relative to that under present-day sunlight environments.

The degradation potential of any UV-B environment is enhanced at higher temperatures and possibly at high ambient humidity. Changes likely to be associated with global warming are therefore expected to increase the propensity of plastic products to undergo solar UV radiation induced degradation. This is even more so for natural materials such as wood that are porous and hydrophilic. Shortening of the outdoor lifetimes of wood and plastics used in construction can place a significant economic burden on developing regions of the world. In considering stabilization technologies it is therefore important to develop and evaluate systems that not only function under UV-B rich solar radiation environments, but also are effective under expected temperature and humidity conditions.

In mitigating the effects of increased UV-B content in sunlight on materials damage, the industry is likely to rely heavily on the use of both conventional and improved photostabilizer systems. Recently reported improvements in synergistic mixtures of stabilizers for polyolefins and studies to better understand the stabilization mechanisms for commodity thermoplastics, are therefore encouraging in this regard. The reports on newer metallocene plastics with superior properties that can be stabilized with conventional stabilizers are also interesting for the same reason. However, the additional cost of these mitigations, especially in relation to the regions where plastics are heavily used has not been adequately assessed.

References

1   A. Torikai, Wavelength sensitivity of the photodegradation of polymers, in *Handbook of Polymer Degradation, Second Edition* ed.: S. H. Hamid, Marcel Dekker, New York, NY, USA, 2000, pp. 573-604.

2   J. F. Rabek, *Polymer Photodegradation*, Chapman and Hall, New York, NY, USA, 1995.

3   M. Johansson and G. Gellerstedt, Chromophoric content in wood and mechanical pulps, *Nord. Pulp. Pap. Res. J.*, 2000, **15**, 282-286.

4   F. G. Lennox, K. M. G., I. H. Leaver, R. G.C. and W. E. Savige, Mechanism of prevention and correction of wool photoyellowing, *Applied Polymer Symposium.*, 1971, 18353-18369.

5   A. Sionkowska, Modification of collagen films by ultraviolet irradiation, *Polymer Deg. Stabil.*, 2000, **68**, 147-151.

6   M. S. Jahan, T. R. Drouuin and R. M. Sayre, Effect of humidity on photoinduced ESR signal from human hair, *Photochem. Photobiol.*, 1987, **45**.

7   F. H. Winslow, W. Matreyek and A. M. Trozzolo, Weathering of polymers, *Soc. Plas. Eng. Tech. Pap.*, 1972, **18**, 766-772.

8   IPCC, Climate Change 2001:The Scientific Basis, IPPC Report No 3.

9   E. B. Rabonavitch, J. G. Queensberry and S. J. W., Predicting heat building up due to sun's energy, *J. Vinyl Tech.*, 1983, **5**, 110-115.

10   J. Fuwape and S. Adedunter, Performance of UV absorbers in plastics and coatings, in *Handbook of Polymer Degradation*, 2 ed. ed.: S. H. Hamid, Marcel Dekker Inc., New York, NY, USA, 2000, pp. 163-190.

11   R. J. Gardner and J. Martin, R,, Humid aging of plastics. Effect of molecular weight on the mechanical properties and fracture morphology of polycarbonate, *J. Appl. Polymer Sci.*, 1979, **24**, 1269.

12   Y. Nagai, T. Ogawa, Y. Nishimoto and f. Ohishi, Analysis of weathering of a thermoplastic polyester Elastomer II. Factors affecting weathering of a polyether-polyester elastomer, *Polymer Deg. Stabil.*, 1999, **65**, 217-224.

13   V. Godard, M. Triboulet, A. Merlin and M. Andre, Photostabilization of natural and weathered wood, *Pint. Acadbadas Ind.*, 2001, **42**, 36-46.

14   C. Hill and N. C., An investigation of the potential for chemical modification and subsequent polymeric grafting as a means of protecting wood against photodegradation, *Polymer Deg. Stabil.*, 2001, **72**, 133-139.

15   A. L. Andrady, Effect of increased solar ultraviolet radiation on materials, *J. Photochem. Photobiol.*, 1998, **46**, 96-103.

16   A. L. Andrady, Wavelength sensitivity in polymer photodegradation, *Adv. Polymer Sci.*, 1997, **128**, 49-94.

17   A. L. Andrady and A. Torikai, Photoyellowing of mechanical pulps III, *Polymer Deg. Stabil.*, 1998, **66**, 317-322.

18   A. Torikai, Wavelength sensitivity in the photodegradation of polymethylmethcrylate: Accelerated degradation and gel formation, in *Science and Technology of Polymers and Advanced Materials* ed.: P. N. Prasad, Plenum Press, New York, NY, USA, 1999, pp. 581-586.

19   A. Torikai and H. Shibata, Effect of ultraviolet radiation on photodeegradation of collagen, *J. Appl. Polymer Sci.*, 1999, **73**, 1259-1265.

20   F. Gugumus, Possibilities and limits of synergism with light stabilizers in polyolefins 1. HALS in polyolefins, *Polymer Deg. Stabil.*, 2002, **75**, 295-309.

21   J. Pan and S. Cui, Study of the photolysis of a commercial hindered amine light stabilizer, *Polymer Deg. Stabil.*, 1993, **40**, 375-378.

22   F. Gugumus, Possibilities and limits of synergism with light stabilizers in polyolefins 2. UV absorbers in polyolefins, *Polymer Deg. Stabil.*, 2002, **75**, 309-320.

23   S. Chmela, P. Hrdlovic and J. Lacoste, Combined oligometric light and heat stabilizers, *Polymer Deg. Stabil.*, 2001, **71**, 171-177.

24   L. Bucsiova, S. Chmela and P. Krdlovic, Preparation, photochemical stability and photostabilising efficiency of adducts of pyrene and hindered amine stabilisers in iPP matrix, *Polymer Deg. Stabil.*, 2001, **71**, 135-145.

25   S. Jipa, R. Setnescu, T. Setnescu and T. Zaharescu, Efficiency assessment of additives in thermal degradation of i-PP by chemiluminescence I, Triazines, *Polymer Deg. Stabil.*, 2000, **68**, 159-164.

26   S. Jipa, R. Setnescu, T. Setnescu and T. Zaharescu, Efficiency assessment of additives in thermal degradation of i-PP by chemiluminescence II, Selenium, *Polymer Deg. Stabil.*, 2000, **68**, 165-169.

27   U. Gesenhues, Influence of titanium dioxide pigments on the photodegradation of poly(vinyl chloride), *Polymer Deg. Stabil.*, 2000, **68**, 185-196.

28   F. Gugumus and N. Lelli, Light stabilization of metallocene polyolefins, *Polymer Deg. Stabil.*, 2001, **72**, 407-421.

29   S. H. Hamid, I. Hussain and K. Alam, Loss of additives from films exposed to harsh outdoor climate of Saudi Arabia, in *4th Chemistry in Industry Conference and Exhibition*, Saudi Arabian Section-American Chemical Society (SAS-ACS), Bahrain, Saudi Arabia, 2001.

30   H. G. Jellinek, *Aspects of degradation and stabilization of polymers*, Elsevier Publishing,, Amsterdam, NL, 1978.

31   A. Davis and D. Sims, *Weathering of Polymers*, Applied Science Publishers, New York, NY, USA, 1983.

32   S. H. Hamid, Role of thermal degradation of polyethylene under natural weathering conditions, in *Proceedings of ANTEC 2000, Society of Plastic Engineers Meeting, Orlando, FL, USA, MAy 7-11, 2000*, Marcel Dekker, New York, NY, USA, 2000, pp. 3768-3769.

33   D. Hon, Degradative effect of ultraviolet light and acid rain on wood surface quality, *Wood Fibre Sci.*, 1994, **26**, 185-191.

34   B. Lindeberg, Improving the outdoor durability of wood by surface treatment, *FATIPEC*, 1986, **2/B**, 589-608

.

LIST OF ABBREVIATIONS

ASL	above sea level
BCC	basal cell carcinoma (s)
Br	bromine (an ozone depleting chemical)
CAS	Chemical Abstracts Service
CC	cortical cataract(s)
CDK	climatic droplet keratopathy
CDOC	colored dissolved organic carbon
CDOM	colored (or chromophoric) dissolved organic matter
CFC	chlorofluorocarbons
CH	contact hypersensitivity
CH_4	methane (a greenhouse gas)
Cl	chlorine (an ozone depleting chemical)
CM	cutaneous melanoma
CO_2	carbon dioxide (a greenhouse gas)
CPD	cyclobutane pyrimidine dimers
DIC	dissolved inorganic carbon
DMS	dimethyl sulfide
DNA	deoxyribose nucleic acid
DOC	dissolved organic carbon
DOM	dissolved organic matter
DTH	delayed type hypersensitivity
DU	Dobson Unit (used for the measurement of total column ozone (1 $DU=2.69 \times 10^{16}$ molecule cm^{-2})
EDUCE	European Database for Ultraviolet Radiation Climatology and Evaluation
EP	Earth Probe (a NASA satellite)
EPA	Environmental Protection Agency
GHG	greenhouse gas
Halon	bromine-containing compound
HALS	Hindered Amine Light Stabilizer
HCFC	hydrochlorofluorocarbon
HFC	hydrofluorocarbon
HIV	human immunodeficiency virus
HPV	human papilloma virus
IL	interleukin
INK4a	human inhibitor of kinase 4a protein (gene in italics)
Ink4a	murine inhibitor of kinase 4a protein (gene in italics)
kda	kilodalton
MAA	mycosporine-like amino acids
NC	nuclear cataract(s)
NaTFA	sodium trifluoroacetate
NCAR	National Centre for Atmospheric Research, USA
NIMBUS-7	a NASA satellite
NMHCs	non-methane hydrocarbons
NO	nitric oxide (an ozone depleting gas)

NO_2	nitrogen dioxide (an ozone depleting gas)
N_2O	nitrous oxide (a greenhouse gas that is also a source of NO_2)
NO_x	nitrogen oxides
NOAA	National Oceanic and Atmospheric Administration, USA
NOEC	no observed effect concentration
OCS	carbonyl sulfide
CDFA	chlorodifluoroacetic acid
ODS	ozone depleting substance(s)
OH	hydroxyl radical (and important atmospheric cleaning agent)
PAR	photosynthetically active radiation, 400-700 nm waveband
PAUR II	Photochemical Activity and solar Ultraviolet Radiation campaign 2
PEC	predicted environmental concentration
POC	particulate organic carbon
PSC	posterior subcapsular cataract(s)
PSC	Polar Stratospheric Cloud (ice crystals which form at high altitudes in Polar regions when the temperature is below a critical threshold)
PNEC	predicted no effect concentration
Ptc	murine 'patch' protein (gene in italics)
PTCH	human 'patch' protein (gene in italics)
QBO	quasi biennial oscillation (a shift in wind patterns - especially over the tropics- with a period of approximately 2.2 years)
RAF	radiation amplification factor (a measure of sensitivity to ozone change)
ROS	reactive oxygen species
SAGE	Stratospheric Aerosol and Gas Experiment, a satellite-based instrument
SCC	squamous cell carcinoma
SZA	solar zenith angle (ie the angle between zenith and the centre of the solar disk)
TFA	trifluoroacetic acid
TFM	the lampricide 3-fluoromethyl-4-nitrophenol
TOMS	Total Ozone Mapping Spectrometer, a satellite-based instrument
Troposphere	lowest part of Earth's atmosphere (0-16 km)
UCA	urocanic acid
UV	ultraviolet
UV-A	electromagnetic radiation of wavelengths in the 315 to 400 nm range
UV-B	electromagnetic radiation of wavelengths in the 280 to 315 nm range
UV-C	electromagnetic radiation of wavelengths in the 100 to 280 nm range
UV index	a standardised unit for providing UV information to the public
VOC	volatile organic compounds
WOUDC	world ozone and UV data centre
XP	xeroderma pigmentosum

APPENDIX. EIGHTEEN QUESTIONS AND ANSWERS ABOUT THE EFFECTS OF THE DEPLETION OF THE OZONE LAYER ON HUMANS AND THE ENVIRONMENT

P. J. Aucamp[a] (coordinator)

[a] *School for Environmental Science and Management, Potchefstroom University for CHE, P.O. Box 915751, Faerie Glen, 0043, South Africa. Email: pjaucamp@iafrica.com*

Introduction

The Meetings of the Parties to the Montreal Protocol appointed three Assessment Panels to review the progress in scientific knowledge on their behalf. These panels are: the Scientific Assessment Panel, the Technological and Economic Assessment Panel and the Environmental Effects Assessment Panel. Each panel covers a designated area and there is very little overlap between their reports. The main reports are published every four years as required by the Meetings of the Parties. All these reports have an executive summary that is distributed more widely than the main report itself. It became customary to add a set of questions and answers – mainly for lay readers – to the report. This document contains the questions and answers prepared by members of the Environmental Assessment Panel. It is based mainly on the 2002 report of the Effects Panel but also contains information from previous assessments. Readers who need more detailed information on any of the questions are referred to these full reports for a more complete scientific discussion.

This set of questions refers mainly to the environmental effects of ozone depletion. The report of the Scientific Assessment Panel contains questions and answers related to the other scientific issues addressed by that Panel. All the reports can be found on the UNEP website (http://www.unep.org/ozone).

Table of Contents

Q1. What is ozone and how do we define ultraviolet radiation?

Ozone is a gas that occurs in the atmosphere. It is formed in the stratosphere by the action of ultraviolet radiation from the sun on oxygen. The ozone molecule contains three atoms of oxygen. It is also formed near the Earth's surface in chemical reactions caused by man-made pollution. Ozone absorbs a part of the ultraviolet radiation from the sun, thereby reducing the potentially dangerous UV-B radiation reaching the surface of the earth.

Ozone is a strong oxidising agent. It will destroy any organic material on contact by oxidising the molecules of the cells. This property is often used to sterilise drinking and swimming pool water. Inhaling ozone can be harmful to mammals in small doses and toxic in large doses. In the lower atmosphere ozone is one of the detrimental components of photochemical smog that is produced as the result of pollution (Bad ozone). However, in the stratosphere, ozone absorbs ultraviolet radiation and protects the environment against the detrimental effects of the UV-B radiation (Good ozone).

The radiation emitted by the sun contains an ultraviolet component. This covers the range with wavelengths from 100 to 400 nm and is divided into three bands: UV-A (315 – 400 nm), UV-B (280 – 315 nm) and UV-C (100 – 280 nm). As the sunlight passes through the atmosphere, no UV-C and approximately 10% of the UV-B is transmitted. They are absorbed mainly by ozone and oxygen. UV-A radiation is less affected by the atmosphere. Therefore, the ultraviolet radiation reaching the Earth's surface is composed of mainly UV-A with a small UV-B component. A decrease in the concentration of ozone in the atmosphere results in increased UV-B levels. DNA and other biological macromolecules absorb UV-B and can be damaged in the process.

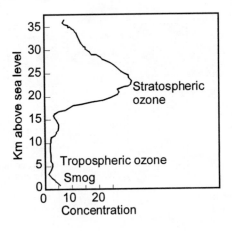

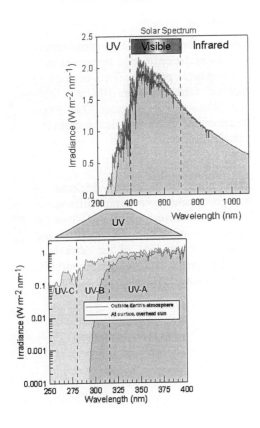

Q2. What determines the level of UV-B at a particular location?

The sun is the origin of ultraviolet radiation reaching the earth. This radiation is absorbed by the components of the Earth's atmosphere including ozone. At higher latitudes the rays of the sun have to take a longer path through the atmosphere before they reach the Earth. In general, the level of ultraviolet radiation is higher at the equator and diminishes towards the poles. The levels increase with elevation above sea level. Clouds, particulate matter and aerosols absorb ultraviolet radiation and diminish ultraviolet levels. The level of the ultraviolet radiation at any particular location is determined by a combination of all these factors.

The UV-B levels vary with the time of day and season. The highest level occurs when the sun is at its maximum elevation, around midday during the summer months. The radiation levels are higher in the intertropical regions.

On average, the highest ultraviolet radiation levels occur on cloudless days. Cloud cover reduces the radiation but it can still be high under partly cloudy conditions when the sun is not obscured. Evidence shows that over the time span of satellite-based ozone measurements, changes in cloud cover have been much less important than stratospheric ozone reductions in causing surface UV changes.

Higher elevations have less atmosphere overhead, as evidenced by the thinner air and lower atmospheric pressure. The increase in UV radiation varies between 10% and 20% for each kilometre of elevation, the exact number depending on the specific wavelength, solar angle, reflections, and other local conditions.

Frequently, other factors besides thickness of the atmosphere cause even larger differences in UV radiation between elevations. Snow is more common at higher elevations, and reflects as much as 90% of the ultraviolet radiation. Dry beach sand reflects about 15% and sea foam about 25%.

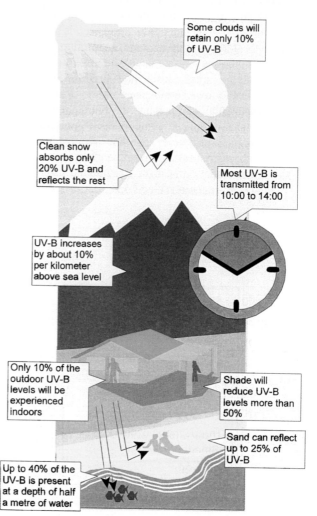

Some clouds will retain only 10% of UV-B

Clean snow absorbs only 20% UV-B and reflects the rest

Most UV-B is transmitted from 10:00 to 14:00

UV-B increases by about 10% per kilometer above sea level

Only 10% of the outdoor UV-B levels will be experienced indoors

Shade will reduce UV-B levels more than 50%

Sand can reflect up to 25% of UV-B

Up to 40% of the UV-B is present at a depth of half a metre of water

Q3. What is the effect of atmospheric pollution on the level of UV-B?

Man-made pollution often contains oxides of nitrogen and sulphur and various hydrocarbons. Chemical reactions between these compounds can form ozone. This mixture of gaseous compounds and particulate matter appear as a brown haze known as photochemical smog. The ozone in the smog will also absorb ultraviolet radiation.

While most of the atmospheric ozone resides in the stratosphere, some ozone is made in the troposphere by the chemical reactions of pollutants such as nitrogen oxides and hydrocarbons. This tropospheric ozone is a component of the photochemical smog found in many polluted areas. Airborne particles (smoke, dust, sulphate aerosols) block UV radiation, but at the same time can increase the amount of scattered light (haze) and therefore increase the UV exposure of side-facing surfaces (e.g., face, eyes). Comparisons of measurements made in industrialised regions of the Northern Hemisphere (e.g. central Europe) and in very clean locations at similar latitudes in the Southern Hemisphere (e.g., New Zealand) indicate the importance of particulate and pollution-related UV-B

reductions. At any particular location there is a direct relationship between UV-B levels and the amount of ozone in the atmosphere. UV-B increases with ozone depletion in the stratosphere but decreases with ozone formation in the lower atmosphere. The natural UV-B variability (e.g., from time of day, or clouds) can be larger, but goes in both directions, up and down. Many detrimental effects of UV-B are proportional to the cumulative UV-B exposure.

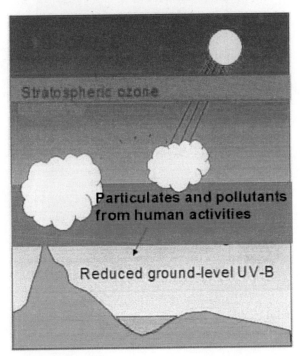

Q4. What is the solar UV index?

The solar UV index (UVI) describes the level of solar UV radiation at the Earth's surface. The values of the index range from zero upward – the higher the index value, the greater the potential for damage to the skin and eye, and the less time it takes for harm to occur. The UV index is computed using forecasted ozone levels, a computer model that relates ozone levels to UV incidence on the ground, forecasted cloud amounts, and the elevation of the forecast cities. Some countries also use ground observations.

The calculation starts with measurements of current total ozone amounts. The data are then used to produce a forecast of ozone levels for the next day at various points. A model is used to determine the amount of UV radiation with wavelengths from 290 to 400 nm reaching the ground. The time of day (solar noon), day of year, and latitude are used. The information is then weighted according to how human skin responds to each wavelength. It is more important to protect people from wavelengths that harm skin than from wavelengths that do not damage the skin.

The weighted irradiances are integrated over the 290 to 400 nm range resulting in a value representing the effect a given UV radiation intensity will have on skin. The estimates are then adjusted for the effects of elevation and clouds. UV at the surface increases by about 10% per kilometre above sea level. Clear skies allow 100% of the incoming UV radiation from the sun to reach the surface, whereas scattered clouds transmit about 90%, broken clouds about 75%, and overcast conditions about 30%. Once adjusted for elevation and clouds, this value is then scaled by a conversion factor. This results in a number that usually ranges from 0 (where there is no sunlight) to the mid teens. This value is called the UV index. Ideally, the computation of the UV index should include the effects of variable surface reflection (e.g., sand, water, or snow), atmospheric pollutants or haze.

Exposure Category	UVI Range
Low	< 2
Moderate	3 – 5
High	6 – 7
Very High	8 – 10
Extreme	11+

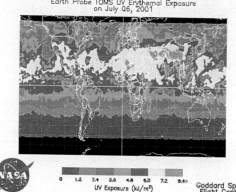

Earth Probe TOMS UV Erythemal Exposure on January 06, 2001

Earth Probe TOMS UV Erythemal Exposure on July 06, 2001

Q5. How does the UV index vary with geographical location and season?

The combination of total ozone and solar zenith angle, which is determined by the geographical position, season and time of the day, can lead to a variety of UV exposure situations.

Modelled noon UV index calculated under clear sky conditions at 20°, 30° and 60°S is shown in the figure. The total ozone column values selected for calculation at 20° and 30° are typical values observed at those latitudes, while the ozone column value used for calculations at 60° are observed under ozone hole conditions. Values around 150 Dobson Units (DU) can be present at 60°S during October, while 200 DU have been observed later in the spring.

The UV index at 60°S under a total ozone column of 200 DU is always lower than the value present at 30°S. On the other hand, the UV index calculated for 150 DU would only exceed those at 30°S if that ozone total column is present at the end of October or later, and exceed those at 20° if present later than the middle of December.

The presence of "patchy" skies or snow-covered ground can result in irradiances larger than those shown in the figure. Altitude can increase the UV index. A good example is the intertropical high altitude desert of Puna de Atacama in Argentina where a UV index of 18 is common in January and December, with a maximum of 20 and even more on certain days. A combination of low solar zenith angle near noon, high altitude, a naturally low ozone total column and very clean atmosphere is responsible for these exceptionally high values.

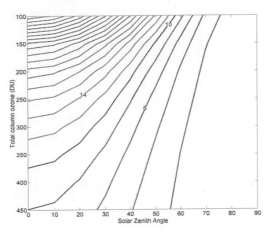

Effect of Solar Zenith Angle on UV Index

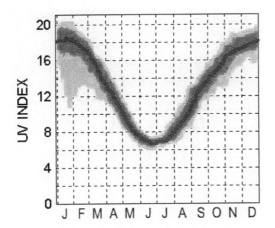

UV Index at La Quiaca (22.11°S, 65.57°W, 3459 m), Argentina

Q6. What is the effect of exposure to UV-B on mammals?

The cells of three different organ systems can be directly exposed to UV radiation—the eyes, the skin, and the immune system. Acute exposure of the eyes to UV radiation causes photokeratitis (snow blindness) and chronic exposure contributes to cataract formation. In the skin, UV irradiation causes sunburn, photoaging, and skin cancer.

Moderate exposure to sunlight in the course of everyday life is essential for health. UV-B radiation is involved in the formation of vitamin D, which is necessary for growth and maintenance of bones and teeth. There is some evidence suggesting that maintaining normal vitamin D levels protects against the development of colon, breast, and prostate cancers. However, very moderate exposure is all that is required, and excessive exposure confers no added benefit.

Skin cancer is found in almost all animals that have been studied in the long-term, for example, cattle, goats, sheep, cats, dogs, guinea pigs, rats, and mice. Direct effects of UV-B radiation on body parts that are covered by thick hair are negligible. However, even furred animals usually have exposed skin around the mouth, nostrils and on other parts of the body. These parts, unless they are heavily pigmented, can be damaged by radiation.

Q7. What is the effect of exposure to UV-B on the skin?

Acute exposure of the skin to UV radiation causes sunburn. The amount of UV required to produce sunburn depends on the absorption in the superficial layers (i.e. the thickness and amount of pigment) of the skin and on other genetic factors. The efficiency with which sunlight produces sunburn depends on the amount of UV-B radiation it contains. For example, more UV-B is present at high altitudes and more is present in noontime sun than at earlier or later hours. Chronic exposure of the skin to UV radiation also causes wrinkling, thinning, and loss of elasticity of the skin (photoaging); however, UV-A radiation may be more important than UV-B radiation in causing these changes.

Sunscreens are designed to protect against sunburn and can be highly effective in this regard. There is also evidence that they reduce the incidence of squamous cell carcinoma and precancerous lesions in the skin. Sunscreens can also provide protection against the photoaging and immunological effects of UV radiation, particularly if they contain chemicals that absorb both UV-B and UV-A radiation. There is no evidence that getting a suntan will help prevent skin cancer. The UV exposure needed to acquire the tan adds to the skin cancer risk. The fact that one is able to tan well does, however, signify that the personal risk is lower (by a factor of 2 to 3) than for people who do not tan. Naturally dark-skinned people have a built-in protection of their skin against sunlight.

Basal and squamous cell carcinomas occur most often and with high frequency in light-skinned Caucasians living in sunny climates. Fortunately, most of these skin cancers are readily treated and are rarely fatal. Cutaneous melanoma is much more dangerous, but occurs with a much lower frequency than the other types. Its relationship to UV radiation is not well understood, but exposure early in life seems to be an important factor in the subsequent development of melanoma. Light-skinned populations have the highest risk of developing melanoma. Although melanoma can occur in highly pigmented persons, such cancers are often not related to sun exposure.

UV irradiation causes skin cancers by altering critical genes that control cell division and cell death. Altered genes result from the ability of UV to make chemical alterations in DNA, the building block of genes. Some of the genes involved in skin cancer development have been identified. These include the p53 tumour suppressor gene (squamous and basal cell carcinomas), the PTCH gene (basal cell carcinomas), the p16 gene (melanomas), and a variety of genes involved in the repair of UV-damaged DNA (all types).

Q8. How does UV-B affect the immune system?

The immune system can be altered by UV irradiation, leading to diminished immune response to infectious agents and some cancers.

Some cells of the immune system, called antigen-presenting cells, reside in the skin. Their function is to capture invading micro organisms and carry them to the lymph nodes, where the immune response is initiated. These cells can be damaged directly by UV radiation and will then no longer be able to initiate an immune response or produce an aberrant one. Other cells in the skin produce chemical mediators that direct the immune response toward either immune suppression or active immunity. Exposing these cells directly to UV-B radiation stimulates the release of mediators that favour the development of immune suppression. Finally, a molecule in the keratin layer of the skin, urocanic acid, undergoes a chemical change in response to UV radiation, which allows it to trigger the release of chemical mediators from mast cells in the skin, which also divert the immune response toward a pathway of immune suppression.

What is the significance of UV-induced immune suppression for human diseases? The answer is not yet clear. Although there are some examples in which UV exposure increases susceptibility to and the severity of an infection, such as with herpes virus infections (cold sores, shingles), the full implications of the immunological effects are unknown. Numerous laboratory animal models of infectious diseases demonstrate that exposure to UV radiation at a critical time during infection can increase the severity and duration of the disease. Also, UV exposure during immunisation can reduce the effectiveness of vaccinations. How these observations may apply to human diseases remains a subject of intense interest and research.

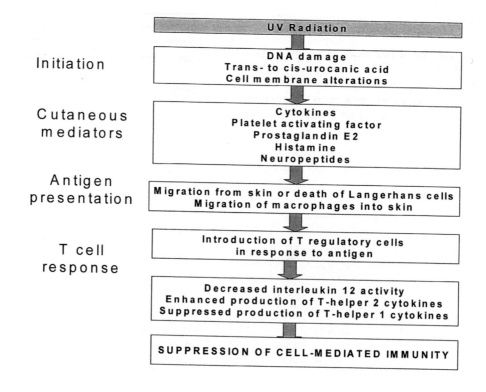

Q9. What are the effects of increased UV-B radiation on crops and forests?

Most plants have UV shielding, but not always sufficient for complete protection. Only a small proportion of the UV-B radiation striking a leaf penetrates into the inner tissues. When exposed to enhanced UV-B radiation, many species of plants can increase the UV-absorbing pigments in their outer leaf tissues. Other adaptations may include increased thickness of leaves that reduces the proportion of inner tissues exposed to UV-B radiation and changes in the protecting waxy layer of the leaves. Several repair mechanisms exist in plants, including repair systems for DNA damage or oxidant injury. The net damage a plant experiences is the result of the balance between damage and protection and repair processes.

There are some UV-B-sensitive varieties of crops that experience reductions in yield. There are also UV-B-tolerant varieties, providing the opportunity to breed and genetically engineer for UV-B tolerant crops. For commercial forests, tree breeding and genetic engineering may be used to improve UV-B tolerance. While many forest tree species appear to be UV-B tolerant, there is limited evidence that detrimental UV-B effects accumulate slowly from year to year in sensitive species. The biochemistry and physiology of plants are influenced by UV-B exposure such as in the accumulation of UV-B pigments. It is not possible to conclude whether or not the changes will have any appreciable impact on the quality of food.

Plants and animals have, during their evolution, adapted to particular environments. They have acquired protection and repair mechanisms appropriate for their particular situations. However, the present rate of global change is so rapid that evolution may not keep up with it, particularly in long-lived plants like trees. Thus, plants adapted to low UV-B environments may suffer even from an increase that is smaller than the difference between natural levels at the equator and higher latitudes. For example, herbaceous plants native to the southern tip of South America (Tierra del Fuego, Argentina) and the Antarctic Peninsula have been shown to be affected by the current ambient UV-B levels. Over long times and many generations, there is the possibility that genetic adaptation can develop.

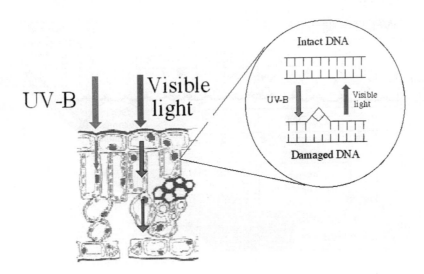

Q10. What is the effect of UV-B exposure on aquatic life?

Pure water is almost transparent to UV radiation. A beam of UV-B radiation can penetrate more than 500 meters through pure water before it is completely absorbed. Natural waters contain UV-absorbing substances, such as dissolved organic matter, that partly shields aquatic organisms from UV-B, although the degree of shielding varies widely from one water body to another.

In clear ocean and lake waters ecologically significant levels of UV-B can penetrate to tens of meters. In turbid rivers and wetlands, however, UV-B may be completely absorbed within the top few centimetres. Most organisms in aquatic ecosystems, such as phytoplankton, live in the illuminated euphotic zone close to the water surface where exposure to UV-B can occur. In particular, UV-B radiation may damage those organisms that live at the surface of the water during their early life stages.

Most adult fish are well protected from excessive solar UV, since they inhabit deep waters. Some shallow water fish have been found to develop skin cancer and other UV-related diseases. The eggs and larvae of many fish are sensitive to UV-B exposure. In the Gulf of Maine, UV penetrates to considerable depth where the embryos and larvae of the Atlantic cod develop. Exposure to UV equivalent to 10 m depth resulted in a significant mortality of developing embryos and a significant decrease in length of larvae. These irradiances occur in many temperate latitudes where these ecologically and commercially important fish spawn. In contrast, lobster larvae seem to be tolerant to UV radiation even though they develop in the surface layers of the water column.

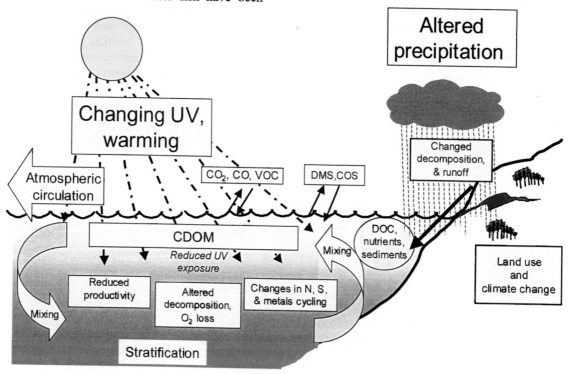

Q11. Does global warming alter the effect of UV radiation on aquatic ecosystems?

Climate change may result in temperature and sea level changes, shifts in the timing and extent of sea ice cover, changes in wave climate, ocean circulation, salinity and altered stratification of the water column. These complex changes are likely to have significant impacts that will vary both spatially and temporally. These changes will affect biological systems (including human marine resources), the global hydrological cycle, vertical mixing and efficiency of carbon dioxide uptake by the ocean. Ozone-related increases in UV-B are an important additional ecological stress that will have both positive and negative impacts in association with the other factors.

Increasing carbon dioxide concentrations will result in warming of the troposphere and simultaneous cooling of the stratosphere, which favours further ozone destruction. One of the possible feedback mechanisms is change in cloud cover and increased rainfall, but this is not well understood. Global warming changes the amount of ice and snow cover in polar and sub-polar areas. Ice and snow strongly attenuate the penetration of solar radiation into the water column.

Therefore, any substantial decrease in ice and snow cover will alter the exposure of aquatic ecosystems to solar UV radiation. Another aspect is the dependence of many physiological responses on temperature. Enzymatic repair mechanisms are inhibited by low temperature, while elevated temperatures may augment enzymatic repair mechanisms.

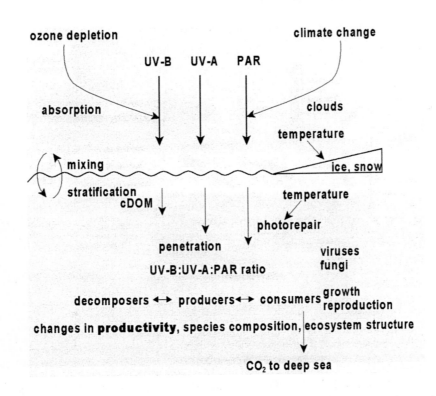

Q12. What are the effects of stratospheric ozone depletion on certain processes and cycles in the environment?

Ozone depletion results in greater amounts of UV-B radiation that will have an impact on terrestrial and aquatic biogeochemical systems. Biogeochemical cycles are the complex interactions of physical, chemical, geological and biological processes that control the transport and transformation of substances in the natural environment and therefore the conditions that humans experience in the Earth's system. The increased UV-B radiation impinging on terrestrial and aquatic systems, due to ozone depletion, results in changes in the trace gas exchange between the continents, oceans and the atmosphere. This results in complex alterations to atmospheric chemistry, the global elemental cycles, such as the carbon cycle, and may have an impact on the survival and health of all organisms on Earth, including humans.

In the figure, UV radiation is shown to influence oceanic primary productivity and the production of trace gases at the surface of the oceans and subsequent transfer to the atmosphere. Once in the atmosphere, trace gases such as CO_2 interact with the physical climate system resulting in alterations to climate and feedbacks in the global biogeochemical system. Since atmospheric CO_2 concentrations play a central role in determining the distribution of heat in the atmosphere, the multiple complex components of the physical climate system such as wind, air-sea momentum, heat exchange and precipitation are influenced. There are also similarly complex interactions between biogeochemical cycling on land and the integrated climate system that have important implications for organisms on Earth. At this stage it is not possible to predict the overall effects of these complex interactions.

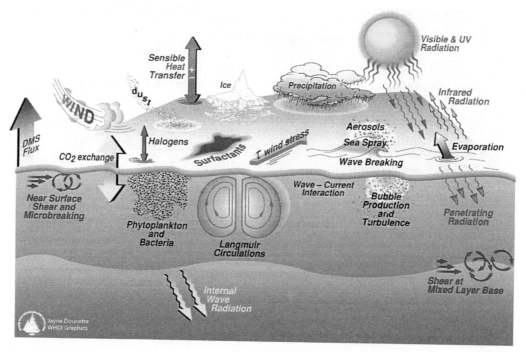

Figure provided by the US Surface Ocean Lower Atmosphere Study (SOLAS) and Woods Hole Oceanographic Institution (WHOI).

Q13. Do increased UV-B levels shorten the lifetime of commercial polymers?

The outdoor service life of commercial plastics is often limited by their UV-stability and weatherability. The outdoor lifetimes of plastics, however, depend on their formulations and specifically on the type and concentration of photostabiliser additives used in them. Information on the lifetimes of unstabilised (virgin) plastic materials is therefore of limited practical value in assessing the UV stability of plastics exposed outdoors.

Available data on the degradation of plastics by UV in sunlight show that for some polymers a portion of the damage is attributable to the UV-B radiation component. As any depletion of the stratospheric ozone layer would increase the UV-B content of the solar radiation reaching the Earth's surface, it is reasonable to expect a consequent increase in the rate of degradation of plastics containing these polymers (and other materials such as wood) under these conditions. The amount by which the service life of materials will be shortened by this phenomenon will of course depend on the type of polymer, location in question, and the light-stabiliser used in the formulation.

Climatic factors, particularly higher ambient temperatures due to global warming, will tend to accelerate UV-induced degradation to an extent depending on the type of plastic and on the location of exposure.

These reductions in service life of plastics can probably be countered by using higher than normal concentrations of existing light stabilisers in the plastic formulation, surface protection of materials (e.g. painting wood) or by selecting different polymeric materials with better UV-resistant materials for outdoor applications. These approaches might be able to retain the service life at present-day levels but may increase the cost of relevant products.

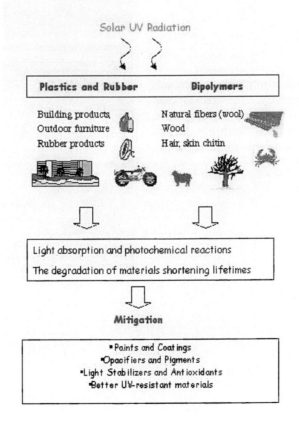

Q14. Will stratospheric ozone depletion change air quality, and how does this relate to global warming?

Stratospheric ozone depletion normally increases the ozone concentration at ground level. In general the impact of stratospheric ozone depletion is smaller than that of local and regional air pollution sources. Increases in the particulates in the atmosphere related to global warming may reduce tropospheric ozone production. Modelling and field studies show that the reduction of ozone photolysis rate and ozone production in the troposphere is expected in the presence of increased amounts of absorbing aerosols in the boundary layer.

Climate change can alter air quality in many ways. Changes in temperature, winds and cloudiness can all be important. Some of these changes will also alter the impact of stratospheric ozone depletion.

As an example, an increase in atmospheric CO_2 concentration would accelerate photosynthesis, which might enhance the emissions of biological volatile organic compounds from forests and other natural ecological systems. Other sources of tropospheric air pollutants may be affected by global warming. It is known that local and large-scale biomass fires, such as are used for land-clearing, are rich sources of nitrogen oxides, carbon monoxide, methane, and other non-methane hydrocarbons, that can lead to enhanced tropospheric ozone production. Climate changes resulting from global warming may increase the risk of large-scale forest and brush fires and so affect concentrations of tropospheric air pollutants. The resulting particulates in the atmosphere can scatter sunlight, thus improving the efficiency of UV-B absorption of the boundary layer ozone and contributing to global warming.

Illustration of the impact of tropospheric aerosols upon atmospheric chemistry. The aerosol can reduce the intensity of radiation, leading to a reduction in ozone production. Such a reduction offsets the impact of stratospheric ozone depletion

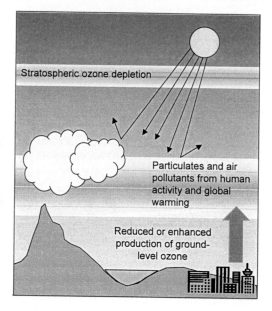

Stratospheric ozone depletion

Particulates and air pollutants from human activity and global warming

Reduced or enhanced production of ground-level ozone

Q15. What risks do the breakdown products of HFCs and HCFCs present to humans and the environment?

The new hydrofluorocarbons (HFCs) and hydrochlorofluorocarbons (HCFCs) replacements for the chlorofluorocarbons (CFCs) are largely degraded before reaching the stratosphere. The final breakdown products are various fluorinated and chlorinated acetic acids. Some of these are rapidly broken down by microbiological activity in water, soil, and sediments. Other breakdown products such as trifluoroacetic acid (TFA) are very persistent but they are very water soluble and chemically non-reactive. Because of their properties, these breakdown products will ultimately collect in aquatic environments. They have low toxicity to aquatic organisms and are very unlikely to adversely affect human health or the environment.

HFCs and HCFCs (CF_3CXYH) break down relatively rapidly to several products including the persistent substances such as trifluoroacetic acid (CF_3COOH) and chlorodifluoroacetic acid ($CF_2ClCOOH$). These are washed from the atmosphere by precipitation and reach surface waters, along with other chemicals washed from the soil. In locations where there is little or no outflow and high evaporation (seasonal wetlands, salt lakes and playas), these products are expected to increase in concentration over time. The concentrations of trifluoroacetic acid and chlorodifluoroacetic acid are expected to increase. While this may present a risk to aquatic organisms, these areas would also experience increases in concentrations of other water-soluble materials such as has already

occurred. The effects of increased concentrations of these naturally occurring salts and other materials would likely be greater and more biologically significant than those of breakdown products of the HFCs and HCFCs.

The results of this interaction with global climate change are judged to be of low significance, since the phytotoxicity of trifluoroacetic acid is not high.

Illustration of the formation of persistent, water-soluble breakdown products of the HFCs and HCFCs (CF_3-CXYH) and their movement and concentration by evaporation, along with other water-soluble salts to surface waters

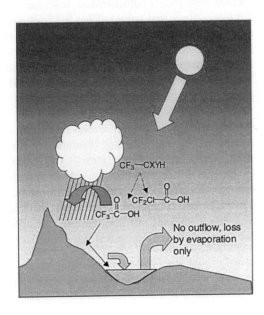

Q16. Is ozone depletion affected by global warming?

The interactions are complex, and not all of them are fully understood (see schematic). In the past, scientists have sometimes stressed the differences between global warming and ozone depletion. Global warming is due to a build-up of gases that absorb outgoing infrared radiation, especially CO_2, while ozone depletion is primarily due to a release of gases that catalytically destroy ozone.

Ozone, the CFCs and their substitutes are minor greenhouse gases. Several other gases involved with the chemistry of ozone depletion are also greenhouse active. These include water vapour, methane (CH_4), and nitrous oxide (N_2O) that are increasing and will ultimately lead to increases in stratospheric gases that catalytically destroy ozone. There are several radiative feedback processes involved. Increases in temperature can lead to changes in cloud cover, rainfall patterns, ice accumulation, surface albedo, and ocean circulation. The direct radiative forcing from increases in UV-B that results from changes in ozone are not significant, since only a small fraction of the incoming solar energy falls within the UV-B range. However, increases in UV radiation at the Earth's surface influence photochemical reactions in the troposphere that would affect the lifetimes of greenhouse gases. It has been suggested that changes in cloud cover can be induced by climate change. Changes in solar output and future volcanic eruptions will influence both global warming and ozone depletion.

It seems that while current ozone depletion is dominated by chlorine and bromine in the stratosphere, in the longer term (~100 years) the impact of climate change will dominate, through the effects of changes in atmospheric dynamics and chemistry. The result is that over the first half of the current century, increases in greenhouse gases may contribute to cooler stratospheric temperatures, since they act as infrared emitters in the stratosphere. This will lead to a decrease in the rate of catalytic destruction of ozone outside Polar regions. In Polar regions however, the cooler temperatures may lead to increased polar stratospheric clouds, thus exacerbating ozone depletion. The temperature changes will lead to changes in atmospheric circulation. These changes may aid the mixing of long-lived CFCs from the troposphere to the stratosphere, which will increase their rate of photochemical destruction, again contributing to a faster recovery of ozone. Changes in polar ozone can also lead to changes in tropospheric circulation patterns, which in turn affect surface climate.

The effects of global warming on UV radiation are twofold. The first effect results from changes in global warming that influence total ozone. The second effect results from climate change effects on other variables such as clouds, aerosols, and snow cover that influence UV directly.

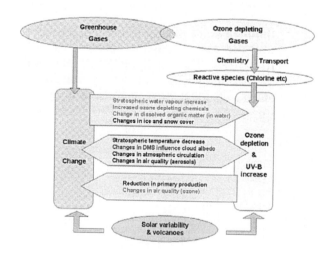

Q17. How did we benefit from the Montreal Protocol?

Several attempts have been made to investigate the economic impacts of the problem of a depleted ozone layer. Such attempts meet with many problems. There are good reasons for concern for effects on humans, animals, plants and materials, but most of these cannot be estimated in monetary terms. Calculating the overall economic impact of such effects is difficult. Economic terms apply only to some of the effects, such as the cost of medical treatments, and the loss of production in fisheries and agriculture, and damage to materials; but how does one calculate the cost equivalent to the suffering of a blind or dying person, or the loss of a rare plant or animal species?

The most comprehensive study was initiated by Environment Canada in 1997 for the 10th anniversary of the Montreal Protocol on Substances that Deplete the Ozone Layer. In this study the costs were calculated for all measures taken internationally to protect the ozone layer, such as replacement of technologies using ozone-depleting substances. The benefits are the total value of the damaging effects avoided in this way. The total costs of the measures taken to protect the ozone layer were calculated to be 235 billion US dollars.

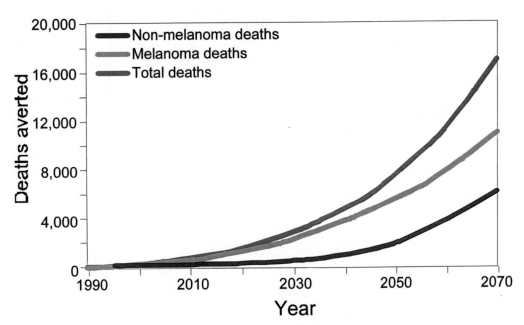

Annual deaths from melanoma and non-melanoma skin cancer averted due to Montreal Protocols (Mean Estimate)

Q18. Where can I get more information about the science and effects of ozone depletion?

There are many websites that contain information on ozone, UV, environmental effects and related topics. However, some are outdated and some may contain incorrect information. The sites mentioned below belong to dependable organisations and contain dependable information. Most of these sites contain links to other sources of information.

UNEP	www.unep.org
WMO	www.wmo.ch
WHO	www.who.int
IPCC	www.ipcc.ch
NOAA	www.al.noaa.gov
EPA	www.epa.gov
NASA	http://jwocky.gsfc.nasa.gov
NIWA	www.niwa.co.nz
Environment Canada	www.ec.gc.ca

List of Panel Members and UNEP Representatives

Environmental Effects of Ozone Depletion and its Interactions with Climate Change:
2002 Assessment

Dr Anthony Andrady
Engineering and Environmental Technology
Research Triangle Institute
3040 Cornwallis Road
Durham, NC 27709
USA
Tel. +1-919-541-6713
Fax +1-919-541-8868
Email: andrady@rti.org *or* andrady@37.com

Dr Carlos L. Ballaré
IFEVA, Facultad de Agronomía,
CONICET and Universidad de Buenos Aires
Avda. San Martin 4453
C1417DSE Buenos Aires
Argentina
Tel. 54 11 4524 8070 or 8071, ext. 8101
Fax 54 11 4514 8730
Email: ballare@ifeva.edu.ar

Dr Alkiviadis F. Bais
Aristotle University of Thessaloniki
Laboratory of Atmospheric Physics
Campus Box 149
GR-54006 Thessaloniki
Greece
Tel. +30-310998 184
Fax +30-310283 752 *or* 30-310248 602
Email: abais@auth.gr

Prof. Lars Olof Björn
Lund University
Department of Cell and Organism Biology
Sölvegatan 35
SE-223 62 Lund
Sweden
Tel. +46-46-22-27797
Fax +46-46-22-24113
Email: lars_olof.bjorn@fysbot.lu.se

Prof. Janet F. Bornman
Department of Plant Biology
Danish Institute of Agricultural Sciences (DIAS)
Research Centre Flakkebjerg
Flakkebjerg
DK-4200 Slagelse
Denmark
Tel. +45 58 11 33 68 (direct) (+45 58 11 33 00)
Fax: +45 58 11 33 01
Email: Janet.Bornman@agrsci.dk

Prof. Martyn Caldwell
Ecology Center
Utah State University
Logan, Utah 84322-5230
USA
Tel. +1-435-797-2555
Fax +1-435-797-3872
Email: mmc@cc.usu.edu

Prof. Terry Callaghan
Abisko Scientific Research Station
S-98107 Abisko
Sweden
Tel. +46-980 40021
Fax +46-980 40171
Email: Terry.Callaghan@ans.kiruna.se
AND
Sheffield Centre for Arctic Ecology
Department of Animal and Plant Sciences
University of Sheffield
Tapton Experimental Gardens
26 Taptonville Road
Sheffield
S105BR
United Kingdom
Tel. +44-114 222 6101
Fax +44-114 268 2521
Email: t.v.callaghan@sheffield.ac.uk

Dr Anthony P. Cullen
School of Optometry, University of Waterloo
Waterloo, Ontario
Canada N2L 3GI
Tel. +1 519 888-4567 ext 3680
Fax: +1 519 725 0784
Email: acullen@uva.uwaterloo.ca

Dr Frank R. de Gruijl
Department of Dermatology
Leiden University Medical Centre
Sylvius Laboratory Room 3038
Wassenaarseweg 72
NL-2333 AL Leiden
The Netherlands
Tel. +31-71-527 19 02
Fax +31-71-527 19 10
Email: F.R.de_Gruijl@Lumc.nl

Dr David J. Erickson
Computational Climate Dynamics Group
Computer Science and Mathematics Division
Oak Ridge National Laboratory
P.O. Box 2008
MS 6367 Oak Ridge
TN 37831-6367
USA
Tel:+1-865-574-3136
Fax+1-865-574-0680
Email: ericksondj@ornl.gov

Prof. D.-P. Häder
Institut für Botanik und Pharmazeutische
Biologie der Universität Erlangen-Nürnburg
Staudtstrasse 5
DE-91058 Erlangen
Germany
Tel. +49-9131-8528216
Fax +49-9131-8528215
Email: dphaeder@biologie.uni-erlangen.de

Dr Margaret L. Kripke
The University of Texas
M.D. Anderson Cancer Center
1515 Holcombe Boulevard
Houston, Texas 77030-4095
USA
Tel. +1-713-745-4495
Fax +1-713-745-1812
Email: mripke@mdanderson.org

Prof. G. Kulandaivelu
School of Biological Sciences
Madurai Kamaraj University
Madurai 625021
India
Tel. +91-452-458485
Fax +91-452-459139
Email: gkplant1@sify.com or
gomathyk@eth.net

Dr H.D. Kumar
214 Saketnagar Colony
Naria
Varanasi - 221 005
India
Tel. +91-542-315-180 (residence)
Email : hd_kumar@yahoo.com

Dr Janice Longstreth
The Institute for Global Risk Research, LLC
9119 Kirkdale Road, Suite 200
Bethesda, MD 20817
USA
Tel. +1-301-530-8071
Fax +1-301-530-1646
Email: tigerr@cpcug.org

Dr Richard L. McKenzie
National Institute of Water and Atmospheric
Research, Lauder
Private Bag 50061 Omakau
Central Otago 9182
New Zealand
Tel. +64-3-440-0429
Fax +64-3-447-3348
Email: r.mckenzie@niwa.co.nz

Prof. Mary Norval
Medical Microbiology
University of Edinburgh Medical School
Teviot Place, Edinburgh EH8 9AG
United Kingdom
Tel +44-131 650 3167
Fax +44-131 650 6531
Email: M.Norval@ed.ac.uk

Dr Halim Hamid Redhwi
King Fahd University of Petroleum and
Minerals
Research Institute
Dhahran 31261
Saudi Arabia
Tel. +966-3-860-3840 or 3810
Fax +966-3-860-2259 or 3586
Email: hhamid@kfupm.edu.sa

Prof. Raymond C. Smith
Institute for Computational Earth System
Science (ICESS) and Department of Geography
University of California
Santa Barbara, California 93106
USA
Tel. +1-805-893-4709
Fax +1-805-893-2578
Email: ray@icess.ucsb.edu

Dr Keith Solomon
Centre for Toxicology, University of Guelph
Guelph, ON
N1G 2W1 Canada
Phone +1-519 837 3320
Fax +1-519 837 3861
Email: ksolomon@uoguelph.ca

Dr Yukio Takizawa
National Institute for Minamata Disease
4058 Hama, Minamata City
Kumamoto 867-0008
Japan
Tel. +81-966-63-3111
Fax +81-966-61-1145
Email: takizawa@nimd.go.jp

Dr Xiaoyan Tang
Peking University
Center of Environmental Sciences
Beijing 100871
China
Tel. +86-10-6275-1925
Fax +86-10-6275-1925 / 27
Email: xytang@ces.pku.edu.cn

Prof. Alan H. Teramura
University of Hawaii, 3860 Manoa Road
Honolulu, Hawaii 96822-1180
USA
Tel. +1-808-988-0456
Fax +1-808-988-0462
Email: teramura@hawaii.edu

Prof. Manfred Tevini
Botanisches Institut II
Universität Karlsruhe
Kaiserstrasse 12
DE-76128 Karlsruhe
Germany
Tel. +49-721-608-3841
Fax +49-721-608-4878
Email: Manfred.Tevini@bio-geo.uni-
karlsruhe.de

Dr Ayako Torikai
Department of Chemistry
Daido Institute of Technology
Takiharu Minami-ku
Nagoya 457-8530
Japan
Tel./Fax +81-52-721-8008
Email: torikaia@msj.biglobe.ne.jp

Prof. Jan C. van der Leun
Ecofys
Kanaalweg 16 G
NL-3526 KL Utrecht
The Netherlands
Tel. +31 30 280 8361
Fax +31 30 280 8301
Email: j.vanderleun@ecofys.nl

Dr Stephen Wilson
Department of Chemistry
University of Wollongong
Northfields Ave.
Wollongong, NSW, 2522
Australia
Tel. +61 2 42 21 35 05
Fax +61 4221 4287
Email: Stephen_Wilson@uow.edu.au

Dr Robert C. Worrest
US Global Change Research Information Office
(GCRIO)
1717 Pennsylvania Avenue NW, Suite 250
Washington, DC 20006-4618
USA
Tel. +1 202 419-3467
Fax: +1 202 223-3064
Email: rworrest@ciesin.columbia.edu
http://www.gcrio.org/

Dr Richard G. Zepp
United States Environmental Protection Agency
960 College Station Road
Athens, Georgia 30605-2700
USA
Tel. +1-706-355-8117
Fax +1-706-355-8104
Email: zepp.richard@epa.gov

Co-authors

Dr. Pieter Aucamp
Environmental Consultant
P.O. Box 915751
Faerie Glenn, 0043
South Africa
Tel. +27-12-365 1025
Fax +27-12-365 1025
Email: pjaucamp@iafrica.com

Stephan D. Flint
Department of Forest, Range and Wildlife
Science
Utah State University
Logan, Utah 84322-5230
USA
Tel. +1 435 797 2474
Fax +1 435 797 3796
Email: sflint@cc.usu.edu

Prof. Mohammad Ilyas
Sheikh Tahir Astro-Geophysical Centre
University of Science of Malaysia
11800 USM Penang
Malaysia
Tel. +604 65 7 7888 /3674
Fax +604-657 91 50
Email: milyas50@hotmail.com

Professor Harry Slaper
National Institute of Public Heath and the
Environment (RIVM)
P.O. Box 1
NL-3720 BA Bilthoven
The Netherlands
Tel: + 31 30 2743488
Email: harry.slaper@rivm.nl

Dr. Prodromos Zanis
Aristotle University of Thessaloniki
Laboratory of Atmospheric Physics
Campus Box 149
Victoria
GR-54006 Thessaloniki
Greece
Tel: +30310998009
Email: zanis@auth.gr

List of Reviewers

Environmental Effects of Ozone Depletion and its Interactions with Climate Change: 2002 Assessment

Dr Jaime F. Abarca
Mardones 0350
Punta Arenas
Chile
Tel. 56-61-213530
Tel/Fax 56-61-211230
Email: drabarca@ctcinternet.cl

Dr Daniel L. Albritton
NOAA Aeronomy Laboratory
Mailstop R/AL, 325 Broadway
Boulder
CO 80305-3328
USA
Tel: 1-303 497 5785
Fax: 1-303 497 5340/5373
Email: aldiroff@al.noaa.gov

Dr Pedro J. Aphalo
Department of Biological and Environmental Science
P.O. Box 35
FI-40014, University of Jyväskylä
Finland
Tel.   +358 14 260 2339
Mobile +358 50 372 1504
Fax   +358 14 260 2321
Email: pedro.aphalo@cc.jyu.fi
http://www.jyu.fi/~aphalo/

Dr Pieter Aucamp
Environmental Consultant
P.O. Box 915751
Faerie Glenn, 0043
South Africa
Tel. +27-12-365 1025
Fax +27-12-365 1025
Email: pjaucamp@iafrica.com

Dr Marianne Berwick
Memorial Sloan-Kettering Cancer Center
Dept of Epidermology and Biostatistics
1275 York Avenue, Box 588
New York, NY 10021
USA
Tel. +1 212 639 8357
Fax +1 212 794 4352
Email:
Berwick_Marianne/mskcc_BIOST@mskmail.mskcc.org

Dr Mario Blumthaler
Institute of Medical Physics
University of Innsbruck
AT-6020
Innsbruck
Austria
Fax +43-512-507-2860
Email: Mario.Blumthaler@uibk.ac.at

Dr Thomas P. Coohill
Siena College
515 Loudon Road
Loudonville, New York 12211
USA
Tel. +1 518-783-2441
Fax +1 518-783-2986
Email: tcoohill@siena.edu

Prof. Edward DeFabo
Department of Environmental and
Occupational Health
School of Public Health and Health Services
George Washington University Medical Center
Ross Hall, Room 113
2300 I St., NW
Washington, D.C. 20037
USA
Tel. 1 202 994 3975
Fax: 1 202 994 0409
Email: drmecd@gwumc.edu

Dr Susana Diaz
CADIC-CONICET
Ruta 3 y Cap.Mutto
C.C. 92
9410 Ushuaia - Tierra del Fuego
Argentina
Tel: +54 2901 422754
Fax: +54 2901 430644
Email: rqdiaz@criba.edu.ar, subediaz@satlink.com

Prof. Nils Ekelund
Department of Natural and Environmental Sciences,
Mid-Sweden University
SE-851 70 Sundsvall
Sweden
Tel. + 46-060-148707
Fax +46-060-148802
Email: nils.ekelund@mh.se

Dr Ernesto Bernardine Fernández
Faculty of Pharmacy
Valparaiso University
Casilla 5001-V Valparaíso
Gran Bretañaa 1111
Valparaiso
Chile
Tel. +56-32-508106
Fax +56 32-508111
Email: ernesto.fernandez@uv.cl

Prof. K. Ganesan
PG and Research Department of Physics
T.B.M.L. College
Bharathidasan University
Porayar
Nagappattinam (Dt)
Tamil Nadu
India 609 307
Tel. + 91 431-660271
Fax + 91 431-660245
Email: sriramnivas_kkl@yahoo.com or
Joansonpyr@rediffmail.com

Prof. Alex E. S. Green
ICAAS Clean Combustion Laboratory
University of Florida
P.O. Box 112050
Gainesville, Florida 32611 - 2050
USA
Tel. 1 352 392 2001
Fax 1 352 392 2027
Email: aesgreen@ufl.edu

Dr Dylan Gwynn-Jones
Institute of Biological Sciences
University of Wales
Aberystwyth
Ceredigion, SY23 3DA
Wales
United Kingdom
Tel. +44 (0)1970 622318
Fax +44 (0)1970 622350
Email dyj@aber.ac.uk

Dr Walter Helbling
Estación de Fotobiología Playa Unión
Casilla de correos N° 153
9100-Trelew
Chubut
Argentina
Tel. +54 2965 498 019
Tel/Fax +54 2965 496 269
Email: whelbling@efpu.com.ar

Dr Shaoshan Li
School of Life Science
South China Normal University
Guangzhou 510631
China
Email: lishsh@scnu.edu.cn
or
li_shaoshan2002@hotmail.com

Dr Yuan Li
Eco-environment Research Institute
Yunnan Agricultural University
Kunming 650201
China
Tel: 86-871-5227550,5227942
Fax: 86-871-5227435
Email: liyuanzu@public.km.yn.cn

Prof. Lawrence E. Licht
York University
Department of Biology
4700 Keele Street
Toronto, Ontario M3J 1P3
Canada
Fax 1 416 736-5989
Email: lel@YorkU.CA

Dr J. Ben Liley
National Institute of Water and Atmospheric
Research
NIWA, Lauder
Private Bag 50061 Omakau
Central Otago 9182
New Zealand
Tel. + 64-3-4400427
Fax +64-3-447-3348
Email: b.liley@niwa.co.nz

Dr Robyn Lucas
The Australian National University
National Centre for Epidemiology and Population
Health
Building 124
Canberra, ACT, 0200
Australia
Tel. +61 2 6125 3448
Fax +61 2 6125 5614
Email: Robyn.Lucas@anu.edu.au

Dr Sasha Madronich
National Center for Atmospheric Research
Atmospheric Chemistry Division
P.O. Box 3000
1850 Table Mesa Drive
Boulder
CO 80307-3000
USA
Tel. +1-303 497 1430
Fax +1-303 497 1400
Email: sasha@ucar.edu

Dr Andy McLeod
Centre for the Study of Environmental Change and
Sustainability
J. Muir Building, The King's Buildings
Mayfield Road
EH9 3JK
Edinburgh
United Kingdom
Tel.: +44-131-6505434
Fax: +44-131-6507214
Email: andy.mcleod@ed.ac.uk

Dr Patrick J. Neale
Smithsonian Environmental Research Center
P.O. Box 28
647 Contees Wharf Rd.
Edgewater MD 21037
USA
Tel. +1 443-482-2285 (Office)/+1 443-482-2329
Fax +1 443-482-2380
Email: neale@serc.si.edu or nealep@si.edu
http://www.serc.si.edu/uvb/uvb_index.htm

Dr Kevin K. Newsham
Biological Sciences Division
British Antarctic Survey
High Cross, Madingley Road
Cambridge
CB3 0ET
United Kingdom
Tel: +44(0)1223 221599 (office) / 221253
(laboratory)
Fax: +44(0)1223 221259 / 362616
Email: k.newsham@bas.ac.uk

Prof. Frances Noonan
Department of Environmental and Occupational
Health
School of Public Health and Health Services
The George Washington University Medical Center
Ross Hall, Room 113
2300 Eye St., NW
Washington DC 20037
USA
Tel: +1202 994 3970
Fax: +1202 994 0409
Email: drmfpn@gwumc.edu

Dr Masaji Ono
Environmental Health Sciences Division
National Institute for Environmental Studies
Onogawa 16-2, Tsukuba 305-8506
Japan
Tel. +81 298 50 2421
Fax +81 298 50 2588
Email: onomasaj@nies.go.jp

Dr V. Luis Orce

Instituto de Investigaciones en Genetica y Biologia
Molecular
INGEBI-CONICET
Obligado 2490 Piso 2
1428-Buenos Aires
Argentina
Tel. 54-1-784-5516
Fax 54-1-786-8578
Email: orce@proteus.dna.uba.ar;
orceluis@hotmail.com

Dr Nigel Paul
Division of Biology Sciences
Institute of Environmental and Biological Sciences
Lancaster University
Lancaster LA1 4YQ
United Kingdom
Tel.. 44 1524-593929
Fax 44 1524-843854
Email: n.paul@lancaster.ac.uk

Dr Rubén D. Piacentini
Instituto de Física Rosario
CONICET-Univ. Nac. de Rosario 9
27 de Febrero 210bis
2000 Rosario
Argentina
Fax +54-341-482 17 72
Email: ruben@ifir.edu.ar

Prof. Henning Rodhe
Department of Meteorology
University of Stockholm
SE-106 91 Stockholm
Sweden
Tel. +46 8 16 43 42
Fax +46 8 15 92 95
Email: rodhe@misu.su.se

Dr Norma D. Searle
114 Ventnor F
Deerfield Beach, Florida 33442
USA
Tel./Fax 1 954 480 8938
Email: ndsearle@aol.com

Prof. Günther Seckmeyer
Institute for Meteorology and Climatology
University of Hannover
Herrenhaeuser Str. 2
DE-30419 Hannover
Germany
Tel. +49-511-762-4022
Fax +49-511-762-4418
Email: Seckmeyer@muk.uni-hannover.de
http://www.muk.uni-hannover.de/~seckmeyer

Dr Richard B. Setlow
Biology Department
Brookhaven National Laboratory
Upton, Long Island, NY 11973
USA
Fax +1 631-344-3398
Email: setlow@bnl.gov

Dr Rajeshwar Sinha
Friedrich-Alexander-Universität
Institut für Botanik und Pharmazeutische Biologie
Staudtstr. 5
DE-91058 Erlangen
Germany
Tel. +49 9131 8528222
Fax +49 9131 8528215
Email: r.p.sinha@gmx.net

Dr Anna Maria Siani
Universita' di Roma "La Sapienza"
Dipartimento di Fisica
Piazzale Aldo Moro, 5
IT-00185 Roma
Italy
Tel. +39-06-49913479
Fax +39-06-4463158
Email: annamaria.siani@uniroma1.it
http://www.phys.uniroma1.it/docs/meteo/hp_gmet.htm

Dr James Slusser
USDA UVB Monitoring and Research Network
Natural Resource Ecology Laboratory
Colorado State University, Fort Collins
CO 80523
USA
Tel. +1 970 491-3623
Fax   +1 970 491-3601
Email: sluss@uvb.nrel.colostate.edu
http://uvb.nrel.colostate.edu/UVB/

Dr Igor Sobolev
Chemical & Polymer Technology
5 Rita Way
Orinda, CA 94563
USA
Tel. 1 925 376-6402
Fax 1 925 376-6402
Email: i.sobolev@worldnet.att.net

Dr J. Richard Soulen
5333 Hickory Bend
Bloomfield Hills, MI 48304
USA
Tel. +1 248 642 6568
Fax   +1 248 258 6769
Email: rsoulen@comcast.net

Prof. Hugh R Taylor
Centre for Eye Research Australia
The University of Melbourne
Department of Ophthalmology
Locked Bag 8, East Melbourne 8002
Australia
Tel.   +61 3 9929 8368
Fax   +61 3 9662 3859
Email: h.taylor@unimelb.edu.au

Prof. H. van Loveren
National Institute of Public Health and the
Environment
P.O. Box 1
NL-3720 BA Bilthoven
Tel   +31(0)30 27 42 476
Mobile +31(0)62 15 55 620
Fax   +31(0)30 27 44 437
Email: H.van.Loveren@rivm.nl

Dr Horacio E. Zagarese
Instituto de Investigaciones Biotecnológicas
Instituto Tecnologico de Chascomus (IIB-INTECH)
CONICET-Universidad Nacional de General San
Martín Camino de Circunvalacion
Laguna Km. 6 CC 164
(B7130IWA) Chascomus
Provincia de Buenos Aires
Argentina
Email: zagarese@infovia.com.ar